ACES HIGH

Most Berkley Caliber Books are available at special quantity discounts for bulk purchases for sales promotions, premiums, fund-raising, or educational use. Special books, or book excerpts, can also be created to fit specific needs.

For details, write: Special Markets, The Berkley Publishing Group, 375 Hudson Street, New York, New York 10014.

Also by the Author

Nonfiction

ACES: TRUE STORIES OF VICTORY & VALOR
IN THE SKIES OF WORLD WAR II
SECRET WEAPONS OF THE COLD WAR
SECRET WEAPONS OF WORLD WAR II

Fiction

A DAMNED FINE WAR
RAPTOR FORCE
RAPTOR FORCE: HOLY FIRE
RAPTOR FORCE: CORKSCREW
INTO THE FIRE

ACES HIGH

The Heroic Saga of the
Two Top-Scoring American
Aces of World War II

BILL YENNE

BERKLEY CALIBER, NEW YORK

THE BERKLEY PUBLISHING GROUP
Published by the Penguin Group
Penguin Group (USA) Inc.
375 Hudson Street, New York, New York 10014, USA
Penguin Group (Canada), 90 Eglinton Avenue East, Suite 700, Toronto, Ontario M4P 2Y3, Canada
(a division of Pearson Penguin Canada Inc.)
Penguin Books Ltd., 80 Strand, London WC2R 0RL, England
Penguin Group Ireland, 25 St. Stephen's Green, Dublin 2, Ireland (a division of Penguin Books Ltd.)
Penguin Group (Australia), 250 Camberwell Road, Camberwell, Victoria 3124, Australia
(a division of Pearson Australia Group Pty. Ltd.)
Penguin Books India Pvt. Ltd., 11 Community Centre, Panchsheel Park, New Delhi—110 017, India
Penguin Group (NZ), 67 Apollo Drive, Rosedale, North Shore 0632, New Zealand
(a division of Pearson New Zealand Ltd.)
Penguin Books (South Africa) (Pty.) Ltd., 24 Sturdee Avenue, Rosebank, Johannesburg 2196,
South Africa

Penguin Books Ltd., Registered Offices: 80 Strand, London WC2R 0RL, England

The publisher does not have any control over and does not assume any responsibility for author or third-party websites or their content.

Copyright © 2009 American Graphic Systems, Inc.
Cover design by Richard Hasselberger
Cover photos (front):inset photos (left): U.S. Air Force; (right): National Archives; airplanes: U.S. Air Force; (back, top):National Archives; (back, bottom, clockwise): Lockheed; U.S. Air Force; Lockheed; Lockheed; Lockheed; spine: U.S. Air Force; National Archives
Book design by Kristin del Rosario

All rights reserved.
No part of this book may be reproduced, scanned, or distributed in any printed or electronic form without permission. Please do not participate in or encourage piracy of copyrighted materials in violation of the author's rights. Purchase only authorized editions.
BERKLEY CALIBER and its logo are trademarks of Penguin Group (USA) Inc.

PRINTING HISTORY
Berkley Caliber hardcover edition / February 2009
Berkley Caliber trade paperback edition / February 2010

Berkley Caliber trade paperback ISBN: 978-0-425-23230-9

The Library of Congress has catalogued the Berkley Caliber hardcover edition as follows:

Yenne, Bill, 1949-
  Aces high : the heroic true saga of the two top-scoring American aces of World War II / Bill Yenne.
    p. cm.
Includes bibliographical references and index.
  ISBN: 978-0-425-21954-6
  1. Bong, Richard I. 2. McGuire, Thomas B., 1920–1945. 3. United States—Army Air Forces—Biography. 4. World War, 1939–1945—Aerial operations, American. 5. World War, 1939–1945—Pacific Area. 6. Fighter pilots—United States—Biography. 7. Medal of Honor—Biography.
I. Title.
  D790. 747 2009.   2008047587
  940'.54—dc22.

PRINTED IN THE UNITED STATES OF AMERICA

10 9 8 7 6 5 4 3

To Cash.
May you grow up dreaming of heroes,
and once grown, may you be regarded as one yourself.

CONTENTS

NOTES ON SQUADRON NOMENCLATURE
AND ORGANIZATION

During World War II, the organizational structure of the U.S. Army Air Forces (USAAF) began at the top with numbered air forces, of which there were sixteen by the end of the war. Both Richard Bong and Thomas McGuire were assigned to the Fifth Air Force for their combat tours. In turn, each of the numbered air forces contained commands, usually a bomber command and a fighter command, among others. These were designated with Roman numerals.

Bong and McGuire were fighter pilots and therefore were in the V Fighter Command of the Fifth Air Force. Generally, the next level down was the group, which usually contained three squadrons.

For most of his combat career, McGuire was assigned to the 431st Fighter Squadron within the 475th Fighter Group, known as "Satan's Angels." From April to December 1944, McGuire was the commander of the 431st.

During his early combat career, Bong was assigned to the 9th Fighter Squadron within the 49th Fighter Group, known as the "Forty-niners." After February 1944, he was assigned directly to the V Fighter Command and allowed to "freelance," attaching himself to various units at his own discretion. These included squadrons within both the 49th and 475th fighter groups.

The USAAF itself was formed on June 20, 1941, as an autonomous component of the U.S. Army. It was the successor to the U.S. Army Air Corps, and it absorbed the functions, assets, and personnel of this organization. In 1947, the USAAF was replaced by the U.S. Air Force, an entity entirely independent of the U.S. Army.

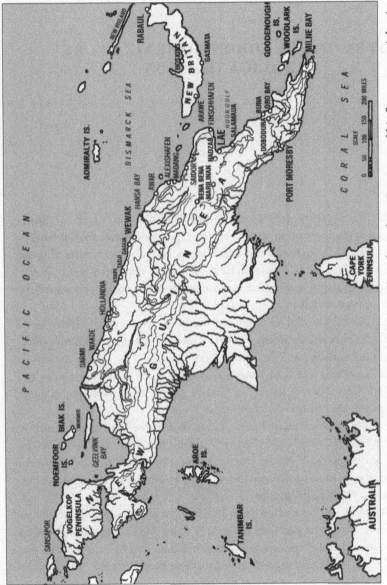

The skies over New Guinea were their battlefield. Flying from bases here, Bong scored his first twenty-eight victories between December 1942 and April 1944, and McGuire scored his first twenty-four between August 1943 and October 1944. (U.S. Army)

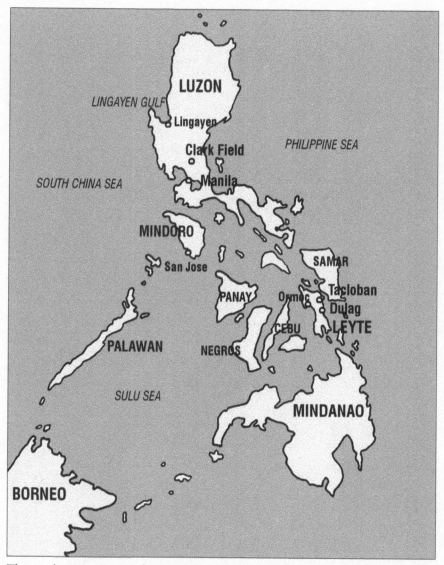

The race between Bong and McGuire reached its crescendo over the Philippines. Bong scored his last twelve victories here between October and December 1944, and McGuire scored his last fourteen here during the same period. (Author's collection)

ACKNOWLEDGMENTS

Anyone who writes of America's two highest-scoring aces must stand on the shoulders of Charles A. Martin, who spent many years compiling original documents related to the life of Tommy McGuire, and Carl Bong, whose privately published collection of his brother's letters are invaluable in both understanding Dick Bong and in tracing his career. In addition to these essential sources, the author wishes to thank Robert Fuhrman, executive director of the Richard I. Bong World War II Heritage Center; Gary W. Boyd, McGuire Air Force Base historian; and U.S. Air Force historian David Chenowith, who supplied photographs. Finally, a tip of the cap to my friend Dan Roam, who urged me and encouraged me to finish this book.

PROLOGUE

Knights of the Air

We sigh for our own lost youth as we think of him, with all the world before him—the medieval world, with all its possibilities of wild adventure and romantic fortune—with knights to overthrow at spear point and distressed damsels to succor and a princess's smile to win at some great tournament. And rank and fame to gain by prowess and hardihood, under the eye of kings, in some great stricken field.

—WALTER CLIFFORD MELLER,
A Knight's Life in the Days of Chivalry (1924)

THE image of the lone warrior is one of the most enduring in human literature. He is the European knight-errant. He is the Japanese samurai. He is the lone rider of the American West. The solitary warrior is a powerful global cultural icon.

General William Tecumseh Sherman famously observed that war is hell, but war is also a paradox. On one hand, it is an all-consuming bloodbath; yet on the other, it is an endeavor that embodies gallantry and heroism that both inspires and excites. It turns the stomach and it stirs the heart. It induces nightmares and it inspires magnificent images that lift the soul.

It is that image of the lone warrior that arouses the imagination that paints warfare not as hell but as glorious. He is not lost among the anonymous dead, but preserved on the pages of great literature or carved in marble for the ages.

Since antiquity, volumes of epic poetry have celebrated Roman equites or medieval knights, whose victories were extraordinary and whose deaths were heroic. Written in the fifteenth century, Thomas Mallory's *Morte d'Arthur* is the classic and often imitated example, but there are vast libraries of others that tell the stories of real people whose heroism was backed by the shedding of real blood.

The warriors whose names are preserved in such epics were often members of an elite warrior class, the knights. In the Middle Ages, admission to knighthood was one of the highest honors that could be bestowed upon a young man, and to be such a warrior carried both immense prestige and immense danger.

"The noblest youths," wrote Tacitus in first-century Rome, "were not ashamed to be numbered among the faithful companies of celebrated leaders, to whom they devoted their arms and service. A noble emulation prevailed among the leaders to acquire the greatest number of bold companions."

The various European words for this special warrior give us a rounded picture of the identity of the man. The word "knight" derives from the Old English *cniht*, meaning a young man who is of service. The German word *ritter* means rider—there being that lone rider on horseback who recurs so often in heroic folklore. Indeed, the French word for knight is *chevalier*, meaning horseman, which is also the root word of chivalry, the code by which the knight lived his life of duty and honor, of courage and service. As in the famous tournaments, which were a sporting event allegory for real warfare, the knights met one another singularly, man on man, in a fight in which the better man always emerged victorious.

To achieve an honor such as knighthood was to achieve membership in a singular warrior class, but just as it carried great prestige, it also carried great responsibility. The institution of chivalry, to which the warrior subscribed, was a system of duty and honor by which the medieval European knight sought to distinguish himself from other warriors.

The times of these singular heroes, both idolized and idealized, eventually faded. The armed and armored rider on his powerful warhorse—facing down another like himself—soon faded from the battlefield, washed over and submerged by the tidal wave of military technology, mass casualties, and a new doctrine of total war in which the code of chivalry no longer played a role.

In August 1914, as Europe went to war, there were still horsemen, still colored banners, and still a sense that among the young men riding forth they would be singular heroes. Soon, however, these young men were ground together in a meat grinder, hamstrung on barbed wire, or chopped apart by machine guns, finding themselves writhing in the stinking mud of Flanders' fields.

Where, the last romantics asked, was chivalry?

Where were the knights?

To these questions, one raised one's eyes to gaze into the skies high above the mud. One heard the sputtering, humming sound of a nine-cylinder Oberursel air-cooled rotary engine, or a nine-cylinder Le Rhône, each carrying a lone rider into battle, man against man.

Just as World War I gave the history of war such dehumanizing doctrines and weapons of mass carnage as trench warfare and poison gas, so those years gave the twentieth century a new caste of knighthood: the fighter pilot. The knights of the war they called the Great War once again fought man against man, but now they were doing it in three glorious dimensions.

Aerial warfare was essentially born in World War I. Balloons had been used for observation in the various conflicts of the nineteenth century and before. The French used observation balloons at the Battle of Fleurus in 1794, and the Union's Army of the Potomac had a Balloon Corps during the Civil War. Airplanes had been used in Italy's war with Turkey in 1911, but World War I was the first war in which airplanes became an integral part of battlefield action. Meanwhile, the necessities of combat led to innovations and advances in aeronautical engineering.

When World War I began, aircraft were flimsy machines that were used primarily for observation. Soon, however, observer pilots started to carry handguns to fire at other observer pilots, and steel darts to drop on troops on the ground. The airplane gave birth to the warplane.

Soon the pilot would truly come to embody all that had been embodied in the medieval notion of the knight. Soon the pilot became the idealized and idolized *ace*.

Fighter pilots became the knights of the air. They were quite literally a breed apart, fighting their battles high above the mud and muck of the battlefield, fighting one another man to man like the knights of the medieval tournament. Just as a special folklore had once existed around the knights of the Middle Ages, and the code of chivalry that defined knighthood contained a special vocabulary, so it was with the knights of the air. Most important in this modern lexicon is the term "ace," which was coined to describe the knight who had achieved a level of expertise beyond that of his fellow knights of the air.

What is an ace?

Technically the term came to be assigned to a pilot of a fighter aircraft who had shot down, or destroyed in the air, a total of *five* enemy aircraft. In other words, an ace was a pilot who had achieved five aerial *victories*. Therefore, an ace also could be described as a fighter pilot who had dueled to the death with five other fighter pilots—and survived.

The term "ace" to describe a victorious knight of the air originated in the French media, where the term *l'as* had been used to describe singularly triumphant sports stars. The first aviator known to have achieved an aerial victory over another was the French daredevil aeronaut turned military pilot Roland Garros, who achieved his victory on April 1, 1915. The first man to be referred to as l'as for downing five airplanes was probably Adolphe Pegoud, although Garros may have been responsible for downing five airplanes earlier than Pegoud.

In 1915, being an ace was truly a feat of skill. Aiming a gun at a moving airplane from a moving airplane was not—and is not—easy. Shooting straight ahead was the best for aiming, but it was hard to do this because it meant shooting through the propeller arc and probably shooting off the propeller. Garros solved this difficulty by having metal deflection plates attached to his propeller. Within weeks, Anthony Fokker and Heinrich Luebbe in Germany developed a system of synchronization in which the machine gun could be made to fire through the arc of the turning propeller only when the blades were *not* in the way. The system was installed on a Fokker Eindecker (monoplane) and suddenly the Imperial German Air Force was virtually—but only momentarily—invincible. Soon the synchronized guns were being used on both sides.

Over time, aviation technology on both sides gave the knights of the air some very potent warhorses, and their victories provided the most—and arguably the *only*—truly heroic headlines of World War I. The aces became the heroes of the Great War, and their names were the true analogs of Sir Lancelot and Sir Galahad. Frenchmen such as Georges Guynemer and René

Fonck, Englishmen such as Mick Mannock, and Canadians such as Billy Bishop were anointed by their media as the greatest names of their era.

While these names are no longer the household words they once were, we can say with little fear of contradiction that the most recognized name of a warrior from World War I is also that of the war's top-scoring ace. Baron Manfred Albrecht Freiherr von Richthofen, possibly better known as the "Red Baron," was the archetypical knight of the air. He was a young and handsome nobleman who also was extraordinarily skilled in the deadly art of aerial warfare.

The eldest son of a Silesian nobleman, von Richthofen was raised in a world where war was glorified and fencing was a way of life. The young aristocrat enlisted in the cavalry of the Imperial German Army and served in both Poland and France in 1914. As the ground war was reduced to static trench warfare, there was little use for cavalry, and many of that service's young officers sought transfer to units where there would be more action. For many, this meant the newly organized air service. Remembered as not having an immediate aptitude for flying, Richthofen served briefly as an observer before applying for pilot training; he shot down his first Nieuport over Verdun in 1915.

Von Richthofen was transferred to the Eastern Front, where he came to the attention of Oswald Boelke, the man credited with molding the German aerial fighter force into an elite and effective weapon. Boelke handpicked von Richthofen for his Jagdstaffel [Fighter Squadron] 2 on the Western Front in September 1916, and within a month Boelke's young protégé was an ace.

Soon von Richthofen had earned a reputation as a skilled fighter pilot and a dangerous adversary, a reputation that also was known in the West after he shot down Lance Hawker, the first ace in Britain's Royal Flying Corps. In January 1917, with nearly two dozen victories, von Richthofen was awarded the Pour le Mérite—the "Blue Max"—and command of Jagdstaffel 11, a unit that scored eighty-nine victories in the Battle of Arras. By June 1917 he was the highest-scoring German ace with fifty-two victories, a dozen more than Boelke himself.

Given command of Jagdgeschwader [Fighter Wing] 1 in June 1917, Richthofen transformed that composite group comprising four squadrons into the most feared unit in the Imperial German Air Force. So that French and

British units would have no doubt about who they were facing, the pilots in Jagdgeschwader 1 painted their airplanes in loud and garish colors, earning them the nickname the "Flying Circus." Von Richthofen painted his own Fokker Dr.I triplane solid red, and thereafter he was known as the "Red Baron." These bright colors were often compared in the media to the brilliant livery that adorned the warhorses of medieval knights.

Despite a head wound that put him out of action for a time, von Richthofen had shot down more than sixty Allied aircraft by the end of 1917, and scored his eightieth victory on April 20, 1918. The following day, during an engagement with No. 209 Squadron of the Royal Flying Corps, a Sopwith Camel flown by Canadian captain Roy Brown got on the Red Baron's tail at treetop altitude over Allied lines in a sector controlled by Australian troops.

The Dr.I crashed and the Red Baron was found dead, a single bullet in his heart. A controversy persists to this day over whether the bullet was Canadian or Australian. As befitting the code of chivalry that had been adopted by World War I airmen, the Allies gave their fallen foe a hero's funeral. No other pilot on either side would top his score of eighty victories during World War I.

The Red Baron never lived to pen his memoirs, but his lasting legacy was written for him in the tributes penned by those with whom he flew—and against whom he flew. An editorial in the British aviation review *Aeroplane*, published in April 1918, as the war still raged, summarized that legacy as well as most when it stated:

> Richthofen is Dead.
> All [Allied] airmen will be pleased to hear that he has been put out of action, but there will be no one amongst them who will not regret the death of such a courageous nobleman.
> Several days ago, a banquet was held in honour of one of our aces. In answering the speech made in his honour, he toasted Richthofen, and there was no one who refused to join. This Englishman honoured a brave enemy.
> Both airmen are now dead; our celebrated pilot had expressed the hope that he and Richthofen would survive the war so as to exchange experiences in times of peace.

The United States was late in entering World War I. It had been raging for thirty-two months when the United States declared war on Germany and its allies, and for thirty-seven months by the time that the U.S. Army Air Service 1st Aero Squadron, an observation unit, reached Europe. It was February 1918 before a U.S. Army squadron entered combat, but American pilots had been flying with Allied units, such as France's all-American Lafayette Escadrille, for a number of years. Indeed, Raoul Lufberry became a top-scoring American ace while flying with the Lafayette Escadrille before the Air Service went into combat.

In World War I, America's "Ace of Aces" was Edward Vernon "Eddie" Rickenbacker, a race-car driver turned pilot. The man who had raced in the Indy 500 four times took his fearless daring into the skies over Europe to become the highest-scoring American ace of World War I and a national hero.

Born in Columbus, Ohio, Rickenbacker came from a background entirely unlike that of the Red Baron. A typical American boy, he grew up with an avid interest in things mechanical and a boy's interest in fast machines. He went on the racing circuit when he was barely twenty and earned a reputation for speed and coolness. When the United States entered World War I, he tried to organize an "aero" squadron composed of his racing pals, but when he enlisted, General John J. "Blackjack" Pershing requested Rickenbacker as his personal driver.

In August 1917, he was finally transferred to the U.S. Army Signal Corps Aviation Section and signed up for flight training. Arriving in France, he flew briefly with a French squadron before joining the 94th Aero Squadron—the legendary "Hat in the Ring" squadron—in March 1918. Rickenbacker scored his first aerial victory on April 29, and his fifth on May 30, making him the first American ace to achieve that status flying with an American unit.

Grounded briefly with an ear infection, he returned to combat in August as his squadron upgraded to the SPAD XIII fighter plane. During the last three months of the war, he distinguished himself by bringing his score to twenty-six, and demonstrating the heroism that earned him the Congressional Medal of Honor and promotion to commander of the 94th Aero Squadron.

As with the knights of old, many of the greatest aces of World War I died young. They died that hero's death before the war ended at the eleventh hour of the eleventh day of the eleventh month of 1918. Like the Red Baron, Oswald Boelke, Roland Garros, Georges Guynemer, Raoul Lufberry, and Mick Mannock, all died their hero's death.

On the other hand, Billy Bishop became the top-scoring of British Empire aces, with seventy-two confirmed victories, and he survived the war. René Fonck, the top-scoring of all Allied aces with seventy-five, also lived to see the armistice.

So, too, did Eddie Rickenbacker, who would go on to an extensive career in American aviation, including service as an executive with American Airways (later American Airlines), North American Aviation, and Eastern Airlines. Unlike the Red Baron, he would also live to write his memoirs, paying tribute to Richthofen in the title *Fighting The Flying Circus*. His book would serve to inspire a generation of aces yet unborn.

On the last page, Rickenbacker, like a true warrior, penned lines entirely reminiscent of those by Walter Clifford Meller with which we began this prologue. The Ace of Aces waxed nostalgically for the thrill of the chase, asking rhetorically:

How can one enjoy life without this highly spiced sauce of danger? What else is there left to living now that the zest and excitement of fighting aeroplanes is gone? Thoughts such as these held me entranced for the moment and were afterwards recalled to illustrate how tightly strung were the nerves of these boys of twenty who had for continuous months been living on the very peaks of mental excitement.

PART I

≡

BOYS

Everything that he ever did...he did by himself. A lone trip across the Atlantic was not impossible for a boy who had grown up in the solitude of the woods and waters....Must we not admit, that this pioneering urge remained to this audacious youth because he had never submitted completely to the repercussions of the world and its jealous institutions?

—JOSEPH K. HART,
from "O Pioneer," a July 1927 article in *Survey Magazine*.
The title was borrowed from Walt Whitman; the subject
was the recent transatlantic flight by Charles Lindbergh
that inspired and infused a generation of young Americans
with a passion for aviation.

CHAPTER 1

The Roaring Twenties and the Lone Eagle

WHEN 1920 began, both Pauline Watson McGuire in New Jersey and Dora Bryce Bong in Wisconsin knew that their first child would be born during the year. However, little did Polly and Dora realize that within a decade, their little babies would grow into boys who would read and consume Eddie Rickenbacker's *Fighting the Flying Circus*. His book would serve to inspire a generation of aces yet unborn.

The year 1920 would be a year of big changes for both Polly and Dora, and indeed for the United States, which was turning over a new leaf. The war was already receding into history, and the United States was looking forward. The most prosperous of the world's economies was ready to move on. It was President Woodrow Wilson who called World War I the "war to end all wars," and many Americans believed him. It seemed to him and to many others that the war had been so terrible that nobody would want to go through that again. It had been the bloodiest war in history, with ten million battle deaths and a like number of civilians killed.

To make sure that World War I really was the war to end all wars, Wilson proposed the League of Nations, a world forum in which war could be replaced by debate. Most of the great nations of the world bought into his concept, but not his own. If World War I was the war to end all wars, most Americans reasoned, then why bother with entangling the United States any further in squabbles within the Old World? The United States had saved the day for Britain and France and was ready to let them pick up the postwar pieces on their own.

The U.S. Congress ratified neither the Treaty of Versailles, which ended World War I, nor membership for the United States in Wilson's League of Nations.

What they did do was turn inward and ratify changes that would deeply and directly change the lives of American citizens. After having amended the Constitution only four times in the entire nineteenth century, Americans had already amended it four times since 1913, and two of those took effect in 1920. One of these, the Eighteenth (passed in 1919 but implemented in 1920), banned the sale of alcohol; the other, the Nineteenth, gave women the right to vote.

The Nineteenth Amendment was a long-awaited step forward. The Eighteenth was a step backward, which sought to legislate morality through Prohibition even as the nation was headed into what F. Scott Fitzgerald called the Jazz Age.

The Prohibitionists who envisioned an era of straitlaced morality were dismayed and horrified when the 1920s turned out to be an era of wild music, wild parties, wild motion pictures, speakeasies, and women showing their legs and smoking cigarettes in public.

These were the Roaring Twenties. Things were changing, but not as the Prohibitionists had long imagined. It was the era described so perfectly by Fitzgerald in *The Great Gatsby*. It was a time of unrestrained materialism and loose morality that was born of unprecedented prosperity. Heavily enforced but almost universally defied, the Eighteenth Amendment would be the only amendment to the Constitution ever to be repealed, although not for fourteen years.

WHEN Americans went to the polls in November 1920 to choose between Warren G. Harding and James M. Cox for president of the

United States, both Pauline Watson McGuire and Dora Bryce Bong were among the first generation of women legally able to cast ballots. By that time, both women also were caring for a newborn son.

Pauline—everyone called her Polly—had married Thomas Buchanan McGuire in New York City on November 24, 1918, less than two weeks after World War I ended. Dora Bryce had married Carl T. Bong in Duluth, Minnesota, half a year later, on July 29, 1919. Thomas McGuire had not served in the war, but Carl Bong had gone overseas to France with the Army Corps of Engineers. Neither couple lived in the state where they were married. The McGuires would live in Ridgewood, New Jersey; the Bongs would live on a farm near Poplar, Wisconsin.

Thomas B. McGuire was American-born of Irish descent, and Carl T. Bong had been born in Islingby, Sweden. He was brought to America when he was seven. Both men married girls whose families had been in America for several generations. Dora Bryce's family was predominantly of Scots-English lineage, and Polly Watson's family had ancestors who included England's Lord Beresford, as well as the Hoffmans, early Dutch settlers of New Amsterdam. Thomas McGuire was a Catholic who married a Presbyterian. The Bongs, like most of their Scandinavian neighbors, were Lutheran.

Dora Bryce's father was a farmer. Polly Watson's father was an industrialist. His Watson Machine Company in Paterson, New Jersey, built steel railroad bridges and the steel skeletons of many New York City skyscrapers—and the American Museum of Natural History in New York as well.

Dora Bryce married a man who ran both a farm near her father's farm and a road construction business that his father had started. Polly Watson married a fast-talking, fast-living car salesman who always was at odds with her parents. They believed that Polly had married beneath herself. Thomas B. McGuire believed himself to be a character from *The Great Gatsby*.

In Ridgewood, on August 1, 1920, Polly Watson McGuire gave birth to her only child, who was named Thomas Buchanan McGuire Jr., after his father. Seven weeks later, on September 24, and half a continent away in Superior, Wisconsin, Dora Bryce Bong gave birth to the first of her nine children. He was named Richard, after his father's younger brother, who had died at age two, and Ira, after Ira Wiley, Dora's uncle, who operated a farm near Carl Bong's place.

Thomas Buchanan McGuire Jr. and Richard Ira Bong, known as Tommy and Dick, respectively, grew up in economically secure families. The Bongs' life was not lavish, but neither did the family want for the necessities. Carl Bong had both a construction business and a farm. All the men in the Bong family were hunters, so during deer season there was always plenty of meat on the table—as well as sausage and jerky preserved for later.

The McGuires could have lived reasonably well on what Tom Sr. made selling Pierce-Arrows, but Polly still had access to her father's seemingly endless credit line at local stores.

Though the McGuires did not want for necessities, nor even luxuries, they did want for domestic harmony. Tom McGuire was displeased by his wife's economic dependence on her father, and Polly's mother never shied away from reminding her daughter that she was displeased by Polly's choice of a husband.

As they grew up, Tommy and Dick both enjoyed the outdoors, as boys had for generations and still do. However, both craned their necks to look into the sky when they heard a sound that had been unheard by boys of earlier generations.

The 1920s were years when aviation touched the lives of Americans everywhere. Powered flight had been born in the United States back in 1903 with the Wright Brothers, but before World War I, the number of airplanes flying in the United States was small. After the war, it was a different matter. During the war, the United States industrial machine had geared up to build enormous quantities of hardware and machinery. Among all this were airplanes in larger numbers than anyone could have imagined in 1914.

The airplane that was produced in the largest numbers of them all was the Curtiss JN series, known familiarly as the "Jenny." Glenn Hammond Curtiss, one of American aviation's first and foremost entrepreneurs, developed and built the most widely produced American design of the World War I era. Through the early 1920s, more examples of the JN series, especially the JN-4, were manufactured than any other American airplane. Nearly 8,500 JN-4s were built, including 2,765 of the JN-4Ds, the most widely produced variant.

The Jenny, like most American-built airplanes during World War I, had been built mainly as a training aircraft. American aces such as Eddie Rickenbacker flew mainly British and French warplanes. Rickenbacker made his mark in a French SPAD XIII. After the war, when the U.S. Army and the U.S. Navy no longer needed their enormous fleets of aircraft, they sold them off. Since they had been used mainly to train pilots in the United States, most of the surplus airplanes remained in the States. Suddenly large numbers of reasonably new planes were on the market. Because it was sturdy, reliable—and now cheap—the Jenny became a familiar sight in the skies over the United States.

The glut of new airplanes on the market by 1920 coincided with a growing fascination with flight among the general public. When pilots with Curtiss Jennies showed up in communities all over the United States to perform stunts and aerobatics, people turned out in droves to see them. As these pilots with their surplus Jennies traveled from place to place, they were known as barnstormers, because they usually operated from farm fields. There were few municipal airports yet, and farm fields offered relatively level and unobstructed ground for takeoffs and landings.

Soon airlines were formed to fly passengers from place to place, and the U.S. Post Office began offering a faster form of service called air mail. The 1920s were an era of change on many levels. F. Scott Fitzgerald may have dubbed the decade the Jazz Age, but it was also the Air Age.

As boys have always been fascinated by machines, Tommy and Dick grew up as part of that first generation of boys to be fascinated by airplanes. They saw them in the sky, and they both were growing up with the heroic exploits of Eddie Rickenbacker as part of their familiar folklore.

When the two boys were just six years old, a momentous event occurred that captured media attention as did few others during the 1920s. For that generation of young boys craning their necks to hear the sound of an airplane engine, it was inspiring to the extreme. It was the seminal event of many young lifetimes. On the morning of May 21, 1927, the world awoke to the news that a young American aviator had become the first person to successfully fly across the Atlantic Ocean alone and nonstop.

Though other fliers had previously crossed the Atlantic, nobody had flown solo from New York to Paris, and Charles Augustus Lindbergh captured the public imagination as no pilot before. Tall and handsome, he represented the best-loved of American archetypes, the daring loner. He was a true knight-errant of the air. He became known as the "Lone Eagle."

Lindbergh's international prominence was sudden and far-reaching. Tens of thousands greeted him in Paris when he made his historic landing in the *Spirit of St. Louis*, and President Calvin Coolidge sent a flotilla of warships to escort him home to America. Once back home, New York City staged a ticker tape parade, and again, tens of thousands turned out to see him. *Time* magazine instituted its "Man of the Year" feature that year so Lindbergh could be "Man of the Year" for 1927.

As Elinor Smith Sullivan, 1930's Best Woman Aviator of the Year, described it, as quoted in *The Century* by Peter Jennings and Todd Brewster, "It's hard to describe the impact Lindbergh had on people. Even the first walk on the moon doesn't come close. The twenties was such an innocent time, and people were still so religious—I think they felt like this man was sent by God to do this. And it changed aviation forever because all of a sudden the Wall Streeters were banging on doors looking for airplanes to invest in. We'd been standing on our heads trying to get them to notice us but after Lindbergh, suddenly everyone wanted to fly, and there weren't enough planes to carry them."

Wrote the *Washington Post* of Lindbergh's appearance in the nation's capital, "He was given that frenzied acclaim which comes from the depths of the people."

"There was something lyric as well as heroic about the apparition of this young Lochinvar who suddenly came out of the West and who flew all unarmed and all alone," said *The Nation*. "It is the kind of stuff which the ancient Greeks would have worked into a myth and the medieval Scots into a border ballad.... But what we have in the case of Lindbergh is an actual, an heroic and an exhaustively exposed experience which exists by suggestion in the form of poetry."

John William Ward, a professor of history and American studies at Amherst College, and a key individual in the Myth and Symbol School of American studies scholarship, eloquently summarized the importance of Lindbergh's accomplishment. "He had fired the imagination of mankind," Ward wrote in his essay on the 1920s *From Prosperity to Collapse*. "From the moment of Lindbergh's flight people recognized that something more was involved than the mere fact of the physical leap from New York to Paris.... Lindbergh gave the American people a glimpse of what they liked to think themselves to be at a time when they feared they had deserted their own vision of themselves.... The newspapers agreed that Lindbergh's chief worth was his spiritual and moral value."

It was not just the poets and the scholars who were dazzled by what Lindbergh had done. It was also—and I would say *especially*—the little boys throughout the United States who had their imaginations stirred by the Lone Eagle. When Lindbergh's book about his record flight, titled *We*, was published by Grosset & Dunlap later in 1927, it found its way into many a boy's Christmas stocking, and its story found its way into many a boy's imagination.

For Tommy McGuire, the first man to personally open the door to the world of aviation was his Uncle Charles. His mother's brother had been one of the many members of the U.S. Army Air Service who had learned to pilot a Curtiss Jenny during World War I. He also had a large collection of model airplanes that captivated his nephew. Charles Watson never gave Tommy an airplane ride, as he might have and probably should have. After he left the army, Charles Watson had given up flying because of the successful nagging of his mother, Dora Watson—whose nagging had been unsuccessful in preventing Polly's marriage to Tom McGuire. Nevertheless, there was nothing to stop Uncle Charles from regaling his eager nephew with stories of flying during World War I.

Soon Tommy McGuire would be making model airplanes of his own. So, too, would that other boy growing up on that farm near Poplar. Young Dick Bong had grown up in the solitude of the woods and waters of Wisconsin, just as Lindbergh had grown up in the solitude of the woods and waters of neighboring Minnesota.

For Dick, his dreams were stoked by the accounts of the Lone Eagle and also by the sight of the planes that carried air mail across the upper Midwest. In the summer of 1928, when Dick was seven, going on eight, President Coolidge was vacationing at Cedar Island, near Superior, Wisconsin. His temporary office, the 1920s version of a "western White House," was at Superior High School. The mail was flown in to him every day, and the mailplane made its approach to Superior directly over the Bong family farmhouse. Every day young Dick would wait for and watch the president's mailplane, mesmerized with the thought of being up there himself.

Tommy McGuire, meanwhile, could imagine that he occasionally had the pleasure of looking up into the sky and actually seeing Lindbergh himself. The Lone Eagle and his wife, Anne Morrow Lindbergh, lived for a time with her parents in Englewood, New Jersey, which was less than twenty air miles northwest of Ridgewood. In the summer of 1927, Uncle Charles took Tommy over to Paterson to watch a preannounced flyover of the Wright Aeronautical Corporation aircraft engine factory by Lindbergh in the *Spirit of St. Louis*. Tommy never forgot that day.

By the time the boys were dreaming of joining Lindbergh, the lack of domestic harmony at Tommy McGuire's house had boiled over. His parents were drifting apart. Tom and Polly had changed. It was the Roaring Twenties, and luxury car salesman Tom McGuire had become the quintessential stereotype of the Jazz Age playboy. He would have easily been at home in the pages of *The Great Gatsby*. One can imagine that he even may have crossed paths with Fitzgerald himself in a Manhattan speakeasy or a country club affair. If one believes in the doctrine of "six degrees of separation," it is easy to surmise that they had acquaintances in common.

Polly, on the other hand, led a more insular life. It was not that she eschewed the pleasures of the Jazz Age. She did take a drink now and then— and eventually it was much more often—but it was usually at a country club rather than at a speakeasy.

Meanwhile, another feature of the 1920s lifestyle would alter Polly's future. At about this time, the well-heeled northern captains of industry were beginning to find it desirable to escape northern winters for Florida. Among these captains was John Roebling of the Roebling Steel Company, who was acquainted with Polly's father, Alfred Watson, who also was in the metal fabricating business.

Roebling and his wife, Margaret, mentioned that they had been wintering at the Spanish colonial-style Kenilworth Lodge in the town of Sebring, a relatively small community in the center of the state roughly between Sarasota and Palm Beach. Designed as a planned development for the upper crust and laid out in a circular pattern around Lake Jackson, the town had been founded in 1912 by Ohio dishwares manufacturer George Sebring, who also built the Lodge four years later. Soon Alfred and Dora were spending a great deal of time in Sebring as well. The Watsons found the climate agreeable, and so did Polly, who took Tommy down to Florida to visit his grandparents.

In 1927, Tommy McGuire's long-bickering parents finally separated. Tom McGuire, who was a Catholic, opposed the idea of a divorce, but Polly insisted on it. Eventually she would get her way, but in the meantime, she decided to do as her parents had, and she moved to Sebring full-time. The Watsons, meanwhile, had purchased a large home with several adjacent buildings not far from the Moorish turrets of the Kenilworth. Polly and Tommy moved south and lived with her parents. She and Tom agreed that Tommy would spend his summers in New Jersey with his father.

Despite the antagonism of Polly and her parents, Tom McGuire still wanted to be part of his son's life, and he did what he could do in his own sort of "Great Gatsby" way. He had wanted to continue to be part of Polly's life as well. For a long time after she moved to Sebring, Tom had continued to send her flowers, but she insisted on refusing them. Eventually he gave up on Polly and went on to a long-term relationship with the young and attractive Joan Mallon. But he never gave up on Tommy.

While Tommy McGuire was growing up in Sebring, the only child of a doting mother and well-to-do-grandparents, Dick Bong was growing up on a farm in Wisconsin with two younger brothers and six younger sisters. The Bong farm was a typical upper Midwest farm, with some horses, as well as cattle, hogs, and chickens. They also raised hay as well as grain on their eighty acres. Like most kids growing up on midwestern farms in the early twentieth century, Dick joined the local 4-H Club, a national farm youth organization started in 1924. The 4-H still exists, and is still administered by the Agriculture Department's Extension Service. One of his 4-H projects was planting, on the family farm, an evergreen windbreak that survived for many decades.

If the urban twenties roared with the sounds of jazz and speakeasies, the rural twenties also were a time of optimism and growing prosperity in their own down-to-home way. Nearly everyone in the cities and farms was better off than their parents, and there was every reason to believe that with the Great War receding, everything would continue to improve indefinitely.

It was not to be.

CHAPTER 2

Changes and Challenges

HARDLY anyone imagined when they awoke on October 24, 1929, that this day was going to mark a turning point in history that would cast a dark shadow across the remainder of the century. That day, ever after called "Black Thursday," was followed five days later by "Black Tuesday" and the catastrophic economic crash that plunged the world into the Great Depression.

For Dick Bong, Black Thursday marked only the one month anniversary following his ninth birthday. The farm made the Bongs reasonably self-sufficient when it came to the basics, and the continued work on paving U.S. Highway 2 kept the Bong Construction Company going.

The center of Dick's world was the family farm. Chores were more than simply milking the cows. The Bong farm was a commercial business, and there was haying to be done. When that was finished, there was harvesting. The Bongs grew and marketed wheat and oats, and they raised potatoes, beans, and peas. Being the oldest, Dick was always in charge, seeing to it that his younger siblings always turned in a good day's work. In the early years, these younger siblings were mainly his sisters Nellie, Betty, and

Geraldine—whom everyone called "Jerry." His next younger sibling, Carl (everyone called him "Bud"), was not born until 1927, so he was not really an able farmhand until Dick was in his early teens. Younger still were Joyce, Barbara, Sue, and Jim.

In the 1930s, and for at least a generation afterward, an important rite of passage for American boys was their first gun, whether it was for hunting, or just target shooting. Tommy McGuire's first gun was a Fox Sterlingworth shotgun, given to him by Uncle Charles when he turned fifteen. In Dick Bong's world, that of a country boy, a big part of that rite of passage was—and still is—when the boy is old enough to go out during hunting season. Dick got his first rifle, Winchester .22-caliber, for his birthday when he turned twelve, and he was soon hunting with a .30-caliber rifle, like his dad. For a country boy, "getting" your first deer is part of coming of age. With Dick Bong, it marked his beginning to discover that he had an uncanny knack for marksmanship.

As for Tommy McGuire, nearly three months into his ninth year when the market crashed, he would later notice that new construction in the housing development that was Sebring sputtered to a halt. At home, he noticed that his lifestyle was impacted more and more. His grandparents still had money, but they had taken a beating in the crash. Over the coming decade, medical bills would sap much of what they still had after the market tanked.

When you are nine years old, you don't really notice what is going on in the world; you notice what is going on around you, what is going on in your own little world. For both boys, there was time with friends, and solitary moments building balsa-wood model airplanes.

For Tommy McGuire, these moments were shared occasionally with his Uncle Charles, who visited from time to time. As was the case with many model airplanes built by boys during the midtwentieth century, the power plant was a tightly wound rubber band that could give a properly built model a range of more than fifty feet.

Every boy's dream, of course, was one of those big models with a small gasoline engine that were advertised on the backs of comic books. Finally, Uncle Charles sent such a model—a SPAD XIII with a "Hat in the Ring" painted on the side—to Tommy. After having spent many hours building it, however, Tommy McGuire lost his prized model with the three-foot wingspan. It went down on a flight that Tommy hoped would do for him and Lake Jackson what the *Spirit of St. Louis* had done for Charles Lindbergh, but alas, Tommy's greatness as an aviator was yet to come.

Then Tommy's grandfather died in 1932, and his grandmother four years later. Meanwhile, his mother, the only other relative Tommy had nearby, was sinking slowly and inexorably into the quicksand of alcoholism. Despite the fact that Highlands County, of which Sebring was the county seat, was a dry county, most people had booze in their homes. Polly drank as drunks usually drink—too much and at awkward and inappropriate times of the day. She often embarrassed herself, but did no real harm to anyone but herself. People whispered about Polly, but they whispered as much about her being a divorcée, as one who drank too much. In moments of sobriety, Polly wore a brave face, and despite the snobbishness of the Sebring blue-bloods—and blueblood wannabes—she was far from being a *total* outcast around Sebring.

IN 1934, Dick Bong and Tommy McGuire entered high school. In the outside world, a world of which the boys were starting to become aware, many things were happening. It was the first full year of the controversial New Deal policies that President Franklin Roosevelt instituted to relieve the effects of the Great Depression. It was the first full year since the Twenty-first Amendment repealed Prohibition, and it was one of the worst years for the climatic disaster that turned America's southern Plains into the Dust Bowl.

Closer to Dick Bong's world, during the spring of 1934, the legendary bandit John Dillinger hid out for a time (and allegedly buried a huge, yet unrecovered, treasure) near the town of Manitowash, Wisconsin, about two hours' drive due east of Poplar.

Four miles from Sebring, Alfred and Dora Watson's friends the Roeblings helped to endow Highlands Hammock State Park, one of Florida's first, which became a major base for Roosevelt's Civilian Conservation Corps (CCC). There was also a large CCC camp near Poplar, Wisconsin.

Tommy McGuire entered Sebring High School, and Dick Bong entered the ninth grade at Poplar High School. It was just a three-year school then, so Dick would spend his senior year at, and graduate from, Central High School in Superior, a dozen miles to the west. Dick had gone into the first grade in 1927, a year later than Tommy, because Dick's parents had wanted both him and his younger sister Nellie to start school together. However, he did so well that he skipped the third grade entirely, and rejoined his peers.

In high school, neither boy went out for football. With Tommy McGuire, it was a matter of his size. At 125 pounds, he wasn't really cut out for the gridiron—although he tried, with inauspicious results. For Dick Bong, it was the fact that Poplar was too small for a team. He did go out for basketball, where, as with a rifle, he was a very good shot. He also played baseball in one of the youth teams sponsored by the American Legion, where he was a natural when it came to pitching. He also was very agile on skates, and he was a good hockey player.

Both Dick Bong and Tommy McGuire joined their high school marching band, and coincidentally, both took up the clarinet. As McGuire's biographer Charles A. Martin points out, he found his niche in the band, where the bandleader, P. J. Gustat, was an important role model for young Tommy. Also, Professor Gustat's son Paul became one of Tommy's closest school friends.

According to Martin, Tommy McGuire had a lot of friends in high school in addition to Paul Gustat. He was a likable, outgoing kid—and he had a car. When he was as young as fourteen, his mother allowed him to drive her car around Sebring. Eventually he was the charioteer of choice when he and his classmates wanted to travel north to nearby Avon Park, where there were dances at the armory.

Tommy was not timid about taking license with the speed limit, something that will always endear a teenage driver to his peers. During his senior year at Sebring High, Tommy drove a Pontiac straight-eight that he had gotten as a Christmas present. The car was the envy of all his friends, especially those who were left in the dust during races on the open road. Tommy also earned a reputation as something of a daredevil with a canoe on Lake Jackson, the large freshwater lake surrounded by some of Sebring's most fashionable homes.

As Professor Gustat filled the function of father figure for Tommy, his own father continued to do his best to fulfill that role himself when Tommy came north to spend his summers. While in northern New Jersey, Tommy would spend time swimming at Lake Hopatcong in Sussex County, where his uncle and aunt, Ted and Stella Tolson, ran a hotel. When Tommy and Paul Gustat traveled north to New Jersey during the summer after their junior year at Sebring High, Tommy's father gave them a gold-plated tour of New York City in a chauffeur-driven limousine that he had arranged through his work as a car dealer. Indeed, he now owned his own Packard dealership, T. B. McGuire Motors, in Ridgewood. Charles A. Martin speculates in his biography of Tommy that Alfred and Dora Watson may have financed the elder McGuire's acquisition of this dealership in exchange for his relinquishing legal custody of his son to Polly. There is no direct evidence of such a transaction, but papers found in Polly's safe deposit box after her death confirm that she was granted full custody not long after the divorce.

Also during the summer after Tommy's junior year, the Sebring High School band won first in its category at the National School Music Competition at Winthrop College in South Carolina. Ironically, while Tommy McGuire was playing first-chair clarinet, and not playing football, Sebring High had a national-award-winning band—led by P. J. Gustat—and a mediocre record in football.

Both Dick Bong and Tommy McGuire earned short-lived nicknames while they were in high school. Bong was known as "Pinky" because his pale Swedish complexion was prone to the effects of the sun, and McGuire was known as "Snotty" or "Honker" because his allergies caused his disproportionally largish nose to run excessively.

Neither boy was a stranger to the occasional schoolboy prank. With Bong, it was setting fire to a pile of stumps at a neighboring farm one Halloween, and wiring a chair at a high school party so that anyone who sat in it got an electrical shock. With Tommy McGuire, most of his high jinks involved driving too fast, and during his senior year, he was also involved in that most essential of high school pranks, defacing the rival team's mascot before the big game. The rival school of the Sebring Blue Streaks was Avon Park High School, whose mascot, a red devil, was represented by a four-foot statue of same at the school. It takes no stretch of the imagination to understand that the annual prank involved blue paint and the darkness of night. Tommy McGuire drove the getaway car.

In 1938, both Bong and McGuire graduated from high school. Both went on to college, with Bong staying close and McGuire going far.

Having attended Central High in Superior, Dick Bong enrolled at Superior State Teachers College in the same town. The school, which has been the Superior campus of the University of Wisconsin system since 1971, was already moving beyond its original mandate for training teachers and getting more and more into general higher education. Dick Bong had a plan, and this suited his plan. He had decided that he wanted to join the U.S. Army Air Corps and be a pilot. However, to be a pilot, Dick needed to be an officer, and at the time, an officer needed more than two years of college. Superior State was a good choice for him. He would be needed on the farm much of the year, but he could easily drive to and from school in the spring or fall, and during the winter, when he wasn't needed so much, he could rent a room in town.

As Dick Bong moved across Superior to a new school, Tommy McGuire was ready to get out of the state. This fact did not please his mother at all, although the fact that she would be visiting Tommy in a city, with its high-end shops and fine restaurants, pleased her cosmopolitan sensibilities. Deep down, she missed the proximity to New York City that she had enjoyed while she lived in Ridgewood. In the present case, the city in question would be Atlanta, and the school was Georgia Institute of Technology.

Tommy McGuire had yet to make a definitive move toward becoming a pilot, but like Bong, he had wanted to fly since he had first heard Charles Lindbergh's name on the radio. Both men had flown in airplanes. Bong had paid for a ride at the State Fair, and McGuire had hitched an excursion in a Ford Trimotor out of Sebring. It was only a matter of time before they had their hands on the controls.

Bong had gone to school as a means of getting into the Air Corps. McGuire picked a top engineering school to study aeronautical engineering. At Georgia Tech, Tommy McGuire also tried out for the marching band, where his experience with the award-wining Sebring High band made him a shoo-in. He also attempted to join the Beta Theta Pi fraternity, which proved more difficult. His fondness for flashy clothes initially turned off some of the members, but he finally made it.

Following the lead of a number of fellow students at Georgia Tech,

McGuire also joined the Reserve Officer Training Corps (ROTC). By the spring of 1939, he had worked his way up to sergeant major of the ROTC Cadet Corps at Georgia Tech and was already looking ahead to an officer's commission—in the Air Corps. By the spring of 1939, war clouds were gathering around the world, and young men were thinking of their future. The college men who joined the ROTC had reasoned that if war came, they would rather join the armed forces as officers than be drafted as privates.

Back when Dick Bong and Tommy McGuire entered high school—that now seemed so long ago—they were largely oblivious to what was going on in the outside world, but when they went off on their own four years later, they were certainly aware that the world beyond America's borders was growing increasingly unstable. In 1938, World War II was still hypothetical, but already the villains of that imminent confrontation were up to the mischief that would drag the world into its first truly global conflict.

CHAPTER 3

A World Goes to War

IT was at about the time when Dick Bong and Tommy McGuire were making the transition from high school to college that the world began to stumble headlong toward the conflagration that would soon be called World War II. Adolf Hitler, the leader of Germany's Nazi Party, had come to power as Germany's chancellor in 1933. He soon began the covert—and later overt—steps that led to the rearmament of Germany in violation of the terms of the Treaty of Versailles, which had ended World War I. In 1936, while Bong and McGuire were sophomores, German armies occupied the German Rhineland, again in direct violation of the Treaty of Versailles. The lack of active opposition by Britain and France only served to encourage the greedy Hitler.

In early 1938, during the latter part of Bong and McGuire's senior year, Germany annexed Austria and the Sudentenland regions of Czechoslovakia, making them part of Hitler's Third Reich. Britain and France complained, and a summit conference was held in Munich. In September, as Bong and McGuire were settling in to their first few weeks of college, Hitler was in Munich promising the prime ministers of France and Britain that Germany would make no further land grabs. To avoid war, Edouard Daladier and Neville Chamberlain acquiesced.

Once again, Hitler was encouraged.

On the last day of September, as Bong was hurrying between farm and school, and as McGuire was concerning himself with pledging for Beta Theta Pi, the headlines in the papers on the newsracks in Superior and Atlanta told the story. Neville Chamberlain had flown home from Munich and had stood outside 10 Downing Street in London to tell the world that his visit to Hitler had been a resounding success.

"My good friends," Chamberlain said happily, "for the second time in our history, a British prime minister has returned from Germany bringing peace with honour. I believe it is peace for our time."

Six months later, German armies swallowed all of Czechoslovakia. The provinces of Bohemia and Moravia became a protectorate of the Third Reich, while Slovakia became a separate pro-Nazi state.

Across the globe, the warlords of the Empire of Japan (Dai Nippon Teikoku) were making land grabs of their own. Their objective as stated at the time was to bring all of East Asia under a Japanese roof in an empire that Japan's prime minister, Prince Fumimaro Konoe, benignly dubbed the Greater East Asia Coprosperity Sphere. Japan had swallowed Korea in 1910, and in 1931, Japanese armies occupied the coal-rich Chinese province of Manchuria, renamed it Manchukuo, and installed a puppet government there.

In the summer of 1937, as Bong and McGuire were getting ready for their last year in high school, Japan had begun a full-scale military offensive against China, beginning the Second Sino-Japanese War (the first was in 1894). The Japanese soon occupied China's big commercial metropolis of Shanghai and attacked Nanking (now called Nanjing), a major city of nearly six hundred thousand. After the fall of Nanking in December 1937, the Imperial Japanese Army began a two-month reign of terror that is known as the Rape of Nanking. The violence and atrocities resulted in an estimated three hundred thousand civilian deaths, and at least as many actual rapes.

Such was the world situation as Dick Bong and Tommy McGuire were on the cusp of adulthood. Midway through their high school senior year, there were sobering headlines datelined in both Europe and the Far East. A year later, things were only that much more ominous. Many people postulated that war was inevitable, but most Americans felt that the United States could avoid being drawn into the conflict, as they had with the Great War a generation earlier.

Whether or not war was inevitable, one thing was considered certain, and that was that aviation would be a key element in the execution of that conflict, both offensively and defensively. By the summer of 1939, discussions of war in Europe no longer contained the word "if." It was now "when." On August 24, 1939, Germany signed a nonaggression pact with the Soviet Union.

On September 1, 1939, eleven months after Chamberlain announced "peace for our time," Germany invaded Poland. Both Dick and Tommy were beginning their second year in college. At this point, Britain and France issued ultimatums because their mutual assistance treaties with Poland called for them. On September 3, Britain and France declared that a state of war had existed for two days.

The "when" of the start of World War II had now been answered.

Those who predicted that airpower would play a central role in the war had their prognostication come true. At the time Germany invaded Poland, Germany's Luftwaffe overall was the best-trained and best-equipped air force in the world. Their stunningly efficient and precisely coordinated air and ground offensive against Poland, known as blitzkrieg (lightning war), was the most rapid and efficient mode of military attack the world had ever seen. The use of fast-moving tanks, mobile forces, dive bombers, and paratroop units all working together as one tight, well-disciplined force stunned the world, especially the Polish defenders. Germany was able to subjugate Poland in just three weeks. The Luftwaffe played such a crucial role in this action that it surprised airpower advocates and airpower skeptics alike.

Having declared war, Britain and France did little in the way of offensive action. A lull in the action of World War II descended over Europe. Throughout the winter of 1939–1940, Allied and German troops sat and stared at one another across the heavily fortified Franco-German border. So little was happening that newspaper writers dubbed the situation the "sitzkrieg," or the "phony war." Meanwhile, in the United States, by an overwhelming margin, the American people wanted to stay out of and as far

away as possible from what the media called "Europe's war." The isolationist contingent within the United States Congress was anxious that the United
States stay out.

For a time, it seemed as though Hitler may have gotten all that he had
wanted, although many people had thought that after he absorbed Austria
in 1938 and occupied Czechoslovakia early in 1939.

Suddenly, those who had asked "What next?" received their answer. On
April 9, 1940, Germany attacked. Sitzkrieg became blitzkrieg again. German troops quickly occupied Denmark and Norway. On May 10, the Germans began a great offensive to the west that duplicated their advance on
Belgium and France in 1914, at the beginning of World War I. By May 28,
Luxembourg, Belgium, and the Netherlands had surrendered, and German
forces were pouring into France. By June 14, Germany had seized control of
Paris, having accomplished in five weeks what it had been unable to do in
four years of protracted fighting in World War I.

When France finally surrendered on June 22, Britain was left to face the
onslaught of Germany's blitzkrieg alone. Only twenty-one miles of English
Channel separated Germany's apparently invincible troops from an army
that had abandoned all of its equipment in France when it barely managed
to escape from the Germans at Dunkirk on the French coast on June 4. As
Hitler's forces prepared for a cross-Channel invasion of Britain, the English
people rallied around Prime Minister Winston Spencer Churchill, who had
taken office on May 10 telling them he had "nothing to offer but blood, toil,
tears, and sweat." He defied Hitler by informing him that his troops would
meet relentless opposition on the beaches, on the streets, and in every village. However, the Luftwaffe commander, Field Marshal Hermann Göring,
insisted that his bombers could easily subdue Britain, making the planned
sea invasion a simple walkover.

On June 18, Churchill told his constituents that the worst was yet to
come. "The Battle of France is over," he said in his address to the nation. "I
expect that the Battle of Britain is about to begin. Upon this battle depends
the survival of Christian civilization. Upon it depends our British life, and
the long continuity of our institutions and our empire. The whole fury and
might of the enemy must very soon be turned on us. Hitler knows that he
will have to break us in this island or lose the war. Let us therefore brace

ourselves to our duties, and so bear ourselves that, if the British Empire and its commonwealth last for a thousand years, men will still say, 'This was their finest hour.' "

The Battle of Britain did, indeed, come next. As it turned out, it was the first major battle in history that was fought entirely in the air.

Late in the summer, the Luftwaffe began its brutal, unremitting bombing assault on Britain's ports, factories, and cities. All that stood in the way of an easy victory were the courageous but vastly outnumbered pilots of the Royal Air Force, specifically of Fighter Command, who met the Germans like gnats attacking crows. Of these Fighter Command pilots, Churchill said, "Never, in the field of human conflict, have so many owed so much to so few."

Among those "few" were a new generation of aces. Soon the stories of men such as Sammy Allard, Alan Christopher Deere, Albert Lewis, and Robert Stanford Tuck were appearing in the papers. James Henry "Ginger" Lacey became a national hero on August 15, 1940, when he shot down a Heinkel He.111 that had bombed Buckingham Palace. Lacey and Sammy Allard went on to be the top-scoring RAF aces of 1940 with twenty-three victories each (although Allard had two shared kills), and there were seventeen Royal Air Force aces with sixteen or more victories.

Meanwhile, the Luftwaffe had a number of aces of their own, as the two best-trained air forces in the world went head to head in the Battle of Britain. Many German pilots came to the conflict with an edge in experience, having honed their skills flying with the Nationalists in the Spanish Civil War of 1936–1939, and flying against the French and Polish air forces earlier in World War II. There were fifteen Luftwaffe aces with twenty or more victories through the end of 1940. Among the notable German aces of the Battle of Britain era was Werner Mölders. Having been the highest-scoring German ace in the Spanish Civil War, he became the first to exceed Baron von Richthofen's World War I score of eighty, and the first ace to top one hundred.

Another high-profile Luftwaffe ace to emerge in 1940 was Adolf Galland, a dashing young hero with movie-star presence, jet black hair, and a pencil-thin mustache. One of the leading aces of the Battle of Britain, Galland became a wing commander, commanding Jagdgeschwader 26, known as the "Abbeville Boys" because they were based at Abbeville in the Pas de

Calais region of northwestern France, just across the Channel from Britain. This placed him in the thick of the action—he shot down two aircraft on his first day with the unit and had scored seventeen victories by August 22.

Galland was a colorful character, the kind of swaggering knight of the air whom one would expect to encounter only in the movies. He was often seen in the company of glamorous women—after all, he was only a couple of hours' drive from Paris. He served gourmet food in his officers' mess, and he liked good wine as well as fine cigars. Galland even had a cigar lighter installed in the cockpit of his Messerschmitt Bf.109.

One of the wildest tales from Abbeville folklore concerns a day when Galland was flying alone, en route to a party hosted by General Theo Oster-kamp, carrying in his fighter aircraft lobster and champagne for the party. Suddenly he was jumped by three British Spitfire fighters. Galland succeeded in outmaneuvering the attackers and shooting down all three. Coinciden-tally, the entire exchange was overheard on the two-way radio at the party. When he landed at the site of the party, the lobster and champagne were shaken but undamaged, and Galland was neither damaged nor shaken. Through the end of 1940, Galland would score fifty-two victories, half of his eventual final tally.

Despite the prowess of the Luftwaffe and its colorful aces, the RAF held Germany at bay and compelled Hitler to abandon his plans for a cross-Channel invasion. Despite the fact that the British had fewer than a thou-sand fighters to face a Luftwaffe onslaught four times as large, the Royal Air Force was able to destroy a dozen bombers for each fighter they lost. Churchill called it the Royal Air Force's "finest hour."

The Battle of Britain was a major setback in Germany's effort toward world domination, but it had not stopped Hitler's armies. Britain remained alone and isolated while the rest of the countries in Continental Europe either allied themselves with Germany, became occupied territories, or waited for a German attack. The war was far from over, but the German onslaught, which had seemed unstoppable earlier in 1940, had met its match. More than anything else, the Battle of Britain had demonstrated the profound and signif-icant role that would henceforth be played by airpower in modern warfare.

It also served to put the term "ace" back into the media lexicon, and into the minds of would-be fighter pilots—especially in the United States.

CHAPTER 4

Americans Prepare

I N the fall of 1940, as it became clear that airpower had been triumphant and decisive in the Battle of Britain, both Dick Bong and Tommy McGuire were on their way to becoming pilots. In the two years since high school, the world had changed immensely, and so, too, had the opportunities for young men who wanted to fly. First and foremost was the Civilian Pilot Training Program, which truly revolutionized pilot training in the United States on the eve of World War II.

Even before Neville Chamberlain made his naive "peace for our time" speech in September 1938, there was an arms race in Europe, with Britain and France on one side, and Germany and Italy on the other. Among the weapons with the highest priority were warplanes. In addition to building new aircraft, these nations, especially Germany, began vigorous pilot training programs.

In the United States, two days after Christmas in 1938, President Franklin Roosevelt announced the Civilian Pilot Training Program as a trial initiative under the provisions of the Civil Aeronautics Act to train pilots. The program took on the ambitious goal of providing flight instruction to twenty thousand college students annually. It was stated that the idea behind the program was to improve the state of general aviation in the United States, but the potential military implications were obvious. As it got under way in 1939, the Civilian Pilot Training Program was available at locations near only eleven American colleges, but it grew quickly to a peak of more than two thousand. The federal government underwrote the cost of a ground school course, as well as of thirty-five to fifty hours of flight instruction per pilot trainee.

A year and a half later, as sitzkrieg turned to blitzkrieg, Roosevelt matched his call for pilots with a call for airplanes. As the German armies swallowed Norway, Denmark, Luxembourg, Belgium, and the Netherlands and swarmed into France, the American people still wanted to stay out of and as far away as possible from "Europe's war." However, many were now starting to worry, and there was a growing realization that this might not be possible.

On May 16, 1940, two days after the Netherlands government had fled in disarray, Hitler's fast-moving blitzkrieg was on the move, and France was teetering on the brink of collapse. On this same day, President Roosevelt went before Congress and raised the ante on military aircraft. Sixteen months earlier, he had floated a trial balloon for ten thousand aircraft, and then asked for just three thousand. Now he came right out and proposed that Congress authorize funding for fifty thousand!

It is not known how Roosevelt arrived at this figure, as it was not then an official War Department proposal. In his memoirs, Secretary of State Cordell Hull took credit for proposing a huge increase in the number of military aircraft on the order books, claiming that he told the president to "aim high" even if it meant increasing American aircraft industry production to more units per month than it had been turning out in a year in the 1930s.

Before the war, such a proposal would have been laughed off as fantasy. In July 1940, with the German armies in control of most of Western Europe, and the first shots in the Battle of Britain being fired, the proposal was taken seriously. Congress decided to make sure that the United States was in a position to defend itself. "National Defense" was the phrase of the moment. It is hard to find a newspaper or print advertising from the era that does not mention the phrase. After what was happening in Europe, National Defense was suddenly considered serious business.

Approving Roosevelt's request, Congress took a page from Rome's Publius Flavius Vegetius Renatus, who wrote in the fourth century, "Let him who desires peace prepare for war."

The American aircraft industry undertook an unprecedented expansion, as had pilot training, to an extent that would have been unthinkable a few years earlier. In May 1940, President Roosevelt had startled the world by calling for 50,000 military aircraft. Between July 1940 and August 1945, the American aircraft industry would deliver 295,959.

By the summer of 1940, with Hitler on the rampage, twenty-twenty hindsight tells us that Roosevelt's prediction was correct, that war between the United States and the Axis (Germany, Japan, and Italy) was inevitable. However, at the time there was, as there has often been during America's wars, an antiwar element within American public opinion who wanted the country to remain uninvolved. In 1939 and 1940, the antiwar movement was called isolationism; their position was to keep America isolated from Europe's war at all costs.

The most vocal of the isolationist groups was America First, formed in September 1940. Most notable among the spokesmen for America First was a boyhood hero of Dick Bong, Tommy McGuire, and countless thousands of American boys their age—Charles Augustus Lindbergh.

The Lone Eagle had come about his isolationism by a circuitous route. The five years after his triumphant flight had been the best he could have hoped for. He married a diplomat's beautiful daughter, Anne Morrow, who loved to fly almost as much as he did. Together they traveled the world by air, sharing adventures that are the stuff of dreams. In 1930 they settled down and had a son, Charles Lindbergh, Jr. Then, in March 1932, their world collapsed. Young Charles was kidnapped and later found murdered in what was known for decades as the "Crime of the Century." The media circus that swirled around the affair was a nightmare for Charles and Anne, and they moved abroad to escape.

Charles Lindbergh visited Germany several times, where he was greatly impressed by German aircraft technology. After his 1938 visit to Germany, in which he met key industry leaders and actually took the controls of the Messerschmitt Bf.109 fighter, Lindbergh reported his technical findings to the U.S. Army Air Corps. Behind the scenes, his report would aid the United

States in national defense, but publicly Lindbergh remained an outspoken opponent of the United States becoming involved in fighting the German war machine. This viewpoint, combined with other of Lindbergh's inopportune and naive remarks, gave many Americans the impression that Lindbergh harbored a sympathy for Nazi political thought.

Having joined America First in 1940, Lindbergh testified before Congress in early 1941, continuing to insist that the United States remain isolated. Meanwhile, the tide of public opinion was rising against isolationism. The majority of the young men who idolized Lindbergh when they were boys broke step with him politically, though the yearning to fly that he had instilled in the boys survived into manhood for many.

Dick Bong had joined the Civilian Pilot Training Program, and like so many young men in 1940, he learned to fly in one of the thousands of bright yellow Piper Cubs that were cropping up at airfields all over the United States. He made his first flight on his twentieth birthday, September 24, 1940.

Tommy McGuire's career as a pilot began two months later, when he signed up for flying lessons at an airport near Atlanta during the last week of November—the week after the Saturday when the University of Florida Gators beat the Georgia Tech Yellowjackets, sixteen to seven. Both Tommy and his old friend Paul Gustat played in the band that day—but on opposite sides. Gustat was a Gator.

As he was working through his flying lessons and his schoolwork at Georgia Tech that winter, McGuire almost took a turn that might have had him flying with the RAF rather than the U.S. Army Air Corps. In the wake of the Battle of Britain, the RAF started forming the first of three "Eagle Squadrons," in which the pilots would be Americans. Like the French Air Force's Lafayette Escadrille in World War I, these units would have Americans flying under a foreign flag in a war that the United States was not yet a belligerent. In February 1941, when the first Eagle Squadron went into action, McGuire read about it in an Atlanta paper and sent to the British consulate for an application. He was turned down. The RAF wrote back that they needed *experienced* pilots.

By the spring of 1941, both Tommy McGuire and Dick Bong—along with thousands of other like-minded young college juniors—had no college degree, but they now did have the requisite number of college credits to get into Air Corps flight school and come out an officer. Tommy McGuire quit Georgia Tech with neither his degree nor the ROTC commission for which he had worked for three years—but he had what he wanted most, a chance to fly, and soon.

After spending a month in New Jersey working for his father at his Packard dealership, McGuire reported to MacDill Army Air Field near Tampa on July 12. He would remain in Florida for just a few days. At the time, the three-month-old MacDill was scheduled to be used not as a training facility but as an air defense base, running antisubmarine patrols off the Florida coastline. For flight training, McGuire and the other fresh new cadets who reported that morning would be sent to bases in Texas.

Dick Bong had enlisted as an aviation cadet in January 1941, and he reported for duty in Wausau, Wisconsin, on May 29. From there, he was ordered to report to California for primary flight training.

To accommodate the large influx of new pilots, the Air Corps then contracted with civilian schools to provide the first sixty hours of flight time for army aviation cadets. Large numbers of these schools were in California, Texas, and the Southwest, where the flying weather was good or excellent most of the year. Both McGuire and Bong began their military careers at such schools.

McGuire was sent to Corsicana Field in Navarro County, Texas, about sixty miles from Dallas. The school at Corsicana was operated by Air Activities, Inc., recently acquired by a partnership of colorful Texas aviation entrepreneurs who included Edward "Doc" Booth, E. D. Criddle, J. O. Womack, and B. W. Woolley. Booth was a West Point graduate who had taken his own Army flight training at Brooks Field and Kelly Field, two of the Air Corps training facilities on the outskirts of San Antonio.

Corsicana Field was typical of the facilities built practically overnight under the heading of "National Defense." In Corsicana's case, the entire base was constructed in forty-five days, opening its doors to its first class of cadets on March 19, 1941.

Bong was one of the cadets who poured into the vast archipelago of training facilities springing to life in California's vast Central Valley. In his case, he arrived at Rankin Aeronautical Academy near Tulare late on June 2. Like Corsicana, it was the brainchild of an aviation entrepreneur, having been started in December 1940 by John Gilbert "Tex" Rankin, one of Hollywood's top aerobatic pilots and the president of the Motion Picture Pilots Association. Also known as Tulare Primary Flying School, Rankin had five auxiliary airfields within a twelve-mile radius, three of which are still functioning general aviation airports. Rankin went on to train more than 10,450 cadets over a period of fifty-four months.

In the meantime, the rapidly growing U.S. Army Air Corps had been reorganized as an autonomous operational organization within the U.S. Army. On June 20, 1941, as part of an army-wide reorganization, the chief of staff, General George C. Marshall, ordered the creation of the U.S. Army Air Forces (USAAF), the first step toward the eventual creation of the independent U.S. Air Force (which finally occurred in 1947).

Over the previous few years, the Air Corps had grown tremendously, and autonomy for America's air arm was long overdue. In 1939, on the eve of World War II, the Air Corps had 23,455 personnel, double the number from a decade earlier, but by the time the service became the USAAF, it had 152,125 people in its uniform. Within a year, that figure would quintuple. Training a sizable number of these people as pilots called for the sort of maximum effort that made countless operations such as Tulare and Corsicana so vital to the war effort.

Going to California was the farthest that Dick Bong had ever been from home. The family had made a travel-trailer trip to Yellowstone National Park in 1936 after his sophomore year in high school, but aside from that, he had been no farther from Poplar than a couple of trips to Milwaukee. On the train trip west, he saw both Chicago and Los Angeles. He found the bright lights of Chicago quite captivating, observing that the Windy City seemed more light at night than in the daytime. Tulare, however, was farm country, and aside from being a good deal flatter than northern Wisconsin, it was a familiar environment.

Though the schools were civilian organizations, the aviation cadets wore military uniforms, and military discipline applied. As with the CCC camps of the 1930s, the routine was like that of an armed forces boot camp, with reveille announcing the dawn, taps calling for lights out, and with marching and saluting marking the time in between. Each cadet paid nearly a third of his monthly flight pay in room and board.

Though many new cadets, including Dick Bong, already had a private pilot's license (thanks to the Civilian Pilot Training Program), they were referred to by upperclassmen as "dodos," implying that they were flightless birds. The upperclassmen insisted on being called "sir," even though they were not commissioned officers.

Primary flight training would take ten weeks, after which the dodos may or may not progress to advanced training and beyond. The whole process took thirty weeks. Primary training was followed by basic training, and finally advanced training. Any dodos who washed out at any point remained dodos and were sent to the infantry or wherever the U.S. Army needed them. Those who made it through the thirty-week course became second lieutenants—and pilots. They might wind up as bomber pilots or they might become fighter pilots. Many of the best would remain behind as instructors.

The aviation cadets were organized into classes based on the month when they were scheduled to become full-fledged pilots. Bong was in Class 42A, because if all went according to plan, he'd graduate in January 1942. McGuire, who arrived in Corsicana a month after Bong reached California, was in Class 42B, scheduled for February.

In addition to standing at attention and paying proper respect to upperclassmen, the daily routine for the cadets consisted of flight time with an instructor in the morning, and ground school in the heat of the afternoon. Ground school included everything from navigation to meteorology and aeronautical engineering. All of the dodos who thought they'd seen the last of algebra when they graduated from high school had a rude awakening. Calisthenics marked the beginning and the end of the dodo's day.

As the rays of blistering summer sun grew more intense and the temperatures in Texas and California moved past ninety degrees, Dick Bong felt his nose begin to redden and peel. Tommy McGuire's hay fever exploded as he stood and marched on Corsicana's grass field, and he battled to keep from snuffling and sneezing during inspection.

A variety of primary trainers were in use by the USAAF and its contractors during World War II. Bong flew a Stearman Kaydett. These aircraft were built by Boeing in Wichita, Kansas, and were designated as PT-13 when powered by a Lycoming engine, and as PT-17 when equipped by a Continental engine. McGuire, meanwhile, began his USAAF career in the cockpit of a Fairchild Cornell. Built by Fairchild in Hagerstown, Maryland, and by other manufacturers under license, the Lycoming engine version was designated as PT-19 and the Continental version was the PT-23. Both aircraft had an open cockpit, and were larger and heavier than the enclosed-cockpit Piper Cub to which Bong and McGuire were accustomed. The engines of the trainers also were a good deal more powerful, delivering about 175 to 220 horsepower, compared to 40 to 65 horsepower for the various engine types used in the Cub.

Gradually the law of natural selection took over and the respective classes of dodos were reduced in number. Classes of about sixty declined by more than 20 percent by the time it came for the cadets to make their first solo flight. The luckier ones dropped out, while the unlucky ones literally crashed and burned. This was a sobering sight for the remaining cadets, underscoring the seriousness of their endeavor.

Dick Bong soloed in his Stearman on June 25, and Tommy McGuire followed in his Cornell on August 5. This was only just the beginning. Before their ten weeks of primary training, they would log more time alone in the open cockpit than with an instructor.

By the time they soloed, they were no longer dodos, but upperclassmen at last. Dick Bong wrote home that it was hard to get used to having the new dodos calling *him* sir. After a few weeks of relishing their promotion to a higher caste, however, it was time to move on to the next phase of their training. With their first ten weeks in the hands of contractors, they would now be under the roof of the USAAF at true military airfields. After primary training now came basic training, the term used in the rest of the Army to denote the entry level of gruntdom. It was like reaching up to touch bottom. As they arrived at their new locations for basic training, they discovered that once gain they were dodos.

Tommy McGuire's new home was Randolph Army Airfield on the edge of San Antonio, Texas. The sprawling, two-thousand-acre base had been constructed in 1930 as the center of flight training for the Air Corps. Then known as the "West Point of the Air," Randolph had (and still has), as its centerpiece, the towering Spanish Revival–style base headquarters that has always deserved its nickname "Taj Mahal."

As McGuire basked in the shadow of the Taj Mahal, Dick Bong had moved about seventy-five air miles due south, to the USAAF's Gardner Army Airfield near Taft, in the California oil country. There was talk of his class going to Texas, but the plethora of new fields cropping up in the Central Valley made that unnecessary. Gardner, which had been open for just a few months, was in the dusty, godforsaken middle of nowhere, but it would evolve into one of the foremost flight training centers in the USAAF. Football star Tom Harmon trained here, as did Chuck Yeager and Richard Miller of Jimmy Doolittle's Tokyo raiders. So, too, did Dick Bong. Back in 1941, though, they were all still dodos.

Having passed his sixty-hour check flight at Rankin Field on August 11, Cadet Bong arrived at Gardner Field on August 20 after a quick weekend trip to Los Angeles with Charles Mohler, a fellow cadet from Southern California who also was bound for Gardner. Tommy McGuire's life as a basic training dodo began at the end of September, as he and a carload of fellow air cadets arrived in San Antonio from Corsicana.

The training would now be in trainers that were larger and more sophisticated than the Stearmans and Fairchilds that Bong and McGuire had been flying during primary training. Basic training went a step beyond learning to loop and roll. Now the cadets were learning air-to-ground and air-to-air radio communications, as well as the intricacies of the Hamilton Standard variable-pitch propeller.

For McGuire, the new aircraft was the North American Aviation BT-9 Yale, and for Bong, it was the Vultee BT-13 Valiant. Both were enclosed-cockpit monoplanes with engines that delivered more than twice the horsepower of the primary trainers. The BT-13, with its tendency to shiver and shake and rattle its canopy as it slowed to stall speed, led to the pilots referring to it as the "Vultee Vibrator."

Bong made his first solo flight in the Vibrator on September 3 and was beginning solo instrument flying at night by the end of the month. In October came long-distance flights up and down the Central Valley. In the meantime, he had his first airplane accident, on September 22. Fortunately, it was a minor one. He clipped another plane while taxiing in his Vibrator, but hit the brakes in time to avoid major damage—or a serious reprimand.

When Bong and the primary air cadets had been at Rankin Field, off-base entertainment included going into Tulare for fried chicken, or attending one of the dances local people staged for the boys in uniform. Dick made a couple of trips to nearby Sequoia National Park, but in the Central Valley, distances are long.

At Gardner Field, however, the cadets were only about 120 tantalizing miles from Los Angeles and Hollywood nightlife. A weekend pass often took carloads of air cadets to venues such as the famous Brown Derby, near the corner of Hollywood and Vine. Meanwhile, the proximity to Los Angeles often brought big-name entertainers to Taft. The Tommy Dorsey and Duke Ellington bands played at the base, as did comedians such as Bob Hope.

Dick Bong's trips south often took him to visit relatives that his family had not seen in years, including his Great-Aunt Lena in Los Angeles and his Aunt Minnie in Anaheim. Usually they traveled straight south on U.S. Highway 99, but in late August, Dick and Charles Mohler crossed over the Coast Range to Santa Barbara and drove to Los Angeles on U.S. Highway 101. Dick Bong saw the Pacific Ocean for the first time, and wrote home that he was unimpressed. The Pacific reminded him of Lake Superior.

Among his other off-base activities while in basic training, Bong found time to join a vocal quartet, singing light classics as a tenor. The group actually made a number of radio appearances, singing live on stations from Maricopa to Bakersfield.

On October 27, Dick Bong left Gardner Field for the last time, having passed basic training, and decided to surprise his family with a home visit. Making his first airline trip, he arrived late the next evening after everyone had gone to bed. He had hoped to be able to rent a Piper Cub while he was home and take some of the younger kids for a ride, but bad weather and poor visibility kept him grounded for the one day he was in Poplar.

A week later, he had all the good flying weather possible as he arrived at Luke Army Airfield, a 1,440-acre training base in Phoenix, Arizona, that the USAAF had opened just five months earlier.

Indeed, the ninety-degree weather and clear skies over Phoenix were welcome after his grueling trip from Wisconsin. Traveling through the night, he reached Minneapolis at dawn on October 30, hoping to fly from there to Los Angeles, because he had to return to Gardner Field to travel to Luke with the rest of his class. However, when the DC-3 from Minneapolis reached

Sioux City, he found the airline flights grounded because of weather. He took a train to Omaha, waited until the wee hours of November 1, then boarded a train for Cheyenne. Finding the airport there closed because of weather, he took a train to Salt Lake City, where he finally got a flight to Los Angeles on United Air Lines on Sunday afternoon. He reached Gardner late that night, then boarded a bus to Phoenix—by way of Los Angeles again—where he finally arrived at 6:30 A.M. on November 4.

As much as he may have yearned to tramp through the snowbanks in the Wisconsin woods looking for whitetail deer, Dick enjoyed the warm weather and the clear skies in Arizona. He did see some snow, but only in the mountains over which he flew on training missions.

Four days after reporting to Luke, Dick Bong was in the cockpit of a North American Aviation AT-6 Texan advanced trainer. With its high-performance 550-horsepower Pratt & Whitney Wasp radial engine, the Texan was by far the hottest aircraft he had yet had the privilege of handling. It had a top speed of more than two hundred miles per hour, nearly twice that of the Stearman he had been flying just five months earlier.

Flying the Texan also offered more in terms of high-altitude training—and it had a gun, a single, .50-caliber machine gun. Though he wrote home that he missed hunting season, Bong would soon have an opportunity for target practice unlike anything he had experienced before.

As 1941 drew to a close, Dick Bong could reflect on the myriad of new experiences that had passed his way during the year. He would soon discover that these would pale in comparison to what the young air cadets and their countrymen were about to experience.

CHAPTER 5

Young Men and War

W ITH virtually no exceptions, no American who was alive and old enough on the morning of Sunday, December 7, 1941, did not remember that day for the rest of his or her life. For the United States, it was unquestionably the single most important turning point of the twentieth century. Soon isolationism would evaporate and the United States would be transformed.

Sunday morning had dawned warm and pleasant in Texas, where Tommy McGuire was winding up his basic flight training, and it had dawned warm and pleasant in Arizona, where Dick Bong was a month into advanced training.

Sunday morning also dawned warm and pleasant in the Hawaiian Islands. As the people of Honolulu went about their business, listening to the radio, getting ready for church, or playing ball, six aircraft carriers of an Imperial Japanese Navy task force stood about two hundred miles to the north-northwest. Aboard the *Akagi, Hiryu, Kaga, Shokaku, Soryu,* and *Zuikaku,* armorers scrambled to load ordnance aboard an armada of Aichi Type 99 dive bombers and Nakajima Type 97 torpedo bombers. Crewmen and pilots of these attack aircraft, as well as of the Mitsubishi A6M "Zero" fighters that would escort the bombers, received their final briefings and climbed aboard. The carriers, escorted by two battleships, three cruisers, nine destroyers, and three fleet submarines, had departed from Japan's Kuril Islands on November 26 and had made their way to within striking distance of the big American naval base at Pearl Harbor, on the western edge of Honolulu.

By this time, Germany had been at war for more than two years, and Imperial Japan had been officially allied with the Nazi regime for more than a year. On September 27, 1940, three days after Dick Bong made his first flight in a Piper Cub on his twentieth birthday, Adolf Hitler celebrated his occupation or control of most of Continental Western Europe by signing the Tripartite Pact with Fascist Italy and Imperial Japan, creating what came to be known as the Rome-Berlin-Tokyo Axis. Together, they imagined that they would conquer and/or control most of the world.

Just as Hitler had done in Europe in 1940, Japan now hoped to do in the Far East. Emperor Hirohito and his military warlords had designs on all of Southeast Asia, from the Philippines through Malaya to the Netherlands East Indies (now Indonesia) and even Australia. First, however, they felt they must deal a decisive blow to American naval power in the Pacific.

By the time the clocks in Honolulu registered 7:00 A.M., it was late morning on the mainland, where Tommy McGuire and Dick Bong went about their business, and 183 Japanese aircraft were airborne. The only people on the ground in Hawaii who knew this were a pair of U.S. Army radar technicians at Opana, north of Pearl Harbor. They weren't sure what the blips on their radar scopes represented. Were they American planes inbound from the West Coast, or something else? Fifteen minutes later, word of the incoming aircraft had reached the duty office of the 14th Naval District, where it was decoded and passed along to Rear Admiral Husband E. Kimmel, commander of American naval forces in Hawaii. Before Kimmel did anything— if he would have done anything anyhow—the snarl of Mitsubishi Kensei and Nakajima Sakae radial aircraft engines was being heard over the sugarcane fields of Oahu's northern shore.

At 7:53 A.M., the first bombs fell on the warships anchored near Ford Island within Pearl Harbor. The sailors aboard the ships anchored on "Battleship Row" near Ford Island were taken completely by surprise. In quick succession, torpedo bombers quickly scored hits on the battleships USS *Oklahoma*, USS *Utah*, USS *California*, USS *Arizona*, and other vessels. A bomb then penetrated the deck of the *Arizona*, exploding within her forward magazine with devastating results. The bombers kept up their attacks on the ships, as well as USAAF aircraft at nearby airfields.

Suddenly the United States was at war, and just as abruptly, the USAAF gave the nation heroes. A pair of 47th Pursuit Squadron fighter pilots were returning to their base at Wheeler Field north of Pearl Harbor after a Saturday night poker game—that had lasted into the early hours of Sunday—when they heard the first shots of the wake-up call that brought America into World War II. Wheeler was under attack, so George Welch and Ken Taylor contacted the Haleiwa auxiliary airfield and asked that two Curtiss P-40B Warhawk fighters be made available, and drove as fast as possible to get into them. It was like a scene out of a movie, and in fact the story has been adapted for several films. The two pilots each made two sorties that morning, downing six Japanese aircraft between them. George Welch would add to his score to become an ace, with sixteen total victories.

As Welch and Taylor were heroically meeting the enemy, Dick Bong was wondering whether he would be getting a furlough so he could go home for Christmas. It was soon obvious that this would be no ordinary Christmas. Most if not all leaves would be canceled. He sat down to write his parents, using that dry, ironic tone that was his trademark. He began, "Well, it seems from the radio this afternoon that we are having a little trouble with Japan."

Bong's class began gunnery training the next day. As the news of the exploits of Welch and Taylor reached the mainland, that gunnery training had to have taken on a whole new meaning. One of Bong's gunnery instructors at Luke that fall was an officer named Barry Goldwater. The future senator from Arizona and 1964 presidential candidate said of him many years later that Bong "was a very bright student. But the most important thing came from a P-38 check pilot who said Bong was the finest natural pilot he ever met. There was no way he could keep Bong from not getting on his tail, even though he was flying an AT-6, a very slow airplane."

As news of Pearl Harbor reached Texas, it was nearing the noon hour.

Tommy McGuire was at the Cadet Club at the Gunter Hotel in San Antonio, where cadets went to hang out, listen to music, and chat up the local girls who went there to meet eligible young men. The Cadet Club was an alternative for the cadets, who could frequent neither the enlisted men's nor the officers' clubs on the USAAF bases around San Antonio. McGuire was there, talking with some friends, when someone walked in, shut down the jukebox, and announced that all military personnel were required to immediately report to their bases.

This, on a Sunday? The men didn't know what was happening until they heard about Pearl Harbor on the car radio as they were headed back to Randolph Field. For some, it was the first time they had ever heard about a place called Pearl Harbor.

If Sunday, December 7, marked a change of immense consequence for the United States, then Thursday, December 11, marked a change of immense consequence for Tommy McGuire. After four days of heightened urgency in their training, McGuire and several of his pals decided they deserved a night on the town. This time they went to the Tower, another nightclub that catered to service personnel unable to visit the officers' clubs. One of Tommy's friends was meeting a young lady named Sidney Bowers, whom he knew from a previous club visit. Sidney was bringing a friend, who she thought might like to meet Tommy.

Sidney's friend was named Marilynn Giesler. Her nickname, "Pudgy," was deliberately paradoxical. Pudgy was as thin as Tommy McGuire. Pudgy was a student at Incarnate Word College (now Incarnate Word University), which was run by the Sisters of Charity of the Incarnate Word, an order founded in 1869 by Claude Marie Dubuis, then the bishop of Texas. According to McGuire's biographer Charles Martin, Marilynn was the playful type of Catholic schoolgirl who once climbed a tree to snoop on the school's indoor swimming pool to see what type of swimsuits the nuns wore.

Whether or not either of them thought in terms of "love at first sight," they definitely made an impression on each other that night. Tommy found Marilynn attractive, and she found him to be an especially skilled dancer. They agreed that they might like to see each other again, but in the meantime, Tommy's basic training was completed and it was time for him to move on.

Dick Bong had been reassigned to another state for his advanced training, but fortunately for Tommy McGuire's budding romance, he was transferred across town. His new home was at Kelly Army Airfield, which, like Randolph, was one of several air bases ringing San Antonio. If the city were a clock face, Randolph would be at two o'clock, Kelly at eight o'clock.

As with Dick Bong, Tommy McGuire's new steed was the North American Aviation AT-6 Texan, which he found very much to his liking after the sluggish primary and basic trainers.

Part of advanced training was formation flying, and it was here that McGuire had his first accident. As with Bong's first accident, he was fortunate that it happened on the ground. As McGuire touched down on Kelly's turf runway, his right wheel hit a soft spot and the Texan veered right. McGuire kicked the left pedal hard to straighten out his trajectory, but he overcompensated and the plane turned hard to the left. It kept turning and McGuire found himself ground-looping into airplanes landing behind him.

He was certain that he was going to hit another Texan. The worst-case scenario, a head-on collision, would have destroyed more than just the two airplanes but also the next one or two in the landing pattern. Amazingly, the Texans coming in after him missed his aircraft, and the only thing injured was McGuire's pride.

Though Christmas leaves were canceled for everyone as the whole armed forces geared up to fight World War II, the cadets did get one day off for Christmas and another for New Year's.

Tommy had dated Marilynn Giesler a few times since December 11, but she was seeing other guys. They weren't going steady yet, but both sensed that it was heading that way. They went to dinner together on New Year's Day and had a few nightclub dates in the days that followed. It wasn't until his advanced training started to wind down at the end of January 1942 that they really became a couple.

In Arizona, Dick Bong finished his advanced training requirements on New Year's Eve with more than two hundred hours of military flight time in his logbook. For him, there would be no celebrating on New Year's Eve because, unlike Kelly, Luke was in "blackout," so nobody could leave the post until noon on January 2.

The graduation date for Class 42A had been set for January 9, and he was trying to help find accommodations at an auto court for his parents, who were planning to drive down to Luke Field from Wisconsin to watch him receive his gold second lieutenant's bars—and his silver pilot's wings. Each cadet was allowed only one guest pass, but he managed to get a second one from a fellow cadet from Illinois who would have nobody coming to see him.

Though it was not official until January 16, Lieutenant Bong already had his next assignment. The Advanced Flying School's commandant, Lieutenant Colonel Ennis Whitehead—later a combat commander in the Pacific Theater—had decided to keep him at Luke as an instructor.

"He made the best score in the rather limited gunnery training which we conducted on ground targets and on towed targets with AT-6 advanced trainers carrying one caliber-30 machine gun mounted in each wing," Whitehead wrote of his decision to keep the skilled marksman from Wisconsin. "Bong could simply fly an AT-6 better than his contemporaries and for that reason made a much better score on tow targets. He was good enough so that we kept him as an instructor for several months. He was a good one."

At the time, Bong resented the assignment. As he watched his 42A classmates headed out to assignments in combat squadrons bound for action against America's enemies, he wanted to be among them. It wasn't until much later that he realized the best way to sharpen your skills as a good pilot is to try to teach someone else to be a good pilot.

Tommy McGuire got his warrior's wish. He was going to be a fighter pilot. On February 6, 1942, he received his gold bars and an assignment to the 50th Pursuit Group at Key Army Airfield near Meridian, Mississippi. He spent his last evening in San Antonio with Marilynn Giesler. They wiled away the hours after dinner dancing at a couple of the clubs around town, including the Tower, on whose dance floor they had danced their first dance nearly two months before.

As Lieutenant McGuire danced his last dance with Pudgy that night, and as Lieutenant Bong prepared to lead a fresh-faced class of dodos into the Arizona skies, the war for which they were preparing was going quite badly for their side.

Even as British prime minister Winston Churchill was visiting President Roosevelt in Washington, D.C., at Christmastime, his armies in North

Africa were being pushed back toward the Suez Canal by Germany's master-ful General (later Field Marshal) Erwin Rommel. Though Hitler's legions had been halted at the gates of Moscow in December, most analysts consid-ered the defeat of the Soviet Union to be just around the corner.

The biggest Allied defeats, however, were coming in the Far East. On the same day that they bombed Pearl Harbor, Imperial Japan attacked in Southeast Asia and the Philippines. By Christmas they had defeated the Brit-ish and captured Hong Kong. On the day after New Year's, as Dick Bong was finding his mom and dad at an auto court in Glendale, Arizona, Manila was surrendered to General Masaharu Homma's Imperial Japanese Army forces. By the time that Tommy and Marilynn danced their last dance at the Tower, Malaya had been swallowed by the Imperial Japanese Army, and the American and Filipino defenders of Bataan were being slowly beaten down. Within days, on February 15, the British would surrender Singapore, mark-ing their biggest defeat yet in World War II.

As Imperial Japan had joined the Axis in September 1940, its military leaders were envious of what Hitler had done in having swallowed most of Western Europe in a few months in the spring of 1940. Now, barely two months into 1942, they had succeeded in emulating him by conquering vir-tually all of Southeast Asia, from the Philippines through Malaya to the Netherlands East Indies.

On the island of Borneo, then mostly part of the oil-rich corner of the Netherlands' overseas empire, the Japanese took possession of the large Royal Dutch Shell refinery complex at Balikpapan. This would be an impor-tant source of petroleum products—and a huge source of aviation fuel—for Japanese forces. As such, Balikpapan would later figure prominently in the story of the air war in the region.

Meanwhile, Thailand had become an ally and supplicant of Japan, and the Imperial forces were beginning to close in on Australia. In February 1942, as General Tomoyuki Yamashita was accepting the humiliating Brit-ish surrender of Singapore, the Japanese under Admiral Shigeyoshi Inoue and General Horii Tomitaro also had captured the port of Rabaul on the island of New Britain (which was part of the Australian Territory of New Guinea) from Australian forces. The Japanese would quickly turn it into the principal forward operating base in the South Pacific for their army, navy, and the air arms of both services.

Once they had been oblivious to world events. Now the young lieutenants throughout the United States followed them with much concern. Once the stories behind the headlines were someone else's problems. Now the young men realized that very soon, nothing, not even the headlines, would stand between them and the Axis forces.

CHAPTER 6

The Daring Young Lieutenants and Their Flying Machines

VOWING never to forget Pudgy, Lieutenant McGuire headed for Mississippi and Key Field to become a fighter pilot. Now East Mississippi Meridian Regional Airport, Key Field was named for Al and Fred Key, a pair of amazing, if now forgotten, aviation pioneers. These barnstorming brothers had figured out a practical method for refueling aircraft in flight, and in 1935 they had succeeded in keeping an aircraft aloft for an incredible twenty-seven days. Their aircraft endurance record has never been beaten.

By 1942, the Key brothers were USAAF officers and bomber pilots headed overseas to distinguished wartime careers. The airfield that bore their name, meanwhile, was one of the places where the USAAF was turning its newly minted second lieutenants into knights of the air.

In was here that Tommy McGuire would get his first taste of a real warplane, a Curtiss P-40E Warhawk, a newer variant of the type that George Welch and Ken Taylor had used in the skies over Pearl Harbor. The Warhawk was the standard front-line fighter in the USAAF at the time. In fact, from 1940 to 1942, more P-40s were produced in the United States than all other fighter types combined.

In May 1941, Curtiss had introduced the P-40E variant, of which more than 2,000 were built. It was powered by an Allison 1,150-horsepower, liquid-cooled V-1710-39 engine that gave it a top speed of 354 miles per hour. It had a service ceiling of 29,000 feet and a range of more than 700 miles. The AT-6 in which McGuire and Bong had taken gunnery training had a single machine gun, but the Warhawk was armed with six wing-mounted .50-caliber machine guns. In the weeks after Pearl Harbor, five outnumbered Warhawk squadrons, most of them equipped with P-40Es, faced the Japanese in the Philippines. It was here that Lieutenant Boyd "Buzz" Wagner had become the first USAAF ace of World War II.

The 50th Pursuit Group to which McGuire was assigned was activated in January 1941 at Selfridge Field in Michigan and moved to Key Field ten months later. Within it were the 81st and 313th Pursuit squadrons, and McGuire was assigned to the latter. The group formed part of the USAAF Fighter Command School, which was based in Florida at Orlando Air Base, the former Orlando Municipal Airport, which had been commandeered two years earlier as an Air Corps base. Shortly after he arrived in Mississippi, McGuire and the 313th got orders to pack their bags and move on to Orlando, where they would be schooled in fighter tactics.

As soon as he arrived in Orlando in late March 1942, McGuire began a grueling training schedule with the 313th. He flew every day, without letup, for three weeks straight. A big part of training was now mock aerial combat, and the Orlando pilots dueled with other USAAF pilots from MacDill Field in the skies over Tampa Bay and the Gulf of Mexico.

Despite the hectic pace, Tommy was pleased to be back in Florida, and only about seventy miles north of Sebring, so he and his mother could trade visits. She was pleased by how handsome her son looked in an officer's uniform, especially with that thin, Errol Flynn mustache that Lieutenant McGuire was starting to grow. They spent more time together than they had since Tommy had gone away to Georgia Tech. They knew it would be short-lived, though, because Tommy was scheduled to be transferred again, to a combat assignment, in early May.

Their renewed relationship remained congenial until the last—until the night when Polly threw a surprise going-away party for him at the hotel in Sebring where she was now living. She showed up very late and very drunk. He packed his bag and headed back to Orlando in disgust.

As Tommy McGuire was learning fighter tactics in a P-40E over Tampa Bay, Dick Bong was getting a taste for the Warhawk's older sibling in the skies over the Grand Canyon State—and the Grand Canyon itself. By the end of February, the AT-6s and other training aircraft at Luke had been augmented by a few Curtiss P-36 Hawk fighters. Older and less capable than the Warhawks, the Hawks were no longer useful to the USAAF in a fighter role but were nonetheless faster and more powerful aircraft than AT-6 Texans. Bong found this to his liking. Throughout the past year, he had been introduced to one aircraft after another, each one incrementally mightier than the last. He liked this. He liked it a lot.

As for the Grand Canyon, he made his first flight over this wonder of the world in an AT-6 on March 4. With his knack for wry understatement, he wrote his mother that it "certainly is a big hole in the ground." He also was amazed at the size of that "big hole" and that he had enough room to loop the Texan and still be completely beneath the 6,860-foot elevation of the rim.

Bong also made his "Hollywood debut" while flying at Luke Field in March and April. Twentieth Century-Fox came to the base to film scenes for *Thunder Birds*, a Technicolor picture about, of all things, USAAF flight training. Directed by Oscar winner William Wellman, it starred John Sutton and Preston Foster, with sultry Hollywood goddess Gene Tierney as their mutual interest in a love triangle. Today, fans squinting at the DVD edition can look for Bong as the pilot of the AT-6s numbered 231 in the mass flyover scene, and 305 in other scenes. He was paid fifty dollars as an extra, which was equal to about a third of his monthly salary.

In his "regular job," movie star Bong was putting in long hours. He flew 32 in the last week of March alone, bringing his aggregate total to 460. During April, his class advanced to longer, cross-country trips, including triangular hops with stops in places such as Albuquerque, Amarillo, and Wichita.

On the first of May, Dick Bong finally received the news that he had been waiting for since January—a transfer to a tactical squadron. His new assignment was to Hamilton Army Air Field in California's Marin County, just across the Golden Gate Bridge from San Francisco. He drove west to Anaheim the next day, and from there he traveled north on U.S. Highway 99 through the Central Valley, in whose skies he had flown during his primary and basic training. It had to have seemed like ages since he had been there.

In Anaheim, Dick tried to look up his relatives, but his Aunt Lena had passed away two weeks earlier, and his Aunt Minnie was out of town. After a quick detour into Yosemite National Park, he was at the Roosevelt Hotel in San Francisco on May 5, and reporting for duty at Hamilton Field the next day.

Unlike the fields where the young lieutenants had been based so far, which were mainly less than two years old, Hamilton had been a military airfield since 1920. It had long been an Air Corps bomber base, but fighter units were now stationed there to aid in the air defense of San Francisco and Bay Area cities. One of the latter outfits was the 14th Fighter Group, containing three fighter squadrons: the 48th, 49th, and 50th. Dick Bong was assigned to the 49th, not to be confused with the 49th Fighter *Group*, with which he would later serve in the Pacific.

The fact that Hamilton Field was two decades old meant that its facilities and its quarters had been built with solid permanence rather than the hurried construction of the other bases that Dick Bong had known. The basketball and handball courts gave him something to write home about, as did the base's six bowling alleys. Bong had become quite a bowler in his spare time, and once he had bowled a score of 191 at a bowling alley in Phoenix. His uncanny sense of aim made him the man to beat at the lanes.

Hamilton Field also was the headquarters air base of the Fourth Air Force, one of four geographical air districts in the United States. Established as Southwest Air District in 1940, it became the Fourth Air Force in 1941. Though the technical headquarters had been moved a few miles south, to the Presidio of San Francisco, to be collocated with the U.S. Sixth Army's headquarters, all Fourth Air Force operations were out of Hamilton.

The Fourth's commander was Brigadier General George Churchill Kenney. Over the next several years he would play a very important role in the lives and careers of both Dick Bong and Tommy McGuire. Kenney was already aware of Bong. Ennis Whitehead had written to Kenney when Bong left Luke Field, telling him to watch out for one of the "hottest pilots" (Kenney's recollection) that Whitehead had seen in years.

At the same time when Bong was wrapping up his Arizona sojourn and moving back to California, Lieutenant Tommy McGuire also was on the move. Two days after the debacle with his mother in Sebring, he left Orlando for Baton Rouge, Louisiana, and his new assignment with the 56th Fighter Squadron of the 54th Fighter Group (the term "Pursuit" was changed to "Fighter" in all USAAF unit designations in May 1942) at Harding Field in Louisiana (later Baton Rouge Metropolitan Airport).

At first McGuire considered his new home an advantage, given that he had moved halfway back toward San Antonio—and Marilynn Giesler. That was the good news. The bad news was that the pilots in the 54th were confined to within a fifty-mile radius of the base. When he phoned her with the bad news, she said that she would make plans to come up to Baton Rouge. However, before that could happen, the 54th was on the move again, this time to March Army Airfield, near Riverside in California.

It was a bitter pill to swallow that Tommy's first fuel stop when he headed west on May 27 was back at Kelly Field, just a few miles from where Marilynn was. He didn't even have time to buzz Incarnate Word College.

Each mile he flew after leaving Kelly Field that day took McGuire farther from Marilynn, and farther west than he had ever been. These miles took him first to March Field, one of the busiest USAAF bases in Southern California, and later on to the Santa Ana Army Airfield, which had opened in February 1942 as the aviation cadet classification center for the West Coast.

He wished that he had been flying the P-40E he had flown in Florida, but in Louisiana, his unit had made the transition from the Warhawk to the Bell P-39 Airacobra.

Tommy McGuire, like many other pilots, considered this a step backward. The Airacobra was born of a noble desire to break new ground technologically, but it was destined to be remembered more as a millstone than as a milestone. Originally designed in 1937, the Airacobra was the first fighter produced in the Unites States to have the engine *behind* the pilot, and a 37mm cannon ahead of the pilot that fired through the propeller hub. The engine's driveshaft ran through the cockpit, between the pilot's feet, to the propeller in the nose. This put the pilot high enough that the Airacobra became the first American fighter to have an automobile-like door on the side of the cockpit. The Airacobra was supposed to have been built with a turbo-supercharged Allison V1710-17, but shortly after the first flight tests in April 1939, the U.S. Army Air Corps decided to save money by revising the specifications and ordering the production aircraft with a non super-charged V1710-37 instead. It was a fateful turning point, for this decision rendered the P-39 worthless at altitudes above 17,000 feet, and thus damned it to mediocrity. Because of this lack of power, the Airacobra was actually dangerous.

The USAAF pilots even had a song to summarize their feelings:

> *Don't give me a P-39,*
> *With an engine that's mounted behind.*
> *It will tumble and roll,*
> *And dig a big hole.*
> *Don't give me a P-39.*

The automobile-like door added to the danger by making it difficult to bail out of a P-39 if it went into a spin, or if it did "tumble and roll." That the P-39 was used at all was due to the fact that when the United States entered World War II, there wasn't much of a choice. The P-39 and the P-40 were really the best single-engine fighters the USAAF had available in reasonable numbers. As a result, the Airacobra saw a good deal of service during 1942 in the South Pacific, North Africa—and Alaska.

In the six months since Pearl Harbor, the war news from the far side of the Pacific was universally bad. In those months, the Imperial Japanese Army had badly mauled Allied warships in repeated engagements, and the Imperial Japanese Army had occupied all of Southeast Asia. When the island fortress of Corregidor fell on May 6, they controlled all of the Philippines.

One month later, the news was even worse. On June 6, Imperial Japanese troops captured the island of Kiska in Alaska's Aleutian chain, and the following day they went ashore on the Aleutian island of Attu. World War II was now being fought on American soil, and there was every reason to believe that mainland Alaska would be next. At the very least, there was a possibility that these islands could be used to launch air attacks against Alaska's major cities and military posts.

Even before the Attu and Kiska disasters, attacks against Alaska had been feared. With this in mind, the P-39s of the 54th Fighter Group were ordered to Alaska immediately, to defend against enemy bombers. Among the P-39 pilots making the move was Tommy McGuire. He had gotten his orders when he reached Santa Ana.

McGuire's first thought was of Marilynn. He had fallen in love when she had been close enough to touch, and close enough to see every day or so, and close enough to dance with at the Tower on Saturday night. But for four months, ever since February 6, they had been kept apart. Even when he thought he'd be closer, they were kept apart. At least they could hear each other's voice over the phone. In Alaska in 1942, however, telephone service was not something you took for granted.

For Tommy McGuire, it was time to get serious.

In medieval times, devotion to a lady was an essential part of chivalry and knighthood. In World War II it was the same. Whether a man was a soldier destined to fight from a slippery, stinking foxhole, or a knight of the air destined to do battle in the clouds, devotion to a lady was of immense import. And this sentiment played out in the many thousands of hurried romances and rushed weddings that took place during those years, in which honeymoons literally came to their tearful ends on the steps of a slowly moving troop train carrying the young knights to their uncertain rendezvous with combat.

It was on one of his visits to Sebring in April that Tommy McGuire had told his mother about Marilynn, and had admitted that he had thoughts of proposing marriage. Polly had been lukewarm on the idea. From her perspective, the rushed wartime romances were a recipe for disaster. Tommy no doubt took it with a grain of salt. Polly's marriage may have been a bit impulsive, but had not been a rushed wartime one—and it had ended badly.

The ensuing weeks had run through his fingers like sand, and he now realized that he had not articulated this sentiment to Marilynn herself. On June 2 he picked up the phone receiver in Santa Ana and asked her to marry him as soon as he got back from Alaska.

She said yes.

They decided that they would be married as soon as possible after Tommy could get back to San Antonio.

Two days later, Tommy McGuire was headed north, toward the 56th Fighter Squadron's new assignment at Nome in Alaska. As he made the first leg of the trip from Los Angeles to Boise, Idaho, his route might have passed near the San Francisco Bay Area, and he may have been, for the first time, flying in the same airspace as Dick Bong.

The two lieutenants were then, of course, just a few of the thousands of young officers the USAAF was then training for war. By the end of June 1942, there were 764,415 people in the growing USAAF, up from 152,125 a year earlier. There was so much more of this story yet to come. By 1944, the number would reach 2,372,292.

CHAPTER 7

Their Warhorse,
Their Fork-Tailed Devil

To the designers who conceived it, this singular breed of warhorse was originally called Atalanta, after a beautiful, fleet-footed maiden of Greek mythology. To the men who developed and built it, the warhorse was the Lockheed Model 22 series. To the U.S. Army Air Forces, who bought more than nine thousand of them, these warhorses were the P-38 series. To just about everyone, this warhorse was the Lockheed Lightning. Its many unofficial nicknames ranged from "Three Bullets on a Knife" to "Twin Boom Angel." The German Luftwaffe fighter pilots who fought against them in Europe called it *der Gabelschwanz Teufel* ("the Fork-Tailed Devil").

When both Dick Bong and Tommy McGuire finally entered combat, they would fly all of their operational missions in one P-38 variant or another, mainly P-38Js and P-38Ls. No account of the P-38 in action in World War II has ever been complete without mention of their names, nor is their story complete without a sketch of this amazing aircraft and how it came to be.

By the time Tommy McGuire was passing through the northern California airspace en route to Alaska in his P-39 Airacobra, Dick Bong had graduated to the P-38, which was then the hottest fighter in the USAAF. By the end of the year, McGuire would saddle up this warhorse as well.

The Lightning had speed—it entered service as the USAAF's fastest operational fighter. It also had range—it could outdistance its predecessors, and with external fuel tanks, it had a ferry range of more than three thousand miles. These external tanks made it ideal for the vast distances the USAAF would encounter in the Pacific Theater, although the aerodynamic characteristics of these tanks did degrade the Lightning's maneuverability. It became a mantra of the P-38 pilots to *always* remember to jettison—the pilots called it "skinning"—the tanks before mixing it up with an enemy fighter in air-to-air combat where maneuverability was the key to victory.

The father of the Lightning was a man whose place in the pantheon of great American aircraft designers is as unique and well deserved as the place of the Lightning in the pantheon of great American warplanes of World War II. His name was Clarence Leonard "Kelly" Johnson, and his workshop was in Burbank, California, just across the Hollywood Hills from Los Angeles. Dick Bong had driven past his gate when he drove to Anaheim to visit his aunts. Tommy McGuire may have flown over his roof when he headed north to Alaska armed with a "yes" from his lady.

The Lockheed Aircraft Company was formed in 1926 by Allan Loughead, who had previously been a partner with his brother Malcolm in the Loughead (pronounced "Lockheed") Brothers Aircraft Company, which dated back to 1912. Since 1926, Lockheed had gone through a series of owners and financial hard times, and was finally acquired in 1932 by a group of investors headed by Robert and Courtland Gross and reconstituted as the Lockheed Corporation. Settling into its Burbank home, the company was focusing its attention on a family of sturdy, twin-engine transport aircraft, including the Model 10 Electra, the Model 12 Electra Junior, and the Model 14 Super Electra. Amelia Earhart had flown her Lockheed Electra on many record-breaking flights before she (and it) disappeared in 1937. Howard Hughes flew his Model 14 in his own record-breaking, three-day, round-the-world flight in 1938. Though Lockheed had done relatively little military work for the American armed forces in the 1930s, the British RAF came to Burbank in 1938 to acquire the Hudson, a military derivative of the

Super Electra. It would be widely used as a patrol bomber during the coming global conflict.

The Model 10 and the aircraft that followed never would have achieved what they did without what was probably the best single decision that Bob Gross ever made. That decision was hiring Kelly Johnson. Nor would the warhorse that Dick Bong and Tommy McGuire took to war have existed without Kelly Johnson.

Johnson grew up around Ishpeming, Michigan, and graduated from the University of Michigan in 1932 with a degree in aeronautical engineering. The following year, at age twenty-three, he began his career with Lockheed, working under chief engineer Hall Hibbard. Johnson helped to design the Lockheed Orion single-engine transport and the Model 10 Electra. He quickly developed a reputation as an ingenious engineer, and in 1937, the Institute of Aeronautical Sciences (now the American Institute of Aeronautics and Astronautics) awarded him the Sperry Award for his design of the Lockheed-Fowler Flap used in the control surfaces of aircraft (including the Lightning). Later in the 1930s, Johnson would direct the engineering effort that led to the design of the revolutionary Lockheed Lightning.

Work on the Model 22 project began in June 1937 after Lockheed won the competition for a U.S. Army Air Corps contract for a high-speed, twin-engine, air-superiority fighter. The requirement was a plane that could climb to twenty thousand feet in six minutes, and that requirement was met. Kelly Johnson and his colleague Hall Hibbard gave the Model 22 an unusual twin fuselage to accommodate its engine.

"It was considered a radically different design—even funny-looking, some said," Johnson later explained in his memoir *Kelly: More Than My Share of It All*. "It wasn't [funny-looking] to me. There was a reason for everything that went into it, a logical evolution. The shape took care of itself. In design, you are forced to develop unusual solutions to unusual problems. For the new fighter, we were required to use the liquid-cooled Allison engine. This meant that we had to have a Firestone radiator. We had a long engine so we had to use a General Electric turbo supercharger. And we had a landing gear that had to retract into the nacelle. By the time we had rung all of that together we were almost back to where the tail should be. So we faired it back another five feet and added the tail. It was a twin-engine airplane, and that produced the characteristic twin-tailed airplane that would go through eighteen versions in all theaters of action in World War II, set some records, and make some design contributions. The use of contrarotating propellers on the P-38 was a new and important feature for fighters. It eliminated the torque effect, or pulling to one side."

Johnson was pushing the edges of the envelope in terms of speed. The Model 22 was the first aircraft to reach the fringes of the sound barrier.

"With the first plane faster than four hundred miles an hour, I knew we would be entering an unknown region of flight and possible trouble," he recalled. "It was the phenomenon of compressibility—the buildup of air ahead of the airplane at high speed. In 1937, in connection with our proposal, I had warned the Air Corps, 'as airplane speeds and altitudes [thinner air] increase, consideration must be given to the effect of compressibility.' "

When he first anticipated the trouble with compressibility, he went to the two best experts in the world on the subject, Dr. Theodore Von Karman and Dr. Robert Millikan at the California Institute of Technology (Cal Tech). He told them what he proposed to do in design, how his team intended to compute performance, and their concern about stability and control.

"We don't know anything different," they said, agreeing with his proposals for dealing with the unknown. "Go ahead."

The unusual design of the Lightning offered many extra advantages. For example, it freed the space ahead of the cockpit for a nose wheel; extra armament; and, in several later versions, specialized radar.

The first XP-38 prototype was secretly constructed between June and December 1938. On New Year's Eve, the finished aircraft was disassembled, wrapped in white canvas, and loaded on three trucks for March Army Airfield near Riverside. The plane arrived just before dawn on the first day of 1939, several hours after its highway travel permit had expired. The flight test phase of the project got off to a bad start when the XP-38 rolled off the end of the runway during taxi tests. Lieutenant Ben Kelsey tried so hard to stop the plane that his foot bent a brake pedal that had withstood a five-hundred-pound static test. The problem, traced to grease on a brake shoe, was quickly corrected.

The XP-38 made its first flight on January 27, 1939, and on February 11, Kelsey took the prototype on a transcontinental flight, during which he attained a cruising speed of 420 miles per hour. He reached Amarillo, Texas, in two hours, forty-eight minutes, and the leg to Dayton, Ohio, took just three minutes less. He arrived at Mitchell Army Airfield on Long Island after seven hours, two minutes of flying time, but lost power on approach and wrecked the prototype when he crash-landed on a golf course.

Nevertheless, the Air Corps placed an order for thirteen service test aircraft under the designation YP-38. These aircraft, which were factory-designated as Model 122, were different from the original Lightning prototype in that they had outward-turning rather than inward-turning propellers. The armament consisted of four .50-caliber machine guns and a 37mm cannon built by Oldsmobile, rather than the two .50-caliber and two .30-caliber machine guns and 23mm cannon that had been provided for in the XP-38.

When World War II began in Europe in September 1939, the Air Corps ordered an additional twenty upgraded YP-38s under the simple designation P-38. Although the first YP-38 was not delivered until March 1941, the first P-38s (Lockheed Model 222) had arrived in service by the time the U.S. Army Air Corps became the U.S. Army Air Forces in June 1941. The armament of the Model 222 was the same as that of the Model 122, but armor protection for the pilot was added.

The only P-38A (actually designated XP-38A) was a P-38 converted by the addition of a pressurized cockpit. Designated as Lockheed Model 622, it served as the prototype for future production-series Lightnings with pressurized cockpits. The USAAF designations P-38B and P-38C were reserved for further conversion projects that never reached fruition, so the P-38D (Model 222) was actually the first fully service-rated Lightning (although only thirty-six were built, with the first of these delivered in August 1941).

In the meantime, the British Royal Air Force had expressed an interest in the Lightning. Since the Allison engine with its supercharger was not cleared for export, the RAF Lightnings were built with a less powerful engine and noncontrarotating propellers. They were designated Lockheed Model 322 and were delivered in December 1941 under the RAF designation Lightning Mk I.

By the time the United States entered the war, the USAAF had taken delivery of the first of 210 P-38Es (Model 222) with improved propellers and avionics systems and with a 20mm Hispano cannon replacing the 37mm Oldsmobile cannon. There were a total of 1,885 Model 222 Lightning fighters delivered to the USAAF under the designations P-38, P-38D, P-38E, P-38F, and P-38G. These models were complemented by 300 Model 222 Lightning photoreconnaissance aircraft delivered to the USAAF under the designations F-4 and F-5.

By April 1943 the Lockheed Model 422, the "ultimate Lightning," was ready for mass production. Equipped with Allison V1710F-15 engines delivering 1,600 war-emergency horsepower, the Model 422 and the similar Model 522 were durable and powerful fighters that earned the Lightning a deserved reputation as one of the best combat aircraft of World War II. The USAAF took delivery of 4,949 Lockheed Model 422s under the designations P-38H, P-38J, P-38K, and P-38L, and 1,960 Model 522s under the P-38L designation. The Vultee Aircraft Company also built 113 P-38Ls for the USAAF under license from Lockheed.

During World War II, the United States, the aircraft industry in general, and Lockheed in particular achieved substantial economies of scale. According to the *USAAF Statistical Digest*, the unit cost of a P-38 was $134,280 before the war, and Lockheed billed the government $97,147 each for much more capable variants in 1944.

The Model 522, which went into production as part of the P-38J series, was an outgrowth of a secret project begun during 1940 to develop a pressurized high-altitude interceptor version of the Lightning. Since the Lightning was still in its YP-38 (Model 122) service test phase, the Model 522 interceptor was ordered under the USAAF designation XP-49. The XP-49 finally made its first flight in November 1942, but its performance was not significantly better than that of the Lightnings already in service. The Model 522 was then developed as part of the P-38J production run, and the XP-49 project was abandoned. The single prototype went to the USAAF research and development center at Wright Army Airfield in Ohio, where it served out the war years as a test bed for experiments with pressurized cockpits.

There were numerous features that made the P-38 superior to earlier USAAF fighters. The twin engines gave it speed, reliability, and stability. The center-mounted armament made it an exceptional and easy-to-use gun platform. Other fighters had wing-mounted guns that were set at an angle to converge on a point ahead of the aircraft. With the center-mounted Lightning guns, a pilot could just bore straight in on an enemy. Around the pilot, the cockpit canopy, with its 360-degree field of view, provided exceptional visibility that was lacking in aircraft such as the P-40 Warhawk.

The Lightning's World War II career began early. Within hours of the United States' declaration of war on Germany in December 1941, an Iceland-based Lightning shot down a German Fw.200 patrol bomber. From there, the Lightning went on to serve with the USAAF on all of the world's battlefronts—from Alaska to the South Pacific, and from North Africa to northern Europe.

Just as every medieval knight yearned for that special maiden to be his lady, he required the accoutrements of battle. He needed, of course, his arms and armor—and he needed his warhorse. Though they were still flying other aircraft in May 1942, the warhorse in which Dick Bong and Tommy McGuire would ultimately go to war was the Lockheed Lightning. It would be not only their warhorse, but their arms and armor as well.

CHAPTER 8

Ups and Downs

BECAUSE the P-38 was a twin-engine aircraft, Bong's initial flight time at Hamilton Field would be spent learning twin-engine flying in a C-40, a light transport aircraft based on the Lockheed Model 12A Electra Junior commercial airliner. Bong was somewhat familiar with this aircraft type from having seen these planes at airports in Duluth and Superior.

By May 12, 1942, he had strapped on a Lightning and felt its power. As his brother Bud recalled later in a memoir of Dick, the young Lieutenant Bong wrote home to his mother about the P-38, declaring, "Wooey! What an airplane. That's all I can say [because of wartime security restrictions], but that is enough."

The young pilots of the 49th Fighter Squadron at Hamilton Field were amazed and thrilled by the Lightning. Its performance was so many orders of magnitude greater than anything they had flown previously that there was no real comparison. However, its ease of handling invited trouble. Pilots were tempted to push it to its limits aerobatically, with occasionally fatal results. In other cases, pilots were pushed by their own adrenaline to a form of hot-rodding that resulted in reprimands.

On June 12, four young lieutenants in the 49th Fighter Squadron were called on the carpet for stunts the previous day that went way beyond the rules. Three of the men had looped their Lightnings under the Golden Gate Bridge. The fourth was Dick Bong. Although many accounts would later include Bong in the bridge loop caper, in all of his own later statements, he insisted that he did *not* fly under the Golden Gate Bridge that day.

A great deal of speculation has swirled around the question of exactly what Dick Bong did that day. His version of the story is that all he had done was make a noisy low-level pass over the home in nearby San Anselmo of a fellow pilot who had recently gotten married. However, in the Dick Bong folklore, there is the story that he not only looped the bridge, but also made a low-level pass over downtown San Francisco.

The latter incident was not mentioned in the San Francisco daily papers that week (in the aftermath of the Battle of Midway there was bigger news to report), but the story does appear in the memoirs of none other than General George Kenney, the Fourth Air Force's commanding officer.

"It was ten o'clock on the morning of July 7, 1942 [three weeks after Bong was grounded], at my headquarters in San Francisco," Kenney wrote, being very specific about the time and place that he first met Bong. "I had just finished reading a long report concerning the exploits of one of my young pilots who had been looping the loop around the center span of the Golden Gate bridge in a P-38 fighter plane and waving to the stenographic help in the office buildings as he flew along Market Street. The report noted that, while it had been extremely difficult to get information from the somewhat sympathetic and probably conniving witnesses, there was plenty of evidence proving that a large part of the waving had been to people on some of the lower floors of the buildings."

Kenney also told of a woman on the outskirts of Oakland, across San Francisco Bay to the east, whose laundry had been blown off her clothesline by a low-flying Lightning piloted by Bong.

In his recollection of reprimanding Bong, Kenney described the young lieutenant as "one of the nicest looking cherubs you ever saw in your life...with a round, pink baby face and the bluest, most innocent eyes—now opened wide and a bit scared."

As Kenney described it, he scolded Bong for a while, reminded him that a court-martial was a serious turn of events, and wound up discussing the low-level handling characteristics of the Lightning with him. With Bong watching, Kenney then tore up the papers that contained the charges on which the young man might have been court-martialed.

A lot of pilots buzzed downtown San Francisco during World War II. Dick Bong may or may not have been one of them, but thanks to the memoirs of the general under whom he later served in combat, the Market Street tale became an indelible part of the Bong folklore.

Whatever had actually happened on June 11, Bong was confined to barracks and grounded for six weeks. His logbook shows that he made no flights between that date and July 26. In the meantime, he was assigned to a desk job at the Early Warning Radar Intercept Board at Fourth Air Force headquarters.

As it turned out, Dick's mother and his oldest sister, Nelda, arrived to visit him on June 12, the same day he was grounded. He had invited them sometime previously, and it was a coincidence that they arrived when they did. Because he was confined to quarters, Dick was not able to see Nelda, although the rules were stretched just enough so he could see his mother. What a disappointment this must have been all around. His mother saw him on the threshold of disciplinary action that could easily have led to a court-martial.

Until his meeting with Kenney, Bong and those around him could readily have perceived that his promising career had ended abruptly and ingloriously. In fact, it was a career that was only just beginning.

The June 11 joyride changed the course of history. Five days later, the 14th Fighter Group and its squadrons, the 48th and 50th, as well as Bong's 49th, were uprooted and sent overseas to Atcham, England, where they would be reassigned to the Eighth Air Force. By November, the 14th Fighter Group had been relocated to Algeria, and it was soon in the thick of the fighting in North Africa and the Mediterranean Theater. Had Dick Bong not impulsively buzzed a friend's house one day, he would have spent the war across the globe from where he achieved his immortality.

As Kenney remembered it, Bong's winding up in the Pacific was a direct result of their first meeting, which Kenney dates to July 7. As it turned out, this was the Tuesday of Kenney's last week as Fourth Air Force commander.

On Saturday he was at USAAF headquarters in Washington, being briefed on his new assignment—to go to Australia as Allied air commander in the South West Pacific Area and commander of the Fifth Air Force. Kenney specifically requested that the fighter forces in his new command be equipped with Lightnings, and that one of them be piloted by Lieutenant Richard Ira Bong.

At the same time that Dick Bong was working the graveyard shift at the Radar Intercept Board and wondering when he would get back into a cockpit, Tommy McGuire was flying in what was technically a combat zone. On June 12, the 42nd Fighter Squadron of the 54th Fighter Group began operating from Kodiak Island, and eight days later the 57th Fighter Squadron began operating from Elmendorf Field, in Anchorage. McGuire's 56th Fighter Squadron was sent to Nome.

Nome is closer to the Arctic Circle and the Soviet Union than it is to Fairbanks or Anchorage. It is a thousand miles from Kiska and just as desolate, though being that distance from Kiska also meant that it was a thousand miles from where the enemy was. The P-39s of the 56th patrolled the skies over the Bering Sea in several-hour shifts every day, but the skies were empty of any aircraft other than themselves. In September, a detachment of 42nd Fighter Squadron P-39s was sent to Adak Island, less than two hundred miles from Kiska, where they began to see some action, in strafing attacks on enemy shipping. However, the 56th remained in Nome, flying endless patrols over empty, open ocean and treeless tundra. Once McGuire thought his patrol had spotted a Japanese submarine, but this was never confirmed.

To describe life in Nome as monotonous would be an understatement. The only thing that the town seemed to have in any abundance was booze, which, when found in the proximity of bored twentysomethings leads to a predictable outcome. Card games were another way to pass the time, and games ran twenty-four hours a day. Having played a lot of cards growing up, this was a pursuit at which Tommy McGuire excelled, as Dick Bong did at bowling.

Just as Dick Bong had been written up in June for unauthorized aerobatics, so, too, was McGuire. Boredom did that to a man. Pilots yearned for some excitement, and found it in the aircraft they flew. On August 10,

McGuire put his Airacobra into a steep dive, and looped it a few feet over the runway. Everyone who saw this death-defying maneuver was impressed—except the squadron commander. McGuire was confined to quarters.

Late in the summer, the tedium was broken a bit by the arrival of a sizable number of Soviet pilots. Under the Lend-Lease program, the U.S. government was starting to supply equipment and other matériel to the Soviets for use against the Germans. One product that was transferred to the Red Air Force in sizable quantities was the P-39 Airacobra. They liked the idea of the nose-mounted cannon for use against the hordes of German tanks swarming across the steppes. The P-39 had a limited service ceiling, but ground attack missions were flown at or below two hundred feet, so the limited ceiling made no difference.

Built in the United States, the aircraft were flown up to bases in Alaska and turned over to Soviet pilots, who flew them across the Bering Strait, across the breadth of the Soviet Union, and into combat.

For the men of the 56th Fighter Squadron, showing the Red Air Force guys how to handle P-39s provided an interesting interruption of the usual routine. So, too, did watching the Red pilots at the local bars. Any American who thought he was especially robust when it came to putting away liquor found himself easily matched and outdone by the Soviets.

Dick Bong had returned to flying P-38s on July 26. He was now attached temporarily to the 84th Fighter Squadron of the 78th Fighter Group because his old squadron had gone overseas while he was grounded. Though the 78th was officially based at Hamilton Field, Bong was now flying out of Oakland Airport, across San Francisco Bay to the southeast. He managed to fly nearly every day during August, but he was in a holding pattern, waiting for word on where and when he would be going on his next assignment. The 78th would be going to England, but Bong didn't know where he would be headed. Though Kenney later stated that he had specifically requested that Bong be sent to Australia, Dick himself would not be told where he was going until the moment he got his orders.

He kept flying, making flights of an hour to three hours every day, ferrying P-38s up and down California, doing training flights and coastal patrols. At least once, his flight flew top cover for a Pan American Airways flight coming into San Francisco from Honolulu. He made arrangements for his pay to be sent to his family while he was overseas and waited. On August 12, he was given two hours to pack for a flight to Australia, but the orders were canceled, and still he waited.

On September 1, 1942, he was still waiting in the dark. The following day, he was on the first leg of an eight-thousand-mile journey across the Pacific to Australia.

Passing through Hawaii and Canton Island—where the U.S. Navy had commandeered the almost-new Pan American Airways seaplane base and hotel—and onward through Fiji, Bong was one of many fighter pilots making the longest trip of his life in a transport plane. Since the war started, the USAAF Air Transport Command had constructed air bridges to connect the United States with world battlefronts and Allied nations where the United States was building up its forces. Some flights went east to England via Canada and Iceland. Others would head southeast by way of Brazil to reach the new battlefronts in North Africa. Others followed the route that Bong took to Australia. Many of the flights were operated under contract by various airlines. In the Pacific, one of the contracts was with a new airline called "Consairways," which had been formed by Consolidated Aircraft Company. Coincidentally, the aircraft flown on this route were LB-30 and C-87 transport variants of Consolidated's biggest-selling product, the B-24 long-range bomber.

After his transpacific odyssey, Bong reached Amberly Field, on Australia's eastern coast near Brisbane, on September 9. If he and the other fresh-faced fighter pilots with whom he shared the flight were imagining that they would soon be in combat, they were wrong. The situation he found at Amberly was analogous to what he had experienced at Hamilton. As Bong arrived, most of the American fighter force consisted of P-40s. General Kenney had asked for P-38s, but they were slower to arrive than their pilots. As September gave way to October, enough of the twin-tailed fighters had finally arrived to equip one squadron, the 39th Fighter Squadron of the 35th Fighter Group.

Dick Bong had been assigned to the 9th "Flying Knights" Fighter Squadron of the 49th Fighter Group, but since it had yet to receive its Lightnings, he would fly temporarily with the 39th Fighter Squadron. At last Bong was getting some P-38 flight time—an hour or two every couple of days—but he was seeing no more combat action than he had in California.

In Alaska, it was essentially the same for Tommy McGuire and the other 56th Fighter Squadron pilots, including his good friend Jack Rittmayer, with whom he would cross paths again two years later, on the other side of the Pacific Ocean.

Aside from the Soviets who blew through from time to time, days were filled with flying and waiting—and chasing shadows in the Bering Sea. By October, as the Arctic days were growing ever shorter, patrols were conducted more and more on instruments. During the Arctic summer, when the sun never set, the pilots could fly most missions under visual flight rules, but as winter approached and the sun disappeared, the world of the pilot flying in Alaska would soon change from one of expansive vistas to one that felt like flying inside a black velvet closet. There were few if any lights outside. Sea and land became one, and instrument skills became essential. With the Alaskan winter, there also came weather that was unimaginable to someone who had grown up in Sebring, Florida.

Finally, there was a light at the end of Tommy McGuire's tunnel. Orders informed him of winds of change blowing his way. Soon he and the other 56th Fighter Squadron pilots would be ordered back to the "lower forty-eight." Though its pilots had spent more time in Alaska than in Louisiana, the 56th and its parent 54th Fighter Group had continued to be officially "based" at Harding Field. The Alaska deployment was technically considered temporary duty. Now they'd be going "home."

McGuire almost never made it.

On October 15, he wrote to Pudgy and told her about the diamond ring he was planning to buy for her. The next morning, his and four other P-39s took off from Nome, heading for Ladd Field, near Fairbanks. Major Bill Litton, the 56th Fighter Squadron's commanding officer, was in the lead. It was a long trip, at the fringe of the Airacobra's normal range, so each plane carried an external fuel tank.

For some reason, nobody in the flight had been briefed on the day's IFF (identification, friend or foe) radio code. When Litton's flight ran into a blizzard, he contacted the tower at Ladd for a compass heading for their instrument approach. He was asked for the daily code. When he didn't have it, the tower refused to give him the heading. For all they knew, Litton was really a Japanese bomber pilot trying to execute an attack. Litton pleaded. The tower refused.

Litton was between the proverbial rock and a hard place. His men were running short of fuel and flying in whiteout conditions. Because of the storm, it would be impossible to find Ladd visually. If one or more aircraft tried to descend beneath the cloud cover, there was the risk of running into one of a myriad of mountain peaks in the area.

Litton decided that they would find a place where the ground was visible and look for an area that was level enough to make an emergency landing before they ran out of fuel and crashed.

After searching, they finally spotted a flat, unobstructed stretch of snow, probably a swamp that had frozen over. When McGuire made it down safely, he counted the airplanes that had bellied in near him on the soft snow and came up one short. These four pilots spent a windy, freezing night in their cockpits, wondering where the fifth man was. He showed up on foot the next day, insisting that he had been stalked by a bear. The other men investigated and found the enormous grizzly tracks that confirmed he was right.

Later in the day, a search party from Fairbanks located the downed Airacobras, and the men were rescued. In retrospect, it was just a twenty-four-hour incident in their lives, but it could have ended very differently.

By the end of October, Tommy McGuire and the men of the 56th Fighter Squadron were at Elmendorf Field, on the northern side of Anchorage, waiting for transportation. It was here that McGuire first got his hands on a P-38. Because of their performance and configuration, Lightnings were considered desirable for the Alaskan environment. As the 56th had nearly found out the hard way with their P-39s, long range was a necessity, and two engines provided a measure of safety when flying long distances over open ocean or trackless wilderness. Though the 56th was rotating out of Alaska by the end of November, its pilots were assigned to be checked out in the new fighters. Tommy McGuire's reaction echoed that of Dick Bong. The P-38 was superior in all respects to any aircraft he had yet flown.

By November 29, three days after Thanksgiving, the 56th was back in the conterminous United States, at Mitchell Field on Long Island. The men were destined to return to their "home base" at Harding Field in Louisiana, but they were given a two-week furlough. Tommy phoned his mother and Marilynn to tell them that he would see them as soon as he could.

The couple had decided to be married as soon as Tommy could get back to San Antonio. At last they were able to set a date: December 4, 1942.

Arranging travel in wartime was an accomplishment easier said than done, so McGuire took advantage of his few days in New York to get over to Ridgewood to see his father and his Uncle Charles. Despite his having already set a date with Marilynn, Tommy found his father lukewarm—at best—about the marriage. There was a lot of talk about "hurrying into things." Tommy was disappointed but not deterred.

Flying to Tampa and hitching a ride on a military flight to Hendricks Field near Sebring, Tommy McGuire finally found himself knocking on the door to the room at the hotel where his mother lived. There was no answer. The increasingly reclusive Polly was not seeing anyone, not even the young second lieutenant who had just flown in from Alaska. According to Charles Martin's biography of McGuire, on his second day in town, she apologetically opened her door. Though she, unlike her ex-husband, supported the idea of her son's impending nuptials, she told Tommy that she didn't feel up to traveling to San Antonio for the wedding. She did, however, help him pick out a diamond ring.

The wedding took place as planned, on December 4. The Spanish-style post chapel at Fort Sam Houston in San Antonio would host a great many such weddings during World War II—weddings in which a passionate couple joined in a holy bond, only to spend just a brief moment as husband and wife before the new husband was pulled away to a distant corner of the globe just days later.

Sidney Bowers, the woman who introduced Tommy and Marilynn, served as maid of honor. None of McGuire's friends was anywhere near San Antonio, so Marilynn and Sidney enlisted a friend, also a young lieutenant, to fill in as best man.

A few days after their wedding, Lieutenant McGuire and his bride arrived in Baton Rouge as he returned to the 56th Fighter Squadron at Harding Field. Finding off-base housing was no easy matter, but they landed at a motor court called the Alamo Plaza, where a number of other married pilots had found lodging. The fact that she had just left San Antonio, home of the real Alamo, to live in a motel called that was an object of great amusement for Marilynn. And the fact that they were among their peers at the Alamo Plaza meant that Tommy and Marilynn would have a good social life.

For two months, their lives in Baton Rouge were that for which every married couple dreams. They had a home, modest as it was; friends with whom to interact; and the usual round of holiday parties at the Harding officers' club. On December 11 they could toast the first anniversary of their first dance and look forward to their lives together.

And so they toasted, but it was wartime, and everything was in flux. At least they'd had those two happy months.

PART II

WARRIORS

It was the *"finis de la Guerre!"* It was the *finis d'aviation*. It was to us, perhaps unconsciously, the end of that intimate relationship that since the beginning of the war had cemented together brothers-in-arms into a closer fraternity than is known to any other friendship in the whole world. When again will that pyramid of entwined comrades—interlacing together in one mass boys from every State in our Union—when again will it be formed and bound together in mutual devotion?

—EDWARD VERNON "EDDIE" RICKENBACKER,
America's World War I "Ace of Aces," commenting
on the U.S. Army Air Service, and the end of World War I
on November 11, 1918

CHAPTER 9

Into the Band of Brothers

O N November 15, 1942, Dick Bong went to war, flying his P-38 up from Amberly Field in Australia to Fourteen-Mile Strip—aka Schwimmer Field—near Port Moresby, on the southeastern corner of New Guinea. His first actual combat air patrol would come one week later, on November 22, over Buna, the Japanese base southeast of Lae and directly across the Owen Stanley Mountains from Port Moresby, where American and Australian forces were locked in a vicious ground battle with the Japanese invaders. New Guinea was then and would continue to be both Dick Bong's home and the central battleground within the South West Pacific Area until 1944.

New Guinea was an improbable slice of real estate to be fought over by the great world powers of the mid-twentieth century. The third-largest island in the world after Australia and Greenland, New Guinea is more than three times the size of the United Kingdom and 20 percent larger than Texas. However, in 1941, when the Japanese first put troops ashore, the vast place had fewer people than the forty-nine square miles of San Francisco. It is a land of impossible terrain that even in the twenty-first century has yet to be bisected by a highway. It is a place of such remoteness that even after World

War II, it was home to multitudes of species not yet cataloged by biologists, and by numerous groups of Stone Age people whose languages had never been heard by anthropologists.

New Guinea was such a difficult place to wage war that the troops who were fighting battles such as the one at Buna had found it a triumph when they managed to march a mile a day through its jungles. The jungles, with their slippery hillsides tangled in forests and foliage where the sun had never shone, and where visibility is often measured in inches rather than yards, were literally hell on earth for most troops who dared to challenge them. Being located barely south of the equator gives New Guinea a climate in which a veritable encyclopedia of tropical diseases can flourish. The troops discovered that malaria was almost routine and that maladies such as dysentery *were* routine.

Strategically, the Japanese high command had decided to occupy New Guinea as a stepping-stone to neutralizing Australia. Since capturing Rabaul on the island of New Britain in February 1942, the Japanese had quickly turned it into the principal forward operating base in the South Pacific for their army, navy, and the air arms of both services. Around Rabaul, major air bases were built at Lakunai, Rapopo, Tobera, and Vunakanau. Rabaul became for the Japanese in World War II what Singapore had been to the British in the previous century, a formidable and heavily fortified keystone to their overall miliary operations—and their empire. By 1943 the Japanese would have more than a hundred thousand personnel stationed at Rabaul.

Taking New Guinea, which the Japanese hoped to execute through the quick seizure of port cities in the Netherlands-administered west and the Australian-administered east, was supposed to have happened as quickly as their earlier swallowing of Malaya and New Britain. It all went according to plan until their invasion fleet, en route to capture Port Moresby, was dealt a serious setback in the Battle of the Coral Sea during the first week of May 1942.

This failure by the Japanese to take Port Moresby and sew up New Guinea set the stage for the vicious fighting that would result in many significant combat actions over the next two years. How is it that New Guinea had become such an essential battlefront of World War II? It was simply because this island—and Guadalcanal, in the Solomon Islands to the east—were the first places where the Allies were finally able to dig in their heels and stop the heretofore relentless Japanese advance.

In early March 1942, the Japanese captured Lae, on the northeastern corner of New Guinea, and established another major air base there. Opposing them, the USAAF units were based at fields across the Owen Stanley Mountains near Port Moresby. These constituted the advance echelon of General Kenney's Fifth Air Force. Commanding this advance echelon would be General Ennis "Whitey" Whitehead, who had been the commander at Luke Field when Bong was in advanced training there.

That intimate relationship between American airmen that Rickenbacker had observed in 1918 had already started to form again among American airmen flying over New Guinea. Many had already been in aerial combat, and many had two or three victories. Captain Buzz Wagner had scored eight.

As Bong had flown west from California in early September, conversation with other fresh, young fighter pilots on the flight had no doubt turned to the military situation in the islands surrounding Australia. The Americans and Australians had finally halted the Japanese offensive, but fierce battles were raging on small islands in the Solomon chain such as Guadalcanal, as well as on New Guinea. Naval battles then raged in the waters between these islands and Australia.

Overhead, there was an equally intense battle for air supremacy over a sprawling war zone equal in area to the continental United States. It had been established since that first day of September back in 1939 that World War II would be a war unlike others. It was the first war in which airpower was not just a novelty, a minor aspect of the action, as it was in Rickenbacker's war, but an essential component of the strategy and tactics of both waging war and achieving victory. Control of the airspace above the battlefield was as important as controlling the ground or the sea-lanes. Airplanes could attack fixed targets, as well as transport ships at sea and troops on the ground. Airplanes could transport personnel and high-value cargo. The only people who could effectively stop an enemy from using airplanes for such things were fighter pilots.

The only people who could effectively stop enemy fighter pilots were *better* fighter pilots. The knights of the air were not a footnote to the overall conflict, but the keystone. That in a nutshell was to be the nature of the war in the skies over the South West Pacific into which Dick Bong and Tommy McGuire would fly as warriors.

WHEN Dick Bong first set foot in New Guinea, that perception—observed by Rickenbacker a generation earlier—that the fighter pilots were becoming a band of brothers was already appearing in New Guinea.

Coincidentally, so, too, was Eddie Rickenbacker.

In October, America's World War I Ace of Aces had been asked by Secretary of War Henry L. Stimson to tour the Pacific Theater to assess the strategic situation and to meet with General MacArthur. Because of a navigation malfunction, the aircraft in which Rickenbacker was traveling went off course between Hawaii and Canton Island, ran out of fuel, and ditched in the ocean. The men in the aircraft survived, but some were injured. They drifted at sea for twenty-four days, running out of food on the third day. On the eighth, Rickenbacker captured a gull that landed on his head. This gave the men a little food and bait with which to catch fish. The men were given up for dead, but only one man died. Rickenbacker and the others were rescued on November 13, two days before Dick Bong went to New Guinea.

Rickenbacker insisted on continuing his mission, and on he went to Australia. Two weeks after his rescue, a still very underweight Rickenbacker sat down for Thanksgiving dinner with General Kenney and his boss, General MacArthur, at MacArthur's own advance headquarters in Port Moresby.

Earlier in the day, Rickenbacker and Kenney had toured the nearby Fifth Air Force fields and had met with some of the pilots. Kenney would remember well the visit to Fourteen-Mile Field, which he called "Laloki," in his memoirs. Dick Bong was there, with fresh experience of flying in a war zone.

The pilots discussed the action they were experiencing, and these younger men stood in awe of this man with twenty-six aerial victories. As Kenney recalled, they guessed that his score would stand for a long while to come. Almost apologetically, Rickenbacker assured them that "of course you have to remember that the Germans were pretty thick on the front in those days. There were always plenty of targets to shoot at."

No one said anything for a few seconds, and then Dick Bong, who had not yet spoken, said, "Captain Rickenbacker, the Japs are pretty thick over here, too."

As everyone laughed, Kenney had a brainstorm of which he was later quite proud.

"Eddie," he said, speaking to Rickenbacker, "I'm going to give a case of Scotch to the first one to beat your old record."

"Put me down for another case," America's Ace of Aces then immediately added.

Few would have guessed that the Wisconsin farmboy whom Kenney described as a "pink-faced cherub" would ultimately be that man.

NOTES ON ALLIED ORGANIZATION
IN THE PACIFIC THEATER

It has been said that sometimes you need a program to sort out technical or organizational details. As we move Bong and McGuire into combat
action in the South West Pacific Area, we provide a brief sketch of Allied and
USAAF organization and order of battle in the Pacific Theater of Operations
(PTO), a sprawling theater that accounted for about a quarter of the Earth's
surface.

Administratively, Allied military commanders viewed the PTO as three
areas:

1. The South West Pacific Area (SWPA), in which Bong and McGuire would
   see action, included Java, Borneo, the Philippines, the Bismarck Archipelago, New Guinea, and Australia. On April 18, 1942, General Douglas
   MacArthur was placed in command of all Allied forces in the South West
   Pacific. MacArthur's headquarters started out in Australia, moving to Hollandia, New Guinea, in October 1944; to Tacloban in the Philippines in
   January 1945; and to Manila in April 1945.

2. The South Pacific Area (SOPAC) contained island chains or islands such
   as the Solomons, the New Hebrides, New Caledonia, and Fiji. In October
   1942, with the growing U.S. Navy presence in SOPAC operations, Admiral
   William F. "Bull" Halsey was given command of this area, though MacArthur, the SWPA commander, commanded U.S. Army and USAAF operations in the SOPAC as well. Meanwhile, the corresponding Japanese
   command, operating out of Rabaul, viewed the South West Pacific Area
   and SOPAC as an integrated area of operations.

3. The Central Pacific, or Pacific Ocean Areas (POA), was a vast, mostly open
   ocean region that contained island chains or islands such as the Carolines,
   Marshalls, Marianas, Iwo Jima, Okinawa, and Japan itself. The battlefield
   was primarily ocean, and the commander was a U.S. Navy officer, Admiral Chester Nimitz.

Farther to the west, the Allied areas adjacent to the PTO were the Southeast Asia Command and the China Burma India (CBI) Theater, whose geo-
graphic perimeters are self-explanatory.

In the PTO, the USAAF assigned one of its numbered air forces to each
area:

1. The South West Pacific was home to the Far East Air Force (FEAF), which was redesignated the Fifth Air Force on February 5, 1942. Its wartime commanders were Major General Lewis Brereton through September 3, 1942; Lieutenant General George Kenney through June 15, 1944; Lieutenant General Ennis Whitehead through June 15, 1945; and Major General Kenneth B. Wolfe through October 4, 1945. Within the Fifth Air Force, there was a V Fighter Command and a V Bomber Command (each designated with Roman numerals). The commands contained fighter groups and bomber groups, which contained fighter squadrons and bomber squadrons, respectively.

2. USAAF assets in the SOPAC would operate closely with U.S. Navy and U.S. Marine Corps aviation units and would be under the direct control of the Joint Chiefs of Staff until the creation of the Thirteenth Air Force in January 1943. Nicknamed the "Jungle Air Force," it was under the command of Major General Nathan Twining through July 27, 1943; Brigadier General Ray Owens through January 7, 1944; Brigadier General Hubert Harmon through June 15, 1944; Major General St. Clair Streett through February 19, 1945; and Major General Paul Wurtsmuth through July 4, 1946.

3. The POA was assigned to the Hawaiian Air Force, which became the Seventh Air Force on February 5, 1942. Its wartime commanders were Major General Willis Hale through April 15, 1944; Major General Robert Douglas through June 23, 1945; and Major General Thomas White through October 19, 1946.

4. A fourth numbered air force in the POA was the Twentieth Air Force, created specifically to conduct a strategic air offensive against Japan using B-29 Superfortress long-range bombers. Beginning in October 1944, it operated from Guam and the Marianas under the direct control of General of the Army Henry H. "Hap" Arnold in Washington, D.C. On-site operational command was under Major General Curtis LeMay.

On June 15, 1944, after the Japanese had been effectively subdued in New Guinea, the Fifth Air Force and the Thirteenth Air Force were operationally merged under the umbrella of an entity called the Far East Air Forces (FEAF) (not to be confused with the earlier Far East Air Force that became the Fifth Air Force). The Far East Air Forces were commanded by General George Kenney, who had previously commanded the Fifth. The Seventh Air

Continued on next page...

Force was also brought under the FEAF umbrella, and this organization provided the USAAF command structure for the entire Pacific Theater.

Meanwhile, in the CBI Theater and Southeast Asia, USAAF assets would
initially be under the Tenth Air Force, but after March 1943 they would be
divided between the Tenth (for India and Burma) and the Fourteenth (for
China) air forces.

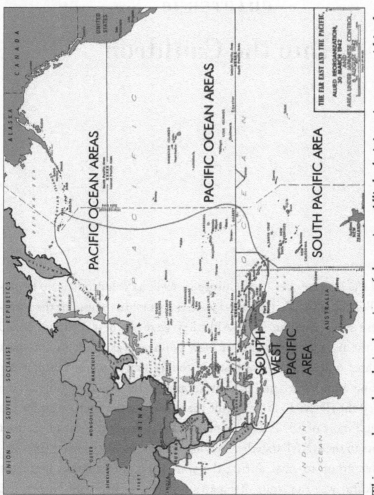

This map shows the relative locations of the various Allied administrative areas within the Pacific Theater. (U.S. Army)

CHAPTER 10

Into the Cauldron

To call the air war over New Guinea in 1942 a "cauldron" is no hyperbole. For the USAAF, those days were the worst of times. For the Imperial Japanese Navy Air Force (IJNAF), they were the best of times. Based at Lae, on the northeastern coast of New Guinea, was probably the most famous fighter unit in Japanese history, the Tainan Kokutai (Tainan Air Group). Named for its original base at Tainan on the island of Taiwan, the group helped the IJNAF to literally rule the skies over the South West Pacific Area through most of 1942. The Tainan Kokutai brought some of the best fighter pilots in the IJNAF together in what was probably the most elite Japanese fighter group to exist during the war. Especially notable about the Tainan Kokutai was that four of Japan's top aces—Hiroyoshi Nishizawa, Saburo Sakai, Junichi Sasai, and Takeo Okumura—were all assigned to it during 1942 and 1943.

Meanwhile, additional and sizable air units were based nearby at the massive Japanese garrison at Rabaul and/or detached to Lae temporarily. These included the Army's 11th Sentai of the Imperial Japanese Army Air Force (IJAAF), and the IJNAF's 582nd Kokutai. The latter was based at

Lakunai, but it operated from Lae after mid-November 1942, about the time Bong arrived in New Guinea.

Like the United States—but unlike Britain and Germany—Imperial Japan did not have an independent air force. While the USAAF gained a large measure of autonomy in the reorganization of June 1941, the IJAAF and the IJNAF remained integrated into their parent services in a support role. For this reason, Allied units operating in the South and Central Pacific were more likely to encounter the IJNAF, because ocean operations were the Imperial Japanese Navy's responsibility, while those Allied units fighting in the China-Burma-India Theater were more likely to encounter the IJAAF, because that was a land war. In the South West Pacific, both Japanese air forces were involved because of large commitments of both ground forces and naval units.

In addition to its cadre of experienced and well-trained pilots, another of the key factors that allowed the IJNAF pilots to rule those tropical skies for at least a year was an incredible aircraft, the Mitsubishi A6M Reisen, best known as the Zero. The most important aircraft to be produced in the first half century of the Japanese aviation industry, the A6M also was arguably the best combat aircraft in widespread service in Asia and the Pacific from 1940 through 1942.

The name Zero came from the developmental designation A6M Type 0, with the "0" being the last digit of the year it was expected to enter service, the Japanese year 2600 (A.D.1940). In Japanese it was known as Rei Shiki Sento Ki (Type Zero Fighter), or Reisen for short. The Allies officially called the aircraft Zeke, but in practice nearly everybody called it Zero.

Because the Japanese names for their aircraft were often hard to pronounce and hard to remember, the Allies gave common English first names to Japanese aircraft. Generally, fighters received male code names, and most other aircraft, including bombers and reconnaissance planes, got female code names. A few reconnaissance aircraft and transports were given male names, but those were exceptions to the rule.

The masterpiece of Mitsubishi designer Jiro Horkoshi, the Zero first flew in April 1939, and from the moment that the first A6Ms went into action in China in July 1940, it was evident that it was the best air-superiority fighter in Asian skies. In the surprise Japanese attack against Pearl Harbor on December 7, 1941, the Zero itself was one of the biggest surprises. American intelligence knew of its existence but drastically underestimated its performance.

The Zero was a lethal weapon in the early part of the war, greatly outclassing and outfighting the USAAF P-40 Warhawks that it met in the Philippines in 1941 and the U.S. Navy F4F Wildcats, with which it did battle in the skies over Guadalcanal. In 1940, American military planners had discounted it as probably an inferior copy of an older American aircraft. But in 1942 the Zero had come to be regarded as an almost mythical secret weapon.

On the IJAAF side, the equivalent to the IJNAF's Zero as the primary army air superiority fighter was the Nakajima Ki-43 Hayabusa, meaning "Peregrine Falcon." Code-named "Oscar" by the Allies, the Ki-43 was roughly the same size as the Zero but was lighter and slightly inferior in performance. Nevertheless, it was an able opponent for the aircraft the Allies were flying during most of 1942.

During their careers, both Bong and McGuire would be as likely to encounter Oscars as Zeros. Indeed, the two aircraft were so similar in appearance that it is not uncommon to find accounts of air battles by various American pilots in which the two names are used almost interchangeably, often for the same enemy aircraft.

During April and May 1942, the various IJNAF Kokutai and IJAAF Sentai flew numerous missions, mainly against Port Moresby, escorting bombers and conducting fighter sweeps aimed at drawing Allied fighters into dogfights. In the latter, the Tainan Kokutai achieved especially decisive victories, even over superior numbers of Allied P-39 Airacobras and P-40 Warhawks. Nishizawa, for example, would be an ace twice over by the summer of 1942, claiming five P-39s between June 1 and July 4 alone. By November he had downed thirty Allied aircraft. He went on to be Japan's top-scoring ace of all time.

Meanwhile, on May 17, in an account that is vividly described by Saburo Sakai in his 1957 memoir *Samurai*, he and Nishizawa brazenly flew a series of aerobatic maneuvers—including six close-formation loops—over Port Moresby. The Allied gunners, apparently stunned by this audacious display, didn't fire a shot at them.

Nishizawa was a man to be reckoned with. A pilot of great skill, he achieved the best record of any ace of any nation in the Pacific Theater in World War II, scoring at least eighty-seven victories. A sullen loner and almost sickly in appearance, he was an unassuming man who was ill at ease on the ground and hardly noticed in a group. But when he got into the air, he suddenly became—as Saburo Sakai remembers—the "Devil." For him, flying was less second nature than *first* nature.

The spring and summer of 1942 would be the best of times for the pilots of the Imperial Japanese Navy Air Force and its Tainan Kokutai. The IJNAF, which still outnumbered the Allied air forces, flew a superior aircraft, had better training, and had the Allied air forces thoroughly outclassed in every regard. Japan was still on the offensive.

As Dick Bong had told Eddie Rickenbacker with his trademark gift for understatement, the Japanese aircraft *were* "pretty thick over here."

The superiority of the Zero, and even the Oscar, over the P-39 and the P-40 was painfully documented, and it wasn't until late in November that the P-38s were ready for action. Though the 39th Fighter Squadron had received them at squadron strength, it took two months to iron out such bugs as self-sealing fuel tanks that were coming apart at the seams. Replacement tanks had arrived from Lockheed, but the wings had to be taken apart to install them.

Dick Bong's baptism of fire came on Christmas Day in 1942.

It was small, but it warranted a larger than usual entry in his logbook. For a week, the 39th had been flying top cover for Fifth Air Force bombers who were attacking Japanese ships running supplies into Buna. As Bong noted tersely in the logbook, he returned from a top cover mission on that Yuletide to find a bullet hole in his aircraft. The lucky round of ground fire did no serious damage. He avoided mention of it in his next letter to his mother.

It must have been strange for the twenty-two-year-old to be celebrating Christmas in a jungle with a bullet hole in his plane and no Christmas presents. Dick's mother had, in fact, sent him a fruitcake. Mail service to America's far-flung battlefronts during World War II was uncertain at best, so Dora had mailed it in October to be sure he received it. He did, but not until July 24, 1943. With fruitcake being as durable as the mail was unpredictable, it survived, and Dick reported that it "tasted mighty good."

On the morning of December 27, Bong was flying as wingman to Captain Tommy Lynch in a P-38F called *Thumper* that was usually flown by fellow pilot—and Bong's tentmate—Lieutenant John "Shady" Lane of Minneapolis. It was not unusual for pilots to trade aircraft.

Lynch's four-ship patrol was north of Buna when they received word that an enemy bomber force had been detected. Some accounts say that they were spotted by coast watchers, but Kenney's recollection is that they were first detected by some P-40s escorting transports. Some accounts state that the force was headed for Port Moresby, but the men of the U.S. Army's 32nd Infantry Division, who were then involved in the ground assault on the approaches to Buna, recall coming under air attack that day and having that attack disrupted by P-38s. In any case, the 39th Fighter Squadron scrambled another eight P-38s to join Lynch's four in the intercept.

Lynch's Lightnings were flying at eighteen thousand feet over Dobodura, near Buna, when they spotted an enemy force of at least twenty-five aircraft. They were a mix of IJNAF Zeros and Aichi D3A "Val" dive bombers, as well as some IJAAF Oscars. The naval force was from the 582nd Kokutai and the Oscars from the 11th Sentai.

As the USAAF fighters dove on the Japanese, Bong did as a wingman is trained to do: he stayed with his leader. Lynch was an experienced fighter pilot who had scored his first victories in May while still flying a P-39, so Bong would be watching him very carefully as the Lightnings raced to intercept the Japanese.

As soon as the two groups of planes came together, and the tracers began arcing through the tropic sky, however, it became a melee.

The Zeros were flying top cover for the Vals, so the Lightnings hit the Zeros first. Bong fired on several, but he was concentrating too hard on remembering textbook precepts rather than getting a feel for combat. He would later kick himself for overanalyzing a situation, rather than reacting quickly and instinctively. Eventually, though, he would come to trust his instincts and a true warrior was born.

Suddenly a Zero slid in behind Lynch, so Bong did his job and opened fire. The Japanese pilot broke off, and Lynch was in the clear. Bong suddenly saw that he was not, and he dove hard to get away from the enemy on his tail.

Pulling out of his dive a treetop level, he found himself free of his pursuer, and staring directly at a slow-moving Val. The Aichi dive bomber, with its fixed landing gear, was not built for tight maneuvering. It was a sitting duck.

Bong thumbed his trigger, giving the Val a short burst.

As he turned away from watching the burning dive bomber tumble into the Bismarck Sea off Samnananda Point, he spotted a Zero in a tight turn moving directly into his sights.

Until the arrival of the P-38 in the war zone, a Zero pilot could more often as not outmaneuver his opposition, but now, things had changed. Dick Bong would discover that day that the Zero, if caught, had some very critical Achilles' heels. As wonderful as the Zero was, its fatal flaw was that it achieved its lightness and maneuverability in part from its having no armor to protect its pilot. American fighters at least had armor plate behind the pilot, the most vulnerable angle in aerial combat. Nor did the Zero have self-sealing fuel tanks.

As he watched the flaming Zero tumble out of the sky, he was feeling pretty good. In fact, he was feeling pretty cocky in that adrenaline-soaked way that a new pilot with two kills experiences when he feels that he can take on the whole enemy air force single-handedly.

As the other eight 39th Fighter Squadron Lightnings joined the fray, Bong took on another Zero, but lost track of him before he crashed. He then locked on to the tail of another Val, but ran out of ammunition before making the kill.

The Americans succeeded in decimating the Japanese strike force, claiming at least a dozen, with the loss of no P-38s, although one was badly damaged. The Americans may have downed as many as nineteen. This was the estimate Bong mentioned in his note to his parents. Lynch shot down two Oscars to bring his score to the magic number of five to make him an ace. Only three Americans scored more than one victory, and Bong was among them.

When the pilots returned to Fourteen-Mile Field, they were greeted at the flight line by General Kenney himself, who had listened to part of the action on the radio. He brought three bottles of Scotch that had been sent to him as a Christmas present by Isaac "Mac" Laddon, the general manager of Consolidated Aircraft Company. Young Dick, who normally did not imbibe, had a glass of whiskey with a splash of soda.

December 27 was especially significant for the Fifth Air Force. The Japanese had held air superiority over New Guinea and the South West Pacific Area for most of 1942, so a decisive victory such as occurred on December 27 was viewed as a big deal. Rarely had the Fifth Air Force had a day like this, and it was now clear that in the P-38 they had a fighter that could hold its own with the Zero. One is tempted to call it a turning point. This may be overreaching in the context of the war in the South West Pacific, but for Dick Bong, it was the biggest so far in his career as a pilot.

On December 28, Eddie Rickenbacker wired his congratulations to Kenney, but queried, "Why in hell did you wait until I left?"

Reflecting on the day, Kenney would recall that he told Whitey Whitehead to "Watch that boy Bong....He just started to work today."

CHAPTER 11

January 1943: The End
of the Beginning

•SCORE•

BONG: 2
McGUIRE: 0

DICK Bong began the year as a combat veteran, while Tommy McGuire was still at Harding Field, and living with his new bride in Baton Rouge. As General Kenney had suggested in his comments on December 27, the work had only just begun. Bong had barely started, and McGuire still awaited a combat assignment.

For the United States and its Allies, the work had only just begun. The Axis had begun 1942 advancing on virtually every front. While those stampede advances had been blunted by the end of the year, the Allies had yet to begin to push back.

One of the greatest victories achieved by the Americans in 1942 had been the defeat of the Japanese fleet at Midway. It had prevented the Japanese from capturing Midway Island and (as far as the Allies knew) possibly Hawaii—but the Japanese remained in control of all they had captured to date.

One of the greatest victories achieved by the British in 1942 was to stop the Germans at El Alamein. It prevented the Germans from capturing the Suez Canal—for the moment—but the Germans still controlled much of

North Africa. Speaking in November 1942 at the lord mayor's luncheon at Mansion House in London, Prime Minister Winston Churchill cautioned that this victory was "not the end. It is not even the beginning of the end. But it is, perhaps, the end of the beginning."

The same could be said of General George Kenney's Fifth Air Force offensive against the Japanese in New Guinea.

The new year began with a major effort by the Japanese to reinforce their base at Lae, and a major effort by the Fifth Air Force to stop them. Lae took on an even more strategic importance for the Japanese as American ground forces were closing in Buna. Using Douglas A-20 attack bombers, as well as larger North American Aviation B-25 and Martin B-26 medium bombers, the Fifth had begun a concentrated effort against Lae and its approaches, as well as against Japanese positions in and around Buna. The 39th Fighter Squadron P-38s took part in this campaign, with some carrying bombs in a fighter-bomber role and others flying top cover to protect the bombers from attacking enemy interceptors.

On New Year's Eve, Dick Bong was flying one of eleven Lightnings flying an escort mission over Lae. As soon as they got a visual on a dozen or so IJNAF Zeros in the area, the Americans went on the offensive. As Bong would recall later, the enemy were "high-grade pilots." It is more than probable that they were the Tainan Kokutai.

Squadron records indicate that the 39th managed to down nine of the enemy. Bong managed to score a hit on one, observing that he had shot a fragment of metal off the engine cowling. He watched the Zero trail off in a shallow dive, but lost track of him. Officially, the engagement gave Bong a "probable," but unconfirmed victory. It counted for naught, and his official score still stood at two.

The first week of January saw a continuation of the New Year's Eve activity, with Fifth Air Force raids against Lae and other Japanese targets. On January 6, coast watchers detected Japanese relief convoys heading toward Huon Gulf, the gateway to Lae's harbor. Kenney planned for a maximum effort against them with his bombers over the next several days. Again, the Lightnings were configured as fighter-bombers.

In attacks against enemy shipping, George Kenney and his aide, Major

Bill Benn, are remembered for having developed a low-altitude bombing technique called "skip bombing." The idea was to release a bomb or cluster of bombs that were delay-fused to explode about five seconds after impact. As Kenney described it, the bomb would "skip along the water until it bumped into the side of the ship. In the few seconds remaining, the bomb should sink just about far enough so that when it went off it would blow the bottom out of the ship. In the meantime, the airplane would have hurdled the enemy vessel and would get far enough away so that it would not be vulnerable to the explosion."

The bomber would approach at altitudes as low as 200 feet above sea level and at speeds ranging from 200 to 250 miles per hour. The 500- or 1,000-pound bombs with their time delay fuses would be released two to four at a time as close as 60 to 300 feet from the side of the target ship. The technique, then in its early stages in January 1943, proved extremely effective. If the bombs did not submerge and explode under the ship, they bounced over it and exploded above it.

A-20s and B-25s, as well as the Bristol Beaufighters flown by the Royal Australian Air Force (RAAF), were the best bombing platforms for skip bombing. As Dick Bong discovered, the P-38 was too fast to be an effective bomber. Nevertheless, Tommy Lynch succeeded in hitting and destroying a Japanese ship with a 1,000-pounder on January 7. As the Lightnings unencumbered themselves of their bombs and resumed their fighter role, their speed became an asset.

On January 7, Bong first arrived over Huon Gulf at about 1:15 P.M., flying a top cover mission for a mixed strike force of Beaufighters and bomb-laden Lightnings. Coming in at an altitude between the bombers and the covering P-38s, about twenty Japanese fighters pounced on the bombers immediately. In turn, the American Lightnings above pounced on the pouncers.

As Dick Bong hurtled into the fight, he found himself diving head on toward an Oscar that turned up to meet him.

The Oscar's pilot fired.

Dick returned fire.

With tracers slashing through the sky in opposite directions, the thought occurred to him that the enemy was going to ram him, so he ducked slightly at the last minute. In the meantime, one of Dick's rounds had obviously found its mark, because the Ki-43 exploded immediately above his head as he raced beneath it.

The scene was repeated again at three-thirty, as Bong was part of a six-ship force covering a group of eight P-38s that came in to bomb Japanese ships in Huon Gulf. Again, the attackers were jumped, by fifteen to twenty Japanese fighters—and again, Dick Bong found himself looking head on into the sights of an Oscar that was rising to meet him.

He opened up with a long burst at forty to sixty yards. Another pilot, Lieutenant Richard Smith, confirmed that the Oscar was on fire after its fatal encounter with Bong, and that it hit the water.

Bong's third and fourth kills were identified as Ki-43 Type 1 aircraft. At the time that Bong first arrived in the South West Pacific, the more heavily armed Type 2 had recently been introduced, but most of the Oscars in service were still Type 1s. Thanks to Bong, there were two fewer at the end of the day on January 7.

The following day, Fifth Air Force operations against the Japanese trying to reinforce Lae continued. The 39th Fighter Squadron flew a total of three top cover missions, the last of which was an escort mission for B-17 Flying Fortress heavy bombers sent to bomb the harbor area at Lae.

Dick Bong and his flight observed an estimated twenty Japanese fighters rise to intercept the bombers, coming up behind them. As the P-38s dove to attack from eighteen thousand feet, Bong noticed that an Oscar had set his sights on a P-38 piloted by Lieutenant Richard Suehr. Bong made two passes at the enemy, who was tenaciously chewing at Suehr's tail.

Having an enemy fighter on your tail is a fighter pilot's worst nightmare. Of all the directions of the compass, the one directly behind, known as the six-o'clock position, is the most vulnerable. Just as having an enemy on your "six" is the hardest situation to escape, being on an enemy at six o'clock is the surest kill. Fighter pilots are always practicing maneuvers to get out from having another aircraft on their six. Failure of a fighter pilot to frequently "check six" is the worst mistake that can be made in combat.

On his second run, Bong got on the Oscar pilot's six and sent him cartwheeling into Huon Gulf. It was one of seven victories to be claimed by the Americans that day. The IJAAF 11th Sentai, however, admitted only one loss, a captain named Tojo, coincidentally the same surname as General Hideki Tojo, the prime minister in Imperial Japan's wartime military government. He may have been Bong's victim.

Dick returned to Fourteen-Mile Field that evening an ace.

The young second lieutenant from Poplar, who had learned to shoot in the Wisconsin woods, had scored a kill at two hundred yards to become an ace. For his actions that day, Bong also would be awarded the Distinguished Flying Cross.

Richard Suehr, whose life Dick Bong saved that day, went on to become an ace himself. He remained in the U.S. Air Force after World War II, and retired as a lieutenant colonel in 1968.

The Japanese convoy managed to reach Lae on January 8, although it had been badly mauled by the Allied bombers. As the ships pulled out on January 9, the bombers continued to harass them. For many of the ships that had survived to deliver their cargo, this would be their last voyage. As the bombers that sent them to the bottom were picked at by Oscars and Zeros, the Lightnings continued to fly top cover, although Dick Bong and Tommy Lynch—whose score as an ace had reached six on January 8—were conspicuous by their absence.

Pleased with their performance, General Kenney rewarded them with some R&R and "a couple of weeks' leave in Australia, where they could rest, get some decent food, and forget about the war for a while."

While Bong enjoyed ice cream and waited for his mail to catch up to him, the war in New Guinea continued. Kenney's bombers continued to attack Japanese shipping, as well as targets around Lae and nearby Finschhafen, as well as farther west along the northern coast of New Guinea. Allied ground troops finally captured Buna on January 22, but Lae remained solidly in the hands of the Japanese.

While Kenney's Fifth Air Force aces were the talk of the South West Pacific Area, the American aces grabbing the headlines were neither in the South West Pacific nor with the USAAF. On Thanksgiving, as Kenney and Rickenbacker were discussing their gifts of Scotch to the first USAAF pilots to break his World War I record, neither was probably thinking that the first American to surpass twenty-six victories in World War II might be a *marine*. By the middle of January 1943, quite a few people had heard Dick

Bong's name, but suddenly every American fighter pilot everywhere in the world was talking about Joe Foss, the American pilot would came out of nowhere to match Rickenbacker's record.

Like Dick Bong, Joseph Jacob "Joe" Foss was a farmboy who grew up dreaming of being a pilot. Born in Sioux Falls, South Dakota, in 1915, Foss took an interest in aviation at age twelve, when he saw Charles Lindbergh perform during one of the Lone Eagle's barnstorming trips through the Dakotas. Foss enrolled at the University of South Dakota in 1934, but it was the trough of the Great Depression, and among the hardest hit of Depression victims were Dakota farmers—and this included the Foss family. Joe Foss left school to help at home, but returned, and finally graduated in 1940. He had learned to fly during his years at the University of South Dakota, and later joined the U.S. Marine Corps Reserve as an aviation cadet. He received his wings and officer's commission in 1941 and was working as a flight instructor when the United States entered World War II.

Initially assigned to a reconnaissance squadron, Foss requested a transfer to a fighter squadron. Because of his advanced age—he was twenty-six—the request was denied. Foss lobbied hard and was finally sent to a marine fighter squadron, VMF-121. In the summer of 1942, as Tommy McGuire was flying over the empty Bering Sea and Dick Bong was making his mythical low-level dash over San Francisco's Market Street, Foss was learning to fly the Grumman F4F Wildcat, then the Marine Corps' standard fighter.

In September, as Dick Bong was flying to Australia, Foss and VMF-121 were following roughly the same route at sea aboard the escort carrier USS *Copahee*, bound for the Solomon Islands, where the Allies were digging in to halt the Japanese advance against Australia. Joe Foss arrived in the Solomons on October 9, and made his first and only carrier takeoff. He landed at Henderson Field, a rugged landing strip hacked out of the Guadalcanal jungle. At this time the marines had captured only part of the island, so Japanese snipers were still active, and Japanese air attacks against Henderson Field also were frequent. This, combined with primitive living conditions, rounded out the difficult situation in which the men of Marine Fighter Squadron VMF-121 found themselves.

Foss flew his first mission on October 13, scored his first victory, and was almost shot down himself. Five days later, he achieved ace status, downing three Zeros in quick succession and knocking down three Mitsubishi G4M Betty bombers. In just nine days of combat, Foss had become an ace, but he would follow this up with three sets of double victories by October 25. On November 4, after shooting down two enemy aircraft, he ditched at sea and nearly died. After swimming part of the five miles to Guadalcanal, he was finally picked up by some local islanders and an Australian mill operator and was repatriated to his squadron the next day.

On January 13, 1943, five days after Dick Bong made ace, Foss shot down three Japanese aircraft, bringing his total score to twenty-six, tieing him with Rickenbacker. At that point, Foss was shipped home. The navy wanted the publicity value of a live hero rather than risking the chance that he might be unlucky one day as he ran up further aerial victories in the Pacific. Back home, the young ace became a high-profile celebrity and the envy of American fighter pilots everywhere.

As for the Japanese, they had to now realize that Churchill was right. The end of 1942, while perhaps not the beginning of the end for the Axis, was certainly a turning point. If the first half of 1942 in the Pacific had belonged to great Japanese aces such as Nishizawa and Sakai, the skies would soon belong to the Americans. Both sides could look at men such as Joe Foss—and at up-and-comers such as Tommy Lynch and Dick Bong—and see it.

As Foss headed home to do his war bond tours, Dick Bong was in Australia taking advantage of his furlough and enjoying an intermission in his budding career as an ace. He was spending five hours a day at the beach near Brisbane, getting sunburned, and trying to get used to swimming in the ocean and the taste of salt water.

"Tastes like the dickens," he wrote his mother.

CHAPTER 12

February 1943: The Calm
Before the Storm

•SCORE•

BONG: 5
McGUIRE: 0

O N February 4, as Joe Foss filled the headlines, Tommy and Marilynn McGuire celebrated their two-month anniversary. For most of those two months, the newlyweds had been living more or less happily at the Alamo Plaza in Baton Rouge. Tommy went to work each day, flying airplanes at Harding Field, then coming home to the Alamo, where several other married pilots lived with their wives.

As they toasted each other on their two-month anniversary, there were winds of change blowing for Tommy and Marilynn—big changes. It was wartime, and few young officers stayed in one place for long. Tommy had gotten his orders. He was headed west to Southern California again, and Marilynn would not be going. There was a severe housing shortage and no room at the inn for wives of married officers. Marilynn was returning to San Antonio to wait for Tommy's return.

Having made a last flight in a P-39 on February 7 at Harding Field, McGuire was being reassigned to the P-38 Lightning. If leaving Marilynn would be a nightmare, getting into a Lightning was a dream come true. Those few days at Elmendorf in Alaska when he'd had the opportunity to try out a P-38 had made an enormous difference. To the USAAF, the fact that this appeared in his logbook meant that McGuire was an ideal candidate for transition to the Lightning.

After a brief stay at the airport in Santa Ana to be familiarized with the new P-38F variant, McGuire and the other pilots making the transition to the Lightning headed up to Muroc Army Airfield—the future Edwards Air Force Base—in the Mojave Desert. Here, in an environment of virtually unlimited runway and excellent flying weather, Tommy McGuire transitioned from a guy who had flown a P-38 a few times into a true Lightning pilot.

Across the globe in the South West Pacific, Dick Bong continued to relish the Lightning experience. He wrote home, extolling the virtues of its speed and bragging about low-level flying down to an altitude of twenty feet or less.

After his furlough in Australia, Bong returned to Fourteen-Mile Field in New Guinea on February 3. By the middle of the month, the 9th "Flying Knights" Fighter Squadron of the 49th Fighter Group—to which he was officially assigned—had received its complement of about two dozen P-38Fs and P-38Gs, so his temporary assignment to the 39th Fighter Squadron ended. Commanded by Lieutenant Colonel Robert Morrissey, the 49th had operated P-40s out of bases in Australia during most of 1942, but had moved up to Port Moresby in October. As the 49th's 9th Fighter Squadron made the conversion to P-38s, its 8th Fighter Squadron continued to operate P-40s.

Beginning on February 17, the Flying Knights began relocating from the busy Port Moresby area to Dobodura—known to the pilots as "Dobo"—on the northern side of the Owen Stanley Mountains near recently captured Buna. General Kenney had ordered both P-38s and B-25s to the northern side so they could be close by Lae and Huon Gulf, and available for operations there when bad weather might have hampered their flying over the Owen Stanleys from Port Moresby.

After the excitement of January, February was a relatively uneventful month for Dick Bong. He flew eight missions between February 10 and 27; some were patrols, others escort missions for transport aircraft. He also flew some alert missions out of the 9th's new home at Dobo.

Strategically, things were deceptively quiet with the enemy in New

Guinea during February, with an emphasis on the word "deceptively." As we
have seen, the Allies had stopped Imperial Japan's previously unstoppable
advance toward Australia. The stopping had been done in places such as
Guadalcanal in the SOPAC and New Guinea in the South West Pacific Area.
The next step, obvious to both sides, would be for Allies to begin rolling the
Japanese back.

The first roll came at Guadalcanal, which the Americans had cleared
of effective Japanese resistance on February 9, 1943. On the scene, General
Alexander Patch, commanding the U.S. Army's Americal Division, proudly
sent a telegram to the chief of staff, announcing "Tokyo Express no longer
has terminus on Guadalcanal."

The Japanese high command, meanwhile, saw that reinforcing and
holding New Guinea was now their most important strategic objective. To
blunt Allied advances on the ground, more troops were needed, and as early
as the end of December, a plan was put in motion to relocate more troops
to Lae from China and Japan. Outside the radius of Fifth Air Force patrols,
Japanese troop convoys were on the move throughout February.

By February 25, General Kenney was aware from intelligence reports
that something big was afoot. On the last day of the month, the Imperial
Japanese Army's 51st Division moved into the Bismarck Sea, having set sail
from Rabaul under a heavy naval escort.

CHAPTER 13

March 1943: A Rising Star

•SCORE•

BONG: 5

McGUIRE: 0

IT was on the first day of March that a Fifth Air Force bomber first glimpsed the Japanese convoy bringing the nearly seven thousand men of General Hidemitsu Nakano's 51st Division to New Guinea. A fresh Japanese division thrown into action in New Guinea would certainly be a serious setback for the Allies. Something had to be done.

The following day, a force of Fifth Air Force B-17 Flying Fortresses located and attacked the convoy in the Bismarck Sea, sinking three of the transports.

On March 3, as the convoy rounded Huon Peninsula near Finschhafen, it came within range of most of the Allied airpower in New Guinea. Fifth Air Force and Royal Australian Air Force units began simultaneous attacks on the convoy, as well as on the Japanese fighter bases around Lae, to suppress enemy air cover for the convoy.

Wave upon wave of Allied bombers struck the convoy from medium altitude and with low-level skip-bombing attacks. By the middle of the day, half of the Japanese transport ships had been sunk, but the others pressed on, steaming desperately through the hailstorm of Allied lead and cordite. During the attack, one B-17 was shot down, and several Zeros made numerous runs at the helpless crewmen as they descended in their parachutes. This incident infuriated the men of the Fifth Air Force.

Overhead, P-38s from both the 9th and 39th fighter squadrons provided air cover in a series of extremely vicious dogfights. This battle began before 9:00 A.M. as the P-38s attacked a group of about two dozen Japanese fighters.

Dick Bong's first action of the battle came at about ten-fifteen, as the 9th Fighter Squadron was flying escort for a group of bombers offshore from Finschhafen. The P-38s were attacked by seven Oscars and turned to engage them. Bong climbed above an Oscar, nailed him with a forty-five-degree deflection shot, and made a second pass just before he hit the water.

Bong then set his sights on another Oscar and made two passes before breaking off the attack with fuel spilling from a ruptured tank in the Japanese aircraft. Dick Bong had scored his sixth confirmed victory that day, while he listed the Oscar with the leaking tank as a "probable."

The P-38s were overwhelmingly successful in aerial combat over the Bismarck Sea, although there are varying claims as to exactly how successful. As General Kenney reported, there were ten Japanese fighters confirmed shot down in aerial combat, plus nine probables. Some of the probables were subsequently confirmed, and the 39th Fighter Squadron claimed ten, while seven were claimed by Dick Bong's 9th Fighter Squadron. The 39th, however, lost three of its pilots that day, including Lieutenant Hoyt Eason, an ace with six victories.

By the morning of March 4, the Battle of the Bismarck Sea was essentially over, with the Fifth Air Force and RAAF having sunk all of the Japanese transport vessels, as well as the destroyers *Shirayuki, Arashio,* and *Tokitsukaze.* The destroyer *Asagumo* was destroyed in a later attack. It was a resounding defeat for the Japanese. The losses seriously impacted their ability to defend positions in New Guinea and throughout the South West Pacific Area. For the Allied airmen, it was a clear demonstration of the capability of airpower to disrupt and destroy a sizable naval force. The battle also was the first really large-scale demonstration of the deadly effectiveness of skip bombing.

Over the ensuing week, Bong flew several intercept missions out of

Dobodura, occasionally shuttling over the mountains to Port Moresby. The Fifth Air Force was gradually building toward air supremacy, but just as Kenney's bombers were able to strike the Japanese air bases, so, too, were the Japanese able to strike the Allied bases. This necessitated having P-38s on strip alert to intercept them. The logbooks of pilots, including those of Dick Bong, are occasionally punctuated by mention of a Japanese air attack that managed to drop a few bombs at or near an American field.

The newly established base at Dobodura, being one of the closest to Lae, was especially irritating to the enemy, and on March 11 the Japanese made a major effort against it. The IJNAF sent an estimated twenty-seven G4M Betty medium bombers, escorted by more than two dozen Zeros, to attack Dobo. Both the 8th and 9th fighter squadrons scrambled fighters to intercept the Japanese. Some of the fighters, including those of Dick Bong and two other members of his flight, took off even as the Bettys were overhead dropping their bombs.

After climbing to twenty-four thousand feet, Bong's flight attacked the bombers as they regrouped and headed back to their base. He had made a pass at the G4M that was bringing up the rear when nine Zeros ganged up on him. He put the Lightning into a steep dive, pushing the throttle hard to 475 miles per hour, nearly 10 percent over the war emergency top speed of the aircraft.

As Bong pulled out of his dive, another gaggle of Zeros hit him, chasing him practically to wavetop altitude. Again, he pushed hard on the throttle, watching in his mirror until he could see only one Zero in pursuit. He stood the Lightning on its wingtip, cranked it around 180 degrees, and headed straight into the Zero, guns blazing.

As he watched his rounds impacting the doomed enemy fighter, he discovered that the sky was again filled with Zeros.

He picked out another potential target, turned slightly to the left, and opened fire. Picking another, he turned ten degrees to the right and fired again. As he banked away to get a look, he could see the first two Zeros in flames, and the third running with smoke pouring out of his engine.

Suddenly three other Zeros hit him from above, tearing up his left engine nacelle. At this point he decided to make a run for it, and he managed to elude his pursuers.

He feathered his left prop and limped back to Dobo, wondering why he had become such a magnet for enemy fighters that day.

In what he readily admitted was his scariest mission since entering combat, Bong had scored two victories and listed the enemy fighter that left the battle in a cloud of smoke as another probable. In his logbook he referred to them as Oscars, but elsewhere he and others call them Zeros.

Including Bong's two, the Flying Knights of the 9th Fighter Squadron managed to shoot down six fighters that day—but only one of the medium bombers. Captain Sidney Woods got the bomber, while Lieutenant Bill Hanning matched Bong's score with two, although his Lightning was damaged and he had to bail out. The 8th Fighter Squadron, meanwhile, shot down four, but lost one of its P-40s. On the ground, Dobodura had taken quite a hit. Three P-38s were destroyed on the ground and several men were killed or wounded.

As his two victories on March 11 brought Bong's score to eight, the Silver Star for which he was recommended after his first double victory on December 27 was working its way through the system. At last, three months later, on March 27, Bong received his medal from Brigadier General Paul "Squeeze" Wurtsmith. He had been commander of the 49th Forty-niners Fighter Group in December, but had been promoted in January to command the V Fighter Command, directly under General Kenney.

The tide was turning. During 1942, the IJNAF and the IJAAF had ruled the skies over the South West Pacific, but things were changing. Dick Bong was more than merely part of that change; he was emerging as one of the star players in the Fifth Air Force. He had a hunter's uncanny sense of marksmanship with moving targets—and he brought a single-minded dedication to duty to his job. Bong celebrated the day of his Silver Star ceremony by flying a four-hour, forty-five-minute patrol. It was uneventful.

Meanwhile, Tommy McGuire had arrived in the South West Pacific. He finished four weeks of training at Muroc in early March, and following the same route that Bong had taken in September, he had made the exhausting, five-day trip across the Pacific to Brisbane. Among the other pilots also traveling west were two of his 54th Fighter Group buddies at Harding Field. Both Jerry Johnson and Wally Jordan had been in Alaska at the same time as McGuire, but not based at Nome.

En route, McGuire and the other fighter pilots had broken the monotony by talking their way onto the flight deck of the big Douglas C-54 transport. The flight crew was glad to have an extra set of trained hands in the cockpit—the copilot sat McGuire down in the right seat and took a nap.

The stopover in Brisbane was short, but Tommy McGuire took the time to wire a dozen roses to the woman in San Antonio who was celebrating their third-month anniversary without him.

The new pilots were hustled aboard a flight that took them north to Townsville, where the V Fighter Command would process them into the 9th Fighter Squadron. Professionally, nothing could have pleased them more. The squadron was developing a reputation as *the* place to be for fighter pilots. Of course, it was a P-38 squadron, and the USAAF had just spent a month training these men in the aircraft.

On March 23, four days before General Wurtsmith pinned the Silver Star on Dick Bong's shirt, McGuire was back in a Lightning. For the next three weeks, while the V Fighter Command waited for more of the Lockheed fighters, the only airspace McGuire would see would be Australian, but at least he was seeing it through the Perspex windshield of a P-38.

During those last two weeks of March, after the big attack on Dobodura, the Japanese continued their assault on Allied bases in New Guinea with a strike on Porlock Harbor and multiple attacks on Oro Bay, a short distance from Dobodura. On March 28, the second of the latter raids brought a major intercept effort from both squadrons of the Forty-niners. The Americans claimed thirteen of the IJNAF aircraft, with the 8th Fighter Squadron losing one P-40. Among the nine Forty-niners getting a kill on March 28 was Walter Markey, a young New Yorker who had flown out to the Pacific on the same LB-30 flight as Bong back in September.

Having flown a long patrol the day before, Dick Bong stood down on March 28, but he was back in the cockpit the next day. They were on patrol near Oro Bay when Dick's wingman, Lieutenant Clayton Barnes, spotted a twin-engine aircraft at ten o'clock high. The rising-sun "meatball" insignia identified it as Japanese. Bong and Barnes skinned their external fuel tanks for maneuverability and climbed to intercept the enemy aircraft.

It turned out to be a Mitsubishi Ki-46, an aircraft known to the Allies as Dinah. Because it had two engines and a female name, the American pilots often referred to the Dinah as a bomber. However, the Ki-46s were used by the IJAAF mainly for longer-range, high-altitude reconnaissance, and like the one with which they crossed paths on March 29, the Dinahs usually flew their missions solo. This particular Dinah was probably flying a poststrike assessment mission over the scene of the previous day's raid.

The Dinah's pilot, knowing his plane was slower than the Lightnings, put the plane into a dive to pick up speed. Bong, being the flight leader, took the shot, making a firing pass from the left at about thirty degrees' deflection. The Dinah's left engine was already belching smoke as Bong banked around for his second go.

Meanwhile, Barnes took a shot at the Dinah, and Bong targeted the Dinah's tail, its six o'clock, on his second pass.

Finally, on his fourth, Bong lined up behind the larger aircraft and peppered it with explosive rounds until the Dinah just blew up.

Operating alone, the Ki-46 was a sitting duck for American Lightnings, and not having a fighter escort was a calculated risk. Both sides often ignored lone enemy aircraft as not worth the bother, but not today. As Dick Bong quipped in his logbook, "No Zeros to interrupt my fun."

CHAPTER 14

April 1943: Deaths in the Families

•SCORE•

BONG: 9
McGUIRE: 0

DICK Bong began April 1943 just one victory from being a double ace and the top ace on the 9th Fighter Squadron Flying Knights. By the end of April he'd have his tenth, and the promotion to first lieutenant for which he had yearned. The 9th itself now celebrated its first full year in combat, and a celebration it was. During the nine months of 1942 that it was in combat, the 9th had averaged just 4.6 aerial victories each month. So far in 1943, the average was 11.3 monthly and climbing.

The Japanese understood that the tables were slowly turning and that the great advances of early 1942 would not continue. But they had begun 1943 believing that the Allies could be kept at bay and prevented from making counteradvances.

The Allies were not making substantial progress on the ground in New Guinea, and the Imperial Japanese Navy was still strong—albeit not nearly as strong as a year before. However, the loss of Guadalcanal to the Americans and the horrendous Japanese defeat in the Battle of the Bismarck Sea delivered hurtful blows to Japanese morale.

In his memoirs, Saburo Sakai recalled the depth of the discouragement felt by the Japanese after the Battle of the Bismarck Sea, writing, "Less than a month after Guadalcanal fell, we were called in for a special officers conference, to hear news of a further disaster. The report remained classified throughout the rest of the war and was never revealed to the Japanese public.... The news carried implications of a disaster greater than Guadalcanal, for it meant that the enemy now dominated the skies as far north as Lae, and that we were helpless to stop his incredibly effective attacks against our shipping."

Admiral Isoroku Yamamoto, commander in chief of Japan's Combined Fleet and the architect of the stunning Japanese success at Pearl Harbor, chose April for his next move. He was undaunted by the Bismarck Sea disaster, feeling that offense was the best course. As he had demonstrated in December 1941, Yamamoto was a big believer in airpower. As such, he understood not only the importance of his own IJNAF but also the danger of the increasing size and power of the American Fifth and Thirteenth air forces. So, too, did Yamamoto's counterpart the Imperial Japanese Army commander in Rabaul, General Hitoshi Imamura.

Yamamoto's plan, code-named "I," was a maximum effort centered around land-based naval airpower and targeting the Allies first in the Russell Islands and the Solomon Islands, then in New Guinea. For I he brought together the assets of his land-based airpower in and around Rabaul, and aircraft from the carriers in his Third Fleet, based at Truk. He even moved his own headquarters from Truk to Rabaul to direct the operation.

On April 1, I began with an attack on Allied positions in the Russells, but the main show came on April 7. The target was an Allied naval task force steaming northwesterly through the Solomons to attack Japanese positions on Vila and Munda. Yamamoto's strike force included 71 bombers escorted by more than 100 fighters. Coast watchers on New Georgia alerted the Allies, and 76 USAAF and U.S. Navy fighters were launched to intercept the enemy. A tremendous air battle erupted in the skies over the Russell and Solomon islands. Allied losses were three ships and seven aircraft. They claimed nearly 40 Japanese aircraft shot down.

It was hardly the payback for the Bismarck Sea that Yamamoto wanted, but his pilots painted a picture that was rosier than the reality, so he slept more soundly that night than he should have.

On April 11 and 12, Yamamoto shifted to the next phase of I with attacks against the allies in New Guinea. The IJNAF sent 22 bombers, escorted by 72 fighters, against Oro Bay, and followed up the next day by sending 43 bombers and 131 fighters across the Owen Stanley Mountains to attack Port Moresby.

Both attacks caught General Kenney off guard. In the big battle on April 7, Yamamoto had targeted an Allied naval force. If he was going to continue to play suit and attack shipping in New Guinea, Kenney reasoned that Yamamoto would target Milne Bay and the easternmost tip of New Guinea, where a lot of Allied ships were concentrated. There were relatively few at either Oro Bay or Port Moresby.

Yamamoto and Kenney were both flummoxed on those two days, the admiral by the paucity of Allied ships and the general by the fact that he had sent most of his fighters to Milne Bay.

Flummoxed, too, was Dick Bong. He was flying among the 9th Fighter Squadron contingent that remained to run a routine patrol over Oro Bay, but before any Japanese aircraft were sighted, his right engine suffered a cracked piston, and he returned to an unscheduled landing at Dobodura.

The fortunes for both Bong and Kenney changed two days later. Bong was airborne again, and Kenney's earlier prediction was borne out. As he put it in his memoirs, "This time I guessed right, but the Japs got a lucky break on the weather, as Dobodura was fogged in and sixty of my fighters there were held on the ground while the raid was on."

Bong was not among those grounded. On April 14, the Japanese headed for Milne Bay with more than eighty aircraft, including at least three waves of G4M Betty medium bombers. They were intercepted by Dick Bong and his wingman, Lieutenant Carl Planck. They had left Dobo as part of a four-ship flight, but the two others had to turn back.

At twenty-six thousand feet over Cape Frere, Bong set one of the bombers afire on his first attack, and then hit another. He had discovered firsthand why the Betty was nicknamed "Flying Cigar." As they had with the Zero, Mitsubishi engineers had taken the calculated risk of trading armor for the lighter weight that made the G4M a reasonably fast aircraft. However, the lack of protection for the fuel tanks made the aircraft prone to going up in flames if hit in the wrong place by a tracer round.

After Bong made his first pass at the bombers, three Zeros made a pass at him, then broke off to chase other P-38s that had arrived on the scene.

Bong then made another firing run at the bombers, and smoke began boiling out of the right engine of one of them. Again Bong was jumped by Zeros, and this time one of them put a cannon shell through his elevator.

He managed to get away and limp back to Dobo, and was not among the pair of losses that the Americans suffered that day. The Japanese reported officially that they lost six bombers and a fighter, while the Americans claimed that it was ten and three.

One of the bombers the Americans claimed was Dick Bong's tenth official victory. He also rightfully claimed one of the other two he hit as a probable. Henry Sakaida, who has written extensively about the South West Pacific air war from the Japanese point of view, believes that there is ample evidence to confirm that all three Bettys hit by Bong on April 14 were among those that failed to return from the mission.

As the I operation officially ended, Admiral Yamamoto was operating under the assumption that his forces had achieved a substantial victory. Based on the reports he received from his IJNAF air crews, he believed that the Allies had lost 28 ships—including a cruiser and a pair of destroyers—and as many as 175 aircraft. In fact, in the entire two weeks, the Japanese sank only 5 ships and destroyed about 24 aircraft.

Yamamoto may never have known the full scope of the overestimate. Four days after the day when Dick Bong sent at least one Betty bomber in flames, another Flying Cigar went down. On the morning of April 18, Yamamoto himself was aboard a Betty flying out of Rabaul toward Bougainville, on an inspection tour of the theater, when he had the opportunity to watch P-38 Lightnings at work—up close.

Allied intelligence had intercepted word of the admiral's travel plans, and President Franklin D. Roosevelt had authorized Secretary of the Navy Frank Knox to "get Yamamoto." The order went back down the chain of command, and eighteen Lightnings from the Thirteenth Air Force's 339th Fighter Squadron were ordered to fly more than four hundred miles from Guadalcanal to intercept an "important high officer."

The intercept was successful, and the admiral was killed in action. Lieutenant Rex Barber and Captain Tom Lanphier both claimed credit for hitting Yamamoto's G4M, but recent examination of evidence and the downed aircraft—still rusting away deep in the Bougainville jungle—indicate that Barber alone shot down the architect of the Pearl Harbor attack. Yamamoto's career ended on the 168th anniversary of the day when Americans celebrated the "midnight ride of Paul Revere," and the first anniversary of Jimmy Doolittle's equally famous "thirty seconds over Tokyo."

In the meantime, Tommy McGuire had finally reached Dobodura. He landed in New Guinea on April 16, but did not make his first flight out of Dobo until April 22, four days after Yamamoto was killed and more than a week after the end of the I operation and Dick Bong's tenth victory.

By now Bong was an ace twice over, while McGuire was a mere rookie. Bong's name was well known to McGuire, but the Irish kid from New Jersey by way of Sebring hardly registered on Bong's radar. Nevertheless, McGuire sought him out. He had a lot to learn about combat flying, and an ace such as Bong obviously knew what he was doing. And so it was that the two men destined for such uncannily parallel greatness met on or about April 18, the same day when the brains behind Pearl Harbor went down. For Bong, it meant just a passing handshake with a new guy such as he had been five months ago. But for McGuire, it was a memorable moment.

B ACK in the States, another memorable meeting was taking place. Marilynn McGuire was in the midst of a five-week first visit to her mother-in-law.

Polly had not been at the wedding, but she and Marilynn had shared a number of increasingly cordial telephone calls, and Marilynn had promised Tommy that she would go to Florida. As Charles Martin writes in his biography of McGuire, Polly was not "feeling well" the day Marilynn arrived. The same thing had happened the last time Tommy had come home to see his mother. However, the following day, Polly sobered up and welcomed her daughter-in-law with open arms and became the perfect hostess. Marilynn, meanwhile, was duly impressed with Polly's apparent standing in Sebring society. They dined in style at the Hotel Sebring, where Polly lived with her Boston bulldog, and visited people all over town. Marilynn was shown pictures of her new husband from the family photo album and filled in on family lore.

Polly also took Marilynn to meet the custodian of her new husband's trust fund, set up years earlier by Dora Watson at the Exchange National Bank in nearby Winter Haven. Before going back to Sebring, Polly stopped to do some "shopping"—buying large quantities of liquor. Marilynn was probably still taken aback even after Polly explained that she had to do it because Sebring was a dry community.

The two women who had Tommy McGuire in common finally parted company with promises that they would soon be together again—and in the company of Tommy.

It wouldn't happen.

Three months later, Marilynn got a phone call.

Polly Watson McGuire was found dead on the floor of her room at the Hotel Sebring on July 22. Marilynn made her return trip to Sebring as quickly as she could.

Polly had not been seen for several days, and there was no response to knocking on her door but the barking of the dog. This was not considered unusual. As both Tommy and Marilynn had discovered firsthand, Polly had a reputation as a recluse who didn't take it lightly when her privacy was disturbed. However, someone had eventually called the fire department to look through the window. It wasn't a pretty sight.

When Marilynn arrived, stories were already being whispered all over town that Polly had drunk herself to death. As insensitive as these cruel innuendoes were, Polly's difficulty with alcohol probably had played a role in her demise. Because Tommy was then in transit somewhere within the South West Pacific and couldn't be reached directly, he was unaware that his mother had passed away. With this in mind, Marilynn's first task was an attempt to keep news of Polly's death out of the papers so he wouldn't find out about it the hard way. The *Sebring American*, predecessor to today's *Sebring News-Sun*, insisted on publishing an obit, but reluctantly agreed to delay sending copies of that issue to troops overseas.

Polly had little in the way of an estate. Most of what she had inherited from her parents, which had once been substantial, had been spent. Marilynn gave the bulldog to the maid, shipped some of Polly's housewares to herself, and returned to San Antonio.

CHAPTER 15

May 1943: Passing in the Night

•SCORE•

BONG: 10
McGUIRE: 0

DICK Bong left Dobodura on May 3, and was gone for more than a week of the month that McGuire would spend there. As a bonus for his double-ace status, Kenney rewarded Bong with a furlough in Australia. He visited Sydney on this trip, but those who knew him recalled that the Wisconsin farmboy cared little for the bawdy nightlife in Australia's largest city. He preferred the beaches around Brisbane for his leisure time.

Bong returned by way of Port Moresby on about May 16, and probably passed McGuire headed south.

There was an ongoing shortage of P-38s in the South West Pacific Area, but when he went to Washington in March, General Kenney had lobbied hard with USAAF commanding general Henry H. "Hap" Arnold for more. After returning to the theater, he continued to prod Arnold for a one-for-one replacement of all the P-39s left in the South West Pacific with P-38s.

Finally, in May, Kenney and General Wurtsmith were sufficiently confident of the increasing flow of equipment from the factory in Burbank that they made good on their plan to form an all-new, all-Lightning fighter group within the Fifth Air Force's V Fighter Command. The 475th Fighter Group was officially activated at Amberly Field in Australia on May 15, along with three constituent squadrons: the 431st, 432nd, and 433rd. The group's commander would be Lieutenant Colonel George Prentice, who had previously commanded the 39th Fighter Squadron when it was the only P-38 outfit in the South West Pacific.

Many of the veteran and recently arrived American P-38 pilots who had earlier been assigned to the 49th Fighter Group were reassigned to the new 475th. Tommy McGuire was one of them. After barely a month of uneventful flying in the same squadron as Dick Bong, McGuire left New Guinea, headed back to Australia as the new outfit was assembled. It would be another three months before he was back in action.

Meanwhile, as the Fifth Air Force was building up its strength and forming new groups, additional Japanese units were coming into the theater. Specifically, the IJAAF brought the 68th Sentai into Wewak, on the northern coast of New Guinea, and the 78th Sentai was deploying to Rabaul. It is important to note that these two sentai were the first to be equipped with the new, high-performance Kawasaki Ki-61 Hien ("Flying Swallow") fighter. Also known within the IJAAF as the Type III Army Fighter, the Ki-61 was given the Allied code name Tony. The major mass-produced Japanese fighter of World War II to use a liquid-cooled inline engine, rather than the circular radial used in Oscars and Zeros, the Ki-61 was a fast and powerful fighter. It compared favorably to the German Messerschmitt Bf.109E, which it resembled, and for which it was occasionally mistaken.

D URING his Australian furlough, Bong had missed two major back-to-back Japanese attacks on Dobo on the night of May 13 and the following day. The big buildup of Japanese airpower from Wewak to Rabaul finally reached critical mass by the second week of May.

Both sides were trading reconnaissance flights. Kenney's Fifth Air Force recon had shown that the Japanese had 116 fighters and 84 bombers at Rabaul alone, and Japanese recon had determined that a large number of Allied supply ships were headed for Oro Bay. Kenney knew that they knew, and he was determined to be prepared; this meant concentrating a large fighter force at Dobo.

"We pushed the fighters across the mountains [from Port Moresby] to Dobodura and waited," Kenney wrote in his memoirs. "During the night six B-17s and four B-24s unloaded incidiaries and fragmentation bombs on Vunakanau [Airfield at Rabaul], where the Jap bombers and some of his fighters were."

The American air crews thought from the number of fires that blazed that they had cut the enemy air strength down considerably. As Kenney recalled, "the next morning it looked as though they had been right."

Kenney went on to say that the Japanese made their attack on May 14 "as we expected, and we took him, [sic] as we had expected. He sent over twenty bombers, two dive bombers, and twenty fighters. We intercepted with forty-three fighters and shot down eight bombers and eight fighters. We lost one P-38 from which the pilot parachuted safely, and one P-40 cracked up on landing. The Jap attack destroyed a few drums of fuel and cut the telephone line between Dobodura and Oro Bay."

It disappointed Bong to have missed such an opportunity for his next score. He was back on patrol on May 17, but May was to be a dry spell for him in terms of aerial combat. He flew one reconnaissance mission over Lae and three bomber escort missions between May 21 and 29, but the Japanese pilots avoided contact with the Forty-niners wherever possible.

A Japanese tactic that did continue through this lull was their sending lone light reconnaissance aircraft over the Allied bases—including Dobodura—in the middle of the night. Nicknamed "Washing Machine Charlie" because of the rattling sound of their small radial engines, the Japanese intruders came in low and escaped quickly over the jungle. Operating low and alone under the cover of darkness, they were hard to detect and hard to chase. Many fighter pilots, including Dick Bong on several occasions, jumped into their aircraft and tried to run them down, but it was virtually impossible.

These "Charlies" were more annoying than dangerous, but they managed to wake everyone up and make it hard to get a decent night's sleep. At other times these Japanese loners interrupted the American troops on nights when they were enjoying a 16mm print of a Hollywood movie. This was especially egregious behavior that truly infuriated the men.

Once in a while the interruption would be of a clarinet recital by Richard

Ira Bong. He had brought his "licorice stick" overseas with him, and occasionally at night he would play for his own amusement, making an effort to imitate Benny Goodman. There are two schools of thought as to whether the interruptions to Bong's playing were bad things. Some accounts complain that he was a really terrible clarinetist, while others recall that people greatly enjoyed his renditions of popular tunes.

CHAPTER 16

June 1943: Into the Interior

•SCORE•

BONG: 11
McGUIRE: 0

T HE clarinet was one of the hobbies that Dick Bong was able to continue in New Guinea, but he missed bowling, and the only hunting
he was able to do was of Japanese aircraft. In his letters home during the
hunting seasons in 1941 and 1942, he had shown a great deal of interest
in the number of deer that his dad, his brothers, and others were bringing
home. Several species of deer, including the rusa, exist in New Guinea, and
are hunted for meat, but there is no evidence that Bong ever went out looking for them. Indeed, with the Imperial Japanese Army in control of much
of New Guinea's trackless jungle, this would have been a more dangerous
pursuit for the deer hunter than for the deer. However, Bong did get a crack
at some indigenous wildlife on June 2.

Returning from a patrol, a fellow 9th Fighter Squadron pilot, Lieutenant
Paul Yeager, suffered an engine malfunction and had to abandon his P-38.
He parachuted into the jungle, and a ground party went out to rescue him.

Because of the established Japanese practice of shooting at downed
pilots, Yeager's squadronmates flew top cover for his rescue. In his book
about his brother, Carl Bong tells that as Dick was circling above the res-

cue boat while it was taking Yeager to safety, he noticed that a crocodile was paying undue attention to the Americans. As Carl Bong related it in his book, telling the tale told by someone who was there, Dick came in low and gave the menacing reptile a burst from his Lightning's nose-mounted arsenal. If the .50-caliber rounds connected, the crocodile was entirely blown away. Blown away as well, in the allegorical sense, were the men in the boat. In his logbook, Bong mentions only a two-hour mission flying "cover for search party."

It was ten days before Dick Bong had his next contact with a somewhat more evenly matched adversary.

Bong's next combat action came against the backdrop of the continued Allied strategy to keep pushing the Japanese back in New Guinea. With his troops marching north along the coast from Buna, General MacArthur had his sights set on Salamaua, then on Lae itself. To support this action from the air, Kenney was determined to establish an advance air base closer to Lae. He wanted his fighters closer because when they flew out of Dobodura, their fuel reserve allowed them to operate over Lae for only about thirty minutes.

For its new base, the Fifth Air Force surveyed a number of level fields in the interior. Kenney favored one near Tsili Tsili, where there was an abandoned grass landing strip that had been used before the war by gold prospectors operating in the area. Another site, at Garoka, near Bena Bena, also was considered. Kenney decided to build his new field near Tsili Tsili, called Marilinan, but to create a diversion at Garoka by pretending to build a base, and doing it so Japanese reconnaissance aircraft would notice. "I wanted a lot of dust raised and construction started on a lot of grass huts."

Kenney preferred the name Marilinan to that of Tsili Tsili, the nearest major town, because Tsili Tsili, when pronounced, sounded like "Silly Silly." He felt this inappropriate for an important base. Nevertheless, the name Tsili Tsili appears in many USAAF records, such as those of the 35th Fighter Group, which later was based there.

While the new primary base would be at Marilinan, Kenney's plan called for a real airstrip at Garoka to be used as an emergency field. Indeed, being closer to the fighting than Port Moresby or Dobodura, both fields would prove their value as emergency fields. By early September, both Dick Bong and Tommy McGuire would owe their lives to being able to land a crippled Lightning at Marilinan.

Building the two bases in literally the middle of nowhere necessitated bringing supplies in to support both the construction crews and the troops who guarded the site. Previous New Guinea bases, such as Dobodura, and those near Port Moresby, were close to the water and could be supported by sealift. In the interior of New Guinea, resupply was entirely dependent on airlift. It was not an easy task to support these bases by air because the interior of New Guinea is crisscrossed by thirteen-thousand-foot ridges with their peaks in the clouds, and the valleys between them are filled with fog.

Then, too, there was the enemy. Because of persistent Japanese air activity, the C-47 transports that hauled the supplies into the interior required fighter escort. Most of these missions were uneventful—until June 12.

At nine thirty-five that morning, as a dozen C-47s were nearing Bena Bena at ten thousand feet, eight IJAAF Ki-46 Oscar fighters were spotted about four thousand feet above. Two flights of 9th Fighter Squadron P-38s were flying escort for the C-47s. There were four Lightnings in Blue Flight, while Green Flight consisted of Captain Sidney Woods, with Dick Bong flying as his wingman. Five of the enemy went after Blue Flight, probably planning to disrupt them into leaving the unarmed transports exposed to attack by other Oscars.

Bong bored in on the five Oscars attacking Blue Flight and hit one. He observed no results with this hit, but as he checked his six, he discovered three Oscars on his tail. Diving through a cloud layer to escape, he picked up airspeed and climbed back into the fray.

He attacked another Oscar head on, spotted an enemy on his tail, and dove again. Climbing back, he launched another attack against an Oscar, at about ten degrees' deflection. This time he saw two explosions in the Japanese fighter. As he raced by, the Oscar was going down.

After making a forty-five-degree pass at yet another Oscar, Bong checked his fuel situation and headed for home. He didn't know exactly how close he was cutting it until he ran out of gas on the taxiway at Dobo.

He also did not realize how close he had cut it with the several Oscars that had been on his tail over Bena Bena until he climbed out of his Lightning and discovered the large cannon holes in the wings.

CHAPTER 17

July 1943: Four in One Day

•SCORE•

BONG: 11
McGUIRE: 0

"J ULY opened the final struggle for air supremacy over New Guinea and the Solomons," George Kenney observed. The Allies were conducting operations around Milne Bay, landing troops on Kiriwina and Woodlark, two islands in the Trobriand chain, as part of Operation Cartwheel, the Allied strategy to tighten a noose around Rabaul. To support these operations, Kenney had used assets other than the 49th Fighter Group, preferring to keep them closer to Lae in case things heated up there suddenly. Also on Kenney's mind in July, if off the operational front burner, was the buildup of Japanese airpower to the west, at the big base at Wewak, on New Guinea's northern coast.

The battle over Bena Bena on June 12 aside, the skies over the Lae area had been relatively quiet for the Forty-niners as the Japanese shifted their air assets eastward, toward Rabaul. The group continued to escort C-47s from Port Moresby to Bena Bena and Marilinan with no further interference from the Japanese. After a battle over Bogadjim on July 3, and some isolated fights on July 8 and 11, the only regular contact with Japanese aircraft for the men at Dobodura seemed to be the nocturnal visits of Washing

Machine Charlie, which did little damage but which was hard to catch. Dick Bong was in Port Moresby on July 3 to pick up a new P-38H Lightning, so he missed that battle. During the early part of the month, he did fly several escort missions for bombers raiding Salamaua, but engaged no enemy fighters. He celebrated the Fourth of July on an uneventful, two-hour weather reconnaissance mission over Lae.

Meanwhile, the advance echelon of the 35th Fighter Group was moving into Marilinan and assuming responsibility for operations there. This left the fighter pilots of the 49th more isolated from the combat action that was ongoing elsewhere during early July. They were anxious for the opportunities for aerial victories, such as they had tasted earlier in the year. They were warriors with a warrior's longing for battle.

As George Kenney wrote, "The 49th Fighter Group kids wanted to know why the Nips didn't come over their way so they could get some of that 'easy meat' and get closer to pulling the cork on their magnum of brandy." (The term "Nip" was a shorthand term for the Japanese that was widely used during World War II. It derives from the term "Nippon," the Japanese word for Japan itself. The Empire of Japan was officially Dai Nippon Teikoku. The term "Nip," like the term "Jap," is today considered derogatory, and we use these only in the context of direct quotes.)

On July 21, the 9th Fighter Squadron finally connected with the enemy in the large-scale air battle for which they had yearned, sharing the action with the Marilinan-based Lightnings of the 35th Fighter Group. The 39th Fighter Squadron of the latter group saw combat again on July 23, scoring 5 victories to bring its cumulative score to 109. During July, the 39th had become the first Fifth Air Force squadron to top 100 victories, and it was the top-scoring USAAF unit in the South West Pacific Area.

Dick Bong and the Flying Knights of the 9th would have their turn a few days later. On July 26, Bong was leading one of three flights of Lightnings making a routine fighter sweep over Lae and Salamaua. They passed over the latter without making contact with any Japanese aircraft and turned inland, flying at sixteen thousand feet over the valley of the Markham River, which flows roughly between Tsili Tsili and Bena Bena. Here the Americans finally met the Japanese.

Dick Bong spotted them first. The Americans initially observed about twenty enemy fighters, but at least another fifteen soon appeared. Estimates of the total enemy force run as high as fifty, which meant the Flying Knights were outnumbered by three or four to one.

The Japanese aircraft were all fighters, including the newly deployed IJAAF Kawasaki Ki-61 Tony. Also present were a roughly equal number of radial-engine fighters that are described in various accounts as IJNAF Zeros or IJAAF Oscars. It would be Bong's first contact with the Ki-61s, with their distinctive inline, water-cooled engines. In his after-action report he referred to them simply as "inline jobs."

Bong's first action upon seeing the enemy was to drop his external fuel tanks to increase his maneuverability, and to bore straight in on the nearest Tony.

Having either missed or done minor damage, Bong put his Lightning into a steep dive to add speed, pulled up, and ran head on into a Zero. He opened fire, immediately setting the enemy aircraft ablaze.

As the Zero went down in flames, Bong found himself above and behind a Tony at about forty-five degrees and opened fire. Having "knocked pieces off his fuselage," Dick moved to another Tony, turning it into a fireball.

By this time Dick Bong was a figurative ball of fire himself, having scored three victories in just minutes. Next he added a fourth, attacking a Zero head on and shooting off the canopy. As he passed his adversary, the engine, or at least the cowling, was coming off the Mitsubishi fighter.

Bong and the others left the battle area to return to Dobodura shortly after 2:00 P.M. The battle had lasted half an hour.

It was a bad day for the Japanese over the Markham River. Along with Bong's outstanding four victories, another six kills were shared by two other 9th Fighter Squadron pilots, Captain Jim Watkins and Lieutenant Jerry Johnson. Of course, as Bong later wryly pointed out, there were so many enemy aircraft in the sky that a fighter pilot "couldn't help but hit something."

Apparently General Kenney didn't agree with Bong's "fish in a barrel" understatement. As a result of his actions that day, Kenney wrote the young pilot up for a Distinguished Service Cross, the second-highest of American decorations for valor, and promoted him from first lieutenant to captain.

Bong's score now stood at fifteen, but he would not have to wait long for his next one.

Two days later, on July 28, Captain Bong was flying one of nine Lightnings that were escorting B-25 medium bombers on what General Kenney would later describe as "a barge hunt in the Cape Gloucester area" on the northern coast of New Britain island. At 8:30 A.M., after two hours in the air, the Americans reached New Britain, and the bombers went to work at low level at Rein Bay. As the fighters circled above at six thousand feet, they were attacked by an estimated fifteen Oscars.

As a pair of Japanese fighters ganged up on him, Dick Bong dove to elude them, then pulled up and made a forty-five-degree head-on pass at another Oscar. Having done no perceptible damage, he attacked yet another broadside and missed.

As he was about to join up with five of his squadronmates, he checked his six and discovered an enemy fighter behind him. Bong recalled feeling the impact of five rounds before he was able to dive out of the Oscar's sights.

The trough of Bong's dive brought him in at forty-five degrees behind another pair of enemy fighters that were sliding in behind one of the B-25s on a bomb run.

He lined up a deflection shot behind one of the Oscars, gave it a long burst, and watched it crash into the Bismarck Sea.

Bong departed the scene of the battle at 9:05 A.M. after thirty-five minutes of fighting. He was pursued by a pair of Oscars but outdistanced them, linked up with the B-25s headed home, and returned to his base just before 10:00 A.M.

The 9th Fighter Squadron had scored seven victories while losing none of their own. Captain Jim Watkins scored three of his eventual total of twelve that day.

Meanwhile, using their skip-bombing skill, the B-25 crews had managed to sink eight supply barges and a pair of large motor launches that morning. Also in the strike package was a B-25 experimentally equipped with a 75mm cannon. The plane was flown by Major Paul "Pappy" Gunn. A prewar bush pilot with extensive service in the South Pacific who had convinced Kenney to give him a commission and allow him to fly combat missions, Pappy was well on his way to becoming a "character" within the South West Pacific and of whom yarns and tall tales would be told for decades. On the July 28 mission, Gunn tried and failed to sink a Japanese destroyer with his gun, but redeemed himself later in the day by using the weapon to blow up an IJAAF transport aircraft that turned out to have contained two generals and three colonels en route to a high-level conference at Wewak.

CHAPTER 18

August 1943: Black Days

•SCORE•

BONG: 16
McGUIRE: 0

JULY had belonged to Dick Bong.

August would belong to Tommy McGuire.

Having scored five victories in less than three days, something that many fighter pilots aspire to accomplish in a whole tour of duty, Dick Bong was treated to a two-week furlough on the beach in Queensland, eating real eggs and drinking real milk instead of just gray powder that was labeled "eggs" or "milk."

After nearly three months of waiting around Amberly Field in Australia for all their factory-fresh P-38Hs to be uncrated, assembled, and tested, the 475th Fighter Group finally began moving north to New Guinea during the first week of August.

Once again, Bong and McGuire passed in the night.

As previously noted, Kenney had earmarked the 475th as the first group whose squadrons were equipped entirely with Lightnings. The 9th, 39th, and 80th fighter squadrons that had been flying the P-38 previously were each assigned to a different Fighter Group. Many of the pilots were newly arrived from Stateside, and they were mixed into the group's three squadrons with the pilots who'd had some experience flying with operational Lightning units in New Guinea.

Tommy McGuire was assigned to the 431st Fighter Squadron as one of the squadron's four flight leaders. By the time its headquarters was officially relocated to New Guinea on August 14, most of the 475th's pilots and aircraft were already on site. That day, Tommy McGuire flew with the 431st in its first combat mission, escorting C-47s to resupply the emergency field at Bena Bena. The following day, the mission was the same, but this time it was a four-hour round trip into Tsili Tsili. On neither day did the Americans cross paths with enemy aircraft.

The pilots typically rotated the missions among themselves, and on August 16 it was the turn of McGuire's flight to stand down. This, however, was the day when the 431st had its baptism of fire over Tsili Tsili.

After two months of being deluded into believing that the primary American base in the interior was the one at Bena Bena, the enemy apparently had finally figured out that Marilinan at Tsili Tsili was the real deal. More than two dozen Japanese aircraft launched an attack on the Marilinan base and wound up tangling with the Lightnings. The 431st claimed half of the Japanese force, mostly fighters, but including two bombers.

Having flown for four months in Alaska and a couple of weeks in New Guinea without combat, McGuire had now missed his squadron's first major action by one day. He had every right to feel as though he were jinxed. Everything would change the next day, though.

A few months earlier, General Kenney had expressed concern about the simultaneous buildup of Japanese airpower in both Rabaul and Wewak, and his fear that the Fifth Air Force was not strong enough to contend with both. "We were not strong enough to handle both Wewak and Rabaul," Kenney wrote. "So it seemed wiser to concentrate on the latter target, which helped both SOPAC and ourselves."

Having observed that "July opened the final struggle for air supremacy over New Guinea and the Solomons," Kenney was about to find August as the crescendo of that struggle.

By August, the Fifth Air Force had the airpower to "handle" Wewak, and Kenney was ready to initiate a sustained bombing campaign against Wewak and the nearby satellite airfields at Borum, But, and Dagua (aka

Dogaw). Reconnaissance showed that the Japanese had at least 225 aircraft based at these fields, and removing them was an important element in the Allied strategy for the South West Pacific Area. The campaign would begin with a two-day maximum effort set for August 17 and 18. The plan was to hit the Wewak airfields with a wave of heavy bombers followed two hours later by a wave of medium bombers, all of which would be escorted by P-38s—and to repeat this the following day.

The predawn opening salvo involved a dozen B-17s and forty-one B-24s hitting the fields in and around Wewak with two hundred tons of ordnance. Two hours later, the thirty-three B-25s swept in to strafe the fields. Overhead, the P-38s flew top cover, ready to engage any Japanese fighters that came up to challenge the bombers.

Incredibly, the Americans found the Japanese aircraft lined up in the same sort of neat rows that the Japanese had come across with USAAF planes at Wheeler Field in Hawaii on December 7, 1941. Whole lines of Japanese aircraft were raked by .50-caliber slugs and set afire by incendiary rounds. As in Hawaii in 1941, the attackers had pulled off a surprise.

For the Fifth Air Force, there would be cause for immense celebrating. No B-25s or P-38s were lost, although two B-34s failed to return from the mission.

In the annals of the Imperial Japanese Army, however, August 17 was a day that would be remembered as the "Black Day." The impact on their air assets, and their ability to engage in offensive operations, had been seriously crippled. More that 150 aircraft had been destroyed, most of them on the ground.

For Tommy McGuire, Tuesday, August 17, was his introduction to the reality of war, the reality of airplanes being blown up, and the reality of bullets being fired *at him* in anger. The sheer scale of the massive air attack had to have been an astonishing experience.

As planned, the Fifth Air Force returned to Wewak the following day, and this time with even larger numbers of fighters and medium bombers. The heavy bombers, twenty-six of them, attacked simultaneously with the fifty-three B-25s. Virtually every airplane caught on the ground was destroyed. However, on the second day, the Japanese managed to get some fighters airborne to challenge the Americans.

On Tuesday, Tommy McGuire had spent as much time over Wewak gawking as strafing, with no contact with enemy fighters. On Wednesday, he didn't even have time to think about aerial combat.

McGuire's flight took off in the predawn darkness and headed north across the rugged hogback ridges and jagged mountains of the New Guinea interior. One of the four Lightnings aborted because of engine trouble, but McGuire led the others across the island and up the coast into Wewak airspace at eight thousand feet as the sun was coming up behind them.

Suddenly a Japanese fighter dove on the P-38s, screaming past them, guns blazing. McGuire instinctively dove after him, sending two bursts of tracers into him. The light, nimble Japanese fighters had a reputation for being able to outmaneuver the big American fighters, but it was suicide to try to outrun a P-38 in a dive. The Japanese pilot committed suicide.

Less than a minute after the beginning of his first aerial engagement, Tommy McGuire had scored his first aerial victory.

As the flaming fighter tumbled from the sky, McGuire's wingman, Lieutenant Francis Lent, screamed at him on the radio to check his six.

He did. As he had killed one Japanese fighter, another was on his tail seeking to do the same to the guy from Sebring.

In a rivet-popping tight left turn, McGuire succeeded in getting out from in front of his enemy, while allowing the Japanese pilot to overshoot. Now it was the enemy who was looking at a Lightning in his six o'clock.

As with the first Japanese pilot whom McGuire had engaged, this man tried to dive to get away. McGuire stayed with him, ripping at his fuselage with .50-caliber claws until the aircraft burst into flames and tumbled toward the airfield at Dagua.

McGuire, now with two victories in his first half hour of air-to-air combat, pulled out of his dive and joined up with Lent.

Another Japanese fighter attacked them. Lent fired a burst and rolled away to avoid a head-on collision. McGuire stayed straight, firing at the enemy as the Japanese pilot fired at him in a deadly game of chicken.

The two adversaries passed so close that both pilots felt the jolt of wingtips colliding. Both aircraft got away from each other, but Tommy was sure he had delivered some good hits.

McGuire and Lent rendezvoused again and made a couple of passes at

Japanese fighters. As the second one turned to escape, Lent turned with him, fired, and made his first score of the day.

McGuire's flight then formed up on the B-25s as they exited the target area to escort them home.

The B-25s had repeated their success of the previous day at the Japanese airfields, doing so much damage that, General Kenney later reported, they had run out of targets. Having done this, they attacked supply dumps at Borum and sank three cargo ships in Wewak Harbor. On Tuesday, no B-25s had been lost. On Wednesday, three went down, including that of Major Ralph Cheli, who earned a posthumous Medal of Honor for leading his squadron through a low-level attack despite severe damage to his own aircraft.

As the P-38s began leading the medium bombers home, more Japanese fighters appeared, intent on taking out another B-25 or two. As Bong and Lent watched, a Kawasaki Ki-61 Tony made a fast pass through the bomber formation.

McGuire gave chase.

The Tony may have been faster than other IJAAF fighters, but it still was a bad idea to try to outrun a Lightning in a dive. Tommy blasted the Tony until it started to belch smoke. The bomber crews later confirmed that they had seen it crash into the jungle below.

Tommy McGuire returned with an amazing three victories from the first mission in which he had fought enemy aircraft. He had scored hits on a fourth, but it was credited to another pilot who also had put rounds into it before it went down.

In all, the 475th Fighter Group, which would adopt the nickname "Satan's Angels," had seriously bedeviled the Japanese, downing thirty-three of their aircraft that day. Nearly half of those were claimed by the 431st Fighter Squadron, nicknamed "Hades." The gunners in the bombers had shot down another eight.

Three aerial victories made Tommy McGuire the toast of the pilots' debriefing at the command post that afternoon, but when he returned to the flight line, the ground crews were more impressed by something else. All eyes were on Sergeant Frank Kish, McGuire's crew chief, as he pointed out the dark green Japanese paint smeared on the left wingtip of "his" P-38.

Another inch or two would have made all the difference between something that the men could laugh about and a collision that would have nipped McGuire's budding career as a warrior in the bud.

IT was General Kenney's plan not to let the enemy rest after those two back-to-back black days. As soon as his fleet had their maintenance done and bullet holes patched, he was sending bombers back to Wewak routinely. Meanwhile, however, the Japanese were not about to roll over and play dead. They had suffered mightily, but they would soon demonstrate that they were ready to throw everything they had left into making things miserable for the Fifth Air Force.

Tommy McGuire's next role in this drama began three days after his remarkable three-victory second combat mission. On August 21, the 431st Fighter Squadron was flying top cover for a medium bomber strike against the Wewak targets when an estimated fifteen enemy fighters attacked.

McGuire immediately lined up one of them at close range and opened fire.

As the first Japanese plane went down, McGuire lined up another. He, too, went down in a twisting, flaming ball of fire.

McGuire had scored his fourth and fifth victories. He had achieved ace status in just two engagements.

As the Japanese interceptors scattered and the tally was made, the 431st pilots realized that they had really overwhelmed the enemy. Both McGuire and Lent had gotten two, while Lieutenant Dave Allen had shot down three.

However, the excitement over their kills was short-lived. The fourth man in the flight, Lieutenant Ralph Schmidt, had gone down. A search-and-rescue effort over the next several days proved unsuccessful. If any environment on earth is truly deserving of the adjective "trackless," it is the steep, thick jungles of New Guinea. Even something as large as a P-38 can fall through its canopy and be lost forever.

New ace Tommy McGuire was written up for a Distinguished Flying Cross for his amazing work, and rewarded with a few days' downtime. In the meantime, Frank Kish brought out some red and white paint, and two more little Japanese flags appeared on the forward fuselage of McGuire's Lightning, right next to the place where McGuire had gotten his airplane's nickname painted. In the spirit of the times, World War II pilots almost always painted names on their precious planes. Sometimes they were named for pop songs, other times for cartoon characters, and often for wives and girlfriends. The name painted on Tommy's Lightning was *Pudgy*.

Tommy wasn't hearing from the real Pudgy as often as he would have liked, although it was not for want of trying by Marilynn. Unfortunately, when they finally reached him, not all the messages were good news. If Tommy McGuire had helped to deliver two "black days" to the Japanese in August 1943, he had one of his own on August 26 as the news of Polly's death reached New Guinea in the form of both a letter and a telegram sent from Sebring a month earlier by Marilynn.

He was devastated.

He would never be able to excitedly explain to his mother the details of his amazing first day in combat. She would never know that he had been written up for the Silver Star and a Distinguished Flying Cross after only three missions behind enemy lines. Now more than ever, Tommy McGuire looked forward to seeing Marilynn and to telling *her* face-to-face about all the things he was experiencing, things he could have imagined in only the most abstract way when he last saw her.

She had said that she would try to meet him on his next furlough, but furloughs that took the men out of combat were only to Australia, and it was essentially impossible for Marilynn to travel that far.

However, McGuire did not have the luxury of time to dwell on his concerns about the loss of his mother, that the woman he loved was a month away by mail, and that an interminable number of months would likely come and go before he saw her again.

His and three other four-ship flights were back over Wewak again with B-25s on August 29 when they were attacked by what the pilots reported as a mix of Zeros and Oscars.

Lieutenant Harry Holze was the first American to engage the enemy, but McGuire was a fast second. He saw a Zero slice through the bomber formation and met it head on as it pulled out of its dive. He put his sights directly on the Zero and hosed it with bullets until it became a fireball.

McGuire next attacked an IJAAF Oscar as it tried to jump the bombers. The two fighters raced toward each other, then slid past each other without having done any serious damage—nor with a wingtip collision, as McGuire had experienced on August 18.

Both planes turned.

McGuire turned tighter and fought to keep the enemy in his sights as it twisted and maneuvered across the sky to escape him. Finally, he saw the smoke and fire beginning to spill from the Oscar.

The next thing McGuire knew, he was being alerted by another Lightning pilot that there were three Zeros on his tail. He had been so engrossed in chasing the Oscar's six o'clock that he neglected to pay attention to his own.

Bad things can happen in a split second during a dogfight.

A hunter can become the hunted in that split second, and this had happened to Tommy McGuire. He had killed two Japanese fighters today in a Lighting, with five Japanese flags already painted on its nose. Here, the Japanese pilots knew, was a dangerous man. They ganged up on him to eliminate him.

A moment earlier, it had been the Oscar twisting and turning like a desperate mouse. But the tables had been turned—now McGuire had *three cats* on his tail.

McGuire maneuvered, watching the streaks of tracers all around him, feeling the occasional machine gun round ping as it hit *Pudgy*.

Suddenly it happened. He felt the jolt of an explosion and saw black smoke pouring from his left engine, just as he had seen smoke pour from enemy fighters.

There was little left for the Japanese to do but finish off this American in the crippled Lightning, but they just waited to see what would happen.

Inside the cockpit, McGuire worked feverishly to feather the left prop and cut off the fuel that was feeding the fire that threatened to burn off his left wing. At last he decided to dive. There was nothing else he could do. If he remained in level flight, the Japanese would start shooting again; if he dove fast enough, the slipstream *might* be enough to blow out the fire, and there was a chance that he could get below the clouds before the Japanese figured out that he wasn't crashing.

McGuire nosed over and went down.

His plan worked. After diving for 2,000 feet, the fire was indeed extinguished, and the Japanese fighters had gone on to other prey, or perhaps their own demise.

That was the good news. The bad news was that he probably couldn't get across the tall mountains and back to Port Moresby on a single engine.

Fortunately, there were now Fifth Air Force fields in the New Guinea interior. He was 250 miles from Marilinan, and that was his best bet. Having limped across the jungle that could have swallowed him forever if he went down, McGuire found himself fighting the torque effect of the single engine as he tried to land a wobbling *Pudgy* on Marilinan's grass strip.

He made it. He survived.

CHAPTER 19

September 1943: Air Supremacy

•SCORE•

BONG: 16
McGUIRE: 7

Tommy McGuire had already experienced more triumphs in combat than many warriors would in a full career. In less than two weeks, he already had an enviable record, having amassed seven aerial victories and being singled out for a Silver Star and a Distinguished Flying Cross—virtually unprecedented for actions in such a short time.

Also accomplished during those two weeks was a major shift in the balance of power between the Allies and Imperial Japan in New Guinea. The "final struggle for air supremacy over New Guinea and the Solomons" that George Kenney had described had finally reached its climax.

Against this backdrop, General MacArthur tightened the noose even further on the Japanese bastion at Lae. On September 4, Allied troops secured Nadzab on the Markham River, scarcely a dozen miles or so northwest of Lae. Several months later, Nadzab would play an important role in Allied air operations as General Wurtsmith moved the headquarters of his V Fighter Command there.

As McGuire's 475th Fighter Group had been tasked with the August operations against Wewak, Dick Bong's 49th Fighter Group would be central in flying top cover for the operations against Lae in September. Bong had spent the early part of August in Australia, and the latter days of the month flying uneventful escort missions. They were uneventful because the C-47s and B-25s whose missions he was covering now went largely unchallenged by Japanese fighters. The balance of power was rapidly shifting away from them, so the Japanese air arms were conserving their assets.

As the Allied ground troops closed in on besieged Lae, the Japanese sent bombers to stifle their advance. A little after noon on September 6, the P-40s of the 8th Fighter Squadron and the P-38s of Dick's 9th Fighter Squadron were on patrol south of Lae when they received word of a Japanese strike force inbound from Rabaul. There were eighteen G4M Betty medium bombers in two waves, with a fighter escort hanging back with the second echelon. Perhaps the plan was to lure the Americans to attack the first group, which appeared to be unescorted.

The 8th Fighter Squadron struck first, intercepting the Japanese bombers over Huon Gulf and downing four aircraft. The 9th then arrived and went after the second wave of nine bombers, which were arrayed in a trio of three-ship elements at about nine thousand feet.

Bong peeled off and closed in on the leader of the element on the left, diving from behind and to the outside.

He closed in and opened fire. He could see his rounds impact the bomber, and it began to slow. The other bombers flew on as the stricken bomber lost altitude. Inside, a desperate pilot fought to keep the bomber from falling, but it was a losing battle.

As the rest of the formation pressed on without this element leader, Bong made another pass, scoring hits along the side of a Betty in the same element. As Bong banked away from the enemy formation, smoke billowed from the Betty's right engine.

So, too, did smoke from Dick's own right engine.

The gunners aboard the bombers had fought back as Bong had bored in, and his P-38 had been hit. As had happened to Tommy McGuire the previous week, Bong's Lightning had taken a serious hit.

The second G4M that Bong had hit had now fallen, and he fought to

keep his P-38 from doing the same. He feathered the prop and began thinking about getting his plane on the ground. As McGuire had, Bong chose
Marilinan Field because it was only about ten minutes away.

They were a very long ten minutes, but at last he felt his tires on terra
firma.

The first two P-38s to be crash-landed by Dick Bong and Tommy
McGuire after a combat mission were now *both* parked at the same small
field in the middle of the New Guinea jungle.

Leaving his damaged Lightning at Marilinan, Bong hitched his way
back to Dobo the next day, believing that he had added two scores to his
tally. He was frustrated to discover that both of his victories had been officially downgraded to probables.

What happened was that both bombers had gone down trailing smoke,
but both had disappeared into a cloud layer clinging to Huon Golf at about
a thousand feet—and none of the pilots in Bong's squadron saw the two
planes actually hit the water.

Whether or not the two bombers were lost or probably lost, the tide was
definitely receding for the Japanese. Lae fell to the Allies on September 16,
and Allied ground troops began moving against enemy positions farther up
the valley of the Markham River.

As Japanese airpower waned, the Fifth Air Force grew stronger. The new
475th Fighter Group that established itself during August was now augmented by another new outfit, the 348th Fighter Group, flying an aircraft new to
the South West Pacific Theater. Like the Lightning, the Republic Aviation P-47
Thunderbolt was a much more formidable aircraft than the earlier-generation
P-39 and P-40 types. Like them, and unlike the P-38, the Thunderbolt was a
single-engine fighter, but its performance was on a par with that of the P-38,
and the USAAF was having good luck with them in the European and Mediterranean theaters. The "Jug," as everyone more or less affectionately called
the Thunderbolt, was powerful and durable. Fiercely loyal to their aircraft, the
P-38 Lightning pilots developed a clever put-down of the P-47, noting that a
Thunderbolt was a "meaningless noise that follows Lightning."

It would be from the ranks of the 348th that Dick Bong would later have his first serious rival for the distinction of top-scoring USAAF ace in the Pacific. This man was Colonel Neel Kearby, coincidentally the commander of the 348th. A Texan from Wichita Falls, Kearby was somewhat elderly for a fighter pilot, being a venerable thirty-two years of age, but he had a younger man's reaction time and was a natural as a fighter pilot.

Kearby had arrived in Australia with the advance echelon of the 348th at the end of June, but the unit was not forward-deployed to Port Moresby until early August, when the bugs were worked out with the P-47. The principal bug, and the real Achilles' heel for the aircraft in the early days, was that its range was inferior to that of the P-38—and range was vital to operations in the sprawling Pacific Theater. The remedy would take development of adequate external fuel tanks, and this would take time. Much of the work was done in the field in Australia.

As Kenney wrote, "I knew it didn't have enough gas but we would hang some more [tanks] on somehow and prove it as a combat plane, especially as it was the only fighter that [USAAF commanding general] Arnold would give me in any quantities for some time. I told Kearby that regardless of the fact that everyone in the theater was sold on the P-38, if the P-47 could demonstrate just once that it could perform comparably I believed that the 'Jug,' as the kids called it, would be looked upon with more favor."

When it came to a demonstration of performance, one turns to the fascinating first meeting of Neel Kearby and Dick Bong. It had taken place on the first of August as Bong was passing through Amberly Field on the nine-day furlough he earned after shooting down five enemy planes in three days.

Colonel George Prentice, commander of the 475th and a staunch Lightning advocate, had flown the P-47 and found it satisfactory, but it was decided that a sure way to reverse the Jug's inferiority complex would be a mock dogfight between a P-47 and a P-38. Kearby would fly a Jug himself in such an exercise. To represent the P-38 pilots, what better man than Dick Bong?

The outcome of the thirty-five-minute duel is subject to the varying perceptions of those who saw it. Some say that Bong was able to outmaneuver Kearby, but barely. Others called it a draw. Bong's own logbook states merely that it took place. In any case, Kearby demonstrated that the P-47 could hold its own with the favorite USAAF fighter in the South West Pacific.

The 348th Fighter Group finally got its fuel tanks, and had its first taste of combat on August 16. Neel Kearby did not score his first aerial victories until September 4, when operations around Nadzab began. He opened with a double, a fighter and a bomber, and he scored his third on September 15. He had openly stated that he planned to be the highest-scoring USAAF ace of World War II, and promised that he would not go home until he had fifty victories.

At the time, though, the man to beat seemed to be Tommy McGuire. There were a number of men with higher scores, but the speed with which he had accumulated his score made him the subject of many conversations at the fighter fields across New Guinea. Was it skill or was it luck? It was probably a combination of the two, but it didn't matter. All that really mattered were results, and he had plenty of those to show.

McGuire spent the early part of September waiting around Port Moresby for a new P-38 to replace the damaged *Pudgy*. He borrowed one, but discovered that the lightbulb was missing from the gunsight, rendering it essentially worthless on a mission. Finally a new P-38H arrived, and by September 9, he had painted the side with the nickname *Pudgy II* and was ready for action. For the next two weeks that action involved routine escort missions in which no Japanese fighters attempted to intercept the American aircraft.

On September 21, the Satan's Angels of the 475th moved across the Owen Stanleys to the growing Fifth Air Force complex at Dobodura, where McGuire had been stationed briefly when he was with the Forty-niners. Once again both McGuire and Bong were at the same base, although their typical day's work was in different quadrants of the Fifth Air Force battle map. The 475th's principal area of operation was on the northern coast of New Guinea in the Wewak area, while the 49th Fighter Group operated mainly in the east, toward New Britain.

It was on one of those Wewak missions that Tommy McGuire had his next taste of combat. Escorting a B-24 raid against Wewak on September 28, his 431st Fighter Squadron went ahead to conduct a fighter sweep of the target area, then returned to escort the bombers. The purpose of the fighter sweep was to draw out the Japanese, luring them into a fight before the bombers arrived, so that the Lightnings could deal with the enemy without having to worry about the bombers.

This tactic usually worked, but this time the Japanese didn't take the bait.

As the fighters joined with the bombers, a single Zero attacked the Lightnings. The Japanese were trying a diversion of their own. The Zero locked onto the tail of one of the P-38s, expecting to lure the other fighters away from the bombers. As another P-38 intervened to chase the Zero, the Japanese pilot broke off his attack and disappeared into a cloud.

Suddenly about thirty Japanese fighters—double the number of Lightnings—attacked as the forty heavy bombers made their bomb run against a munitions stockpile in Wewak.

McGuire made a pass at one Zero, checked his six, and saw that he and his wingman each had a Zero lining up behind him. McGuire ordered a fast break to the outside, and he and his wingman turned hard in opposite directions.

Now in the clear, McGuire headed for another target, a Zero that was attacking an American plane. The Japanese pilot turned, but McGuire had anticipated the turn, and he watched the plane fly directly into his gunsight.

As one burning Zero tumbled earthward, McGuire looked for other prey. Again he saw a Zero on the attack, again he closed to close range to open fire, and again a Zero cartwheeled out of the sky trailing smoke and fire.

McGuire looked for a third target, checked his six, saw that he was being followed, and dove to escape. In so doing, McGuire crossed the Zero's gunsights and a few rounds hit his left engine.

He managed to get away from the Zero, but for the second time in a month, he was nursing a crippled Lightning across 250 miles of New Guinea wilderness. There is no better illustration of one key advantage of the P-38 over the P-47 than this. McGuire had feathered his prop and cut off fuel to a damaged engine, yet he still flew on his second engine. Had this happened in a single-engined Jug, McGuire would have had to bail out, and would have found himself hanging in a parachute harness in a triple-canopy jungle where his chances of ever being found were remote at best.

It must have felt like déjà vu all over again as McGuire landed *Pudgy II* on a single engine at Marilinan. This time he borrowed a recently repaired Lightning, and the top-scoring ace in the 475th Fighter Group was able to get himself back to Dobodura.

CHAPTER 20

October 1943: Down in Flames

•SCORE•

BONG: 16
McGUIRE: 10

I F General Douglas MacArthur needed assurance that his troops were winning the war, and that airpower was a key part of it, he needed to look nor farther than Wewak. By October the Japanese had essentially abandoned the four major air bases in the area, using them only for emergency landings and refueling stops. In the west, Lae had fallen to the Allies, and nearby Finschhafen, once another important Japanese base, was captured two weeks later. The Fifth Air Force had pushed the IJAAF and IJNAF farther back up the coast to Hollandia (now Jayapura, Indonesia), on the northern coast of New Guinea.

To the east, George Kenney's airmen continued to attack the Japanese on New Britain, hitting airfields to gradually wear down their aircraft strength, and attacking shipping to make resupply of the island increasingly difficult.

On October 2, medium bombers set out to attack the port of Cape Hoskins on the northern shore of New Britain, escorted by fourteen 9th Fighter Squadron Lightnings. As the strike force passed west of Gasmata, on New Britain's southern shore, at fifteen thousand feet and prepared to turn north, Dick Bong, flying one of the P-38s, spotted a lone Japanese aircraft. It was a Mitsubishi

Ki-46 Dinah reconnaissance aircraft, such as he had shot down on March 29, and it was headed south, straight toward the American force. In his after-action report, Bong guessed by the slow turn the Dinah made that the pilot hadn't yet noticed that he was about to come face-to-face with dozens of American airplanes. In any case, his turn brought Ki-46 into Dick Bong's sights. Moments later, the flaming aircraft was tumbling out of the sky.

A few days later, Bong was on furlough in Australia again, at Southport, which he described in a letter to his mother as a beach town south of Brisbane. It was spring in Australia, and starting to get warmer, but back home it was fall, and Dick asked his mother to save him some apples. It had been thirteen months since he had been home, and he wondered whether he might get enough leave to go home for Christmas.

While Bong was away, Neel Kearby's career as a fighter pilot was beginning to take off. On October 11, bad weather that had socked in the northern coast of New Guinea for more than a week finally cleared. Kearby was leading a four-Jug reconnaissance patrol that day, with Major Raymond Gallagher, commander of the 342nd Fighter Squadron, as his wingman. Near Wewak, they observed a lone Oscar below them.

Kearby attacked, converting his altitude advantage to speed, and destroyed the Japanese fighter. Japanese records examined in later years suggest that the pilot of the lone Japanese plane was probably Lieutenant Colonel Tamiya Teranishi, commander of the 14th Sentai, who was flying ahead of a force that had been launched from the Wewak area to intercept the Americans.

Gallagher peeled off to pursue another lone Japanese fighter to the north, over the Pacific. The other three Americans continued west, making a pass over Wewak, then turned back. Suddenly they spotted a large number of Japanese aircraft below them. General Kenney reports that there were a dozen fighters and three times that number of bombers, while other accounts reverse the proportions. Among the fighters were Ki-43 Oscars and Ki-61 Tonys, and possibly some A6M Zeros as well.

Despite the enemy's numerical superiority, Kearby figured that surprise would convert to even odds, so he ordered an attack. In his first high-speed pass, Kearby claimed three, while Bill Dunham and John Moore each scored singles.

Kearby then ordered his patrol to break contact and return to base, but he spotted Gallagher under attack by a pair of Tonys. He dived into the fray, guns blazing. At that point Dunham and Moore observed Kearby fighting six Ki-61s. He probably downed at least one of these, if not two.

As Kearby returned to Port Moresby from the mission, both General MacArthur and General Kenney were on hand to greet him. By coincidence, they were both at the base to discuss the large air operation against Rabaul that Kenney was planning for October 12. Kearby thus had a chance to tell his story, not only to the commander of the Fifth Air Force, but also to the highest-ranking U.S. Army officer in the Pacific. For his part, the chance meeting gave Kenney the opportunity to proudly show off a remarkable fighter pilot to his boss.

"I remarked to General MacArthur that the record number of official victories in a single fight so far was five," Kenney recalled of the meeting. He added that it had been "credited to one of the Navy pilots," and that the man had been awarded a Congressional Medal of Honor for the action. In fact, Kenney was thinking about Joe Foss of the Marine Corps, who had shot down five in one day over Guadalcanal a year earlier and who was awarded the Medal of Honor. In the meantime, a U.S. Navy pilot, Stanley "Swede" Vejtasa of VF-10 aboard the carrier USS *Enterprise*, had shot down *seven* Japanese aircraft during the Battle of Santa Cruz, also in October 1942— and he was *not* awarded the Medal of Honor. Foss received the medal for a series of actions and for a cumulative score of twenty-six, not for five in one day, as Kenney remembered.

Parenthetically, the best single-day records of all time were scored by pilots with Germany's Luftwaffe during World War II. Emil "Bully" Lang scored eighteen victories in one day against the Red Air Force on the Eastern Front, and Hans-Joachim Marseille scored seventeen victories in one day against the Royal Air Force in North Africa.

In any case, Kenney was determined to get the Medal of Honor for Kearby. If aces who scored five in a day deserved Medals of Honor, one of his "boys" who downed seven certainly should have one.

"I added that as soon as I could get witnesses' statements from the other three pilots and see the combat camera-gun pictures, if the evidence proved that Kearby had gotten five or more, I wanted to recommend him for the same decoration," Kenney said. "The General [MacArthur] said he would approve it and send it to Washington recommending the award. We both congratulated Kearby and I left for Fighter Command Headquarters to get the evidence. The testimony of the rest of his flight, and the pictures, confirmed the first six victories beyond a doubt. At the time Kearby got the seventh, however, the other three pilots had been so absorbed in extricating themselves from combat that they had not watched his last fight and, much to my disgust, the camera gun had run out of film just as it showed Kearby's tracer bullets begin to hit the nose of the Jap plane. I wrathfully wanted to know why the photographic people hadn't loaded enough film, but they apologetically explained that this was the first time anyone had ever used that much. They hadn't realized that enough film to record seven separate victories was necessary but from now on they would see that Kearby had enough for ten."

The six confirmed victories brought Kearby's overall total to nine, and eventually he would be awarded the Medal of Honor.

October 11 also saw Tommy McGuire back in action, if not in combat. While the Jugs of the 348th were cutting a huge swath through the IJAAF, McGuire was finally reclaiming *Pudgy II*, which had been repaired after the September 28 shoot-out. The following day, McGuire and *Pudgy II* participated in what was the largest bombing raid yet conducted in the Pacific Theater. Once upon a time, if the Fifth Air Force sent 50 aircraft against a target, a force of this size was considered substantial. On October 12, in a maximum effort against Rabaul, Kenney launched 349 aircraft, including 87 B-17 and B-24 heavy bombers and 114 B-25 medium bombers. There were 125 P-38s, as well as Australian Beaufighters. The first wave achieved a surprise attack.

Although antiaircraft fire was stiff, the response of the Japanese fighter force was feeble, and McGuire saw no air-to-air combat. The bombers, however, dealt a serious blow to the enemy. More than 100 Japanese aircraft were destroyed on the ground, while nearly 50 transport ships and more than 70 smaller craft were sunk in Rabaul's harbor. Three destroyers were among the vessels listed as damaged.

Expecting that a raid of this magnitude might be the harbinger of an Allied invasion of New Britain, the Japanese responded in kind three days later. Scraping together between 60 and 95 aircraft, they made an early-morning attack on Allied shipping in Oro Bay, just offshore from Dobodura.

Tommy McGuire heard the scramble siren at 8:30 A.M. and dashed to *Pudgy II*. The Japanese strike force was met by roughly 75 Lightnings, which prevented them from sinking any of the Allied ships. The Japanese also turned home without at least 21 of their dive bombers and 15 of their fighters. Some intelligence reports reported that as few as 6 Japanese planes made it back to Rabaul without major damage. Among the 10 Japanese aircraft claimed by the 431st Fighter Squadron was Tommy McGuire's own tenth, making him a double ace. The ground crews at Dobo, who usually never saw such a spectacle in their own skies, greatly enjoyed the show.

Two days later, the Japanese tried again, and again Tommy McGuire responded to the scramble siren. However, *Pudgy II* was down for maintenance, so McGuire had to improvise. He "borrowed" the P-38 belonging to Major Franklin Nichols, commander of the 431st Hades Fighter Squadron, who was over at Port Moresby for the day, attending a conference.

Even though Nichols had a standing rule about no one touching his Lightning, McGuire figured that the boss wouldn't mind if his plane was used for just a couple of hours. Or would he?

McGuire didn't take much time to wonder as he strapped himself into the aircraft.

The Lightnings intercepted the Japanese strike force at twenty-eight thousand feet over open water before the force reached Oro Bay. McGuire picked out a fighter at the edge of the formation and poured lead into it until it started to smoke and fall. He followed it down, throwing short bursts into it until he was sure it was a goner. Then he returned to the fight above.

As he climbed through twenty-one thousand feet, he saw two Zeros about to attack some Lightnings from his flight. Shouting a warning over his radio, he opened fire on the enemy. However, as he checked his own six, he saw that four enemy fighters were swarming to attack him.

As was his trademark in such situations, he put the Lightning into a steep dive. As usually happened, the enemy broke off the attack rather than follow him down, and Tommy was alone as he pulled out at near wavetop level.

Again, he climbed into the action, and again he found Zeros on his tail. This time one of the Zeros followed him into his dive, managing to put several rounds through the Perspex canopy of the purloined P-38. However, having just cheated death by inches, McGuire escaped yet again.

Back at twelve thousand feet, McGuire observed the sickening sight of seven Zeros closing in to finish off a damaged Lightning that was limping toward Dobodura. Knowing that without drastic measures this American would die, Tommy McGuire went into action.

It was not a difficult decision to attack the Zeros, but it was a difficult angle from which to attack. He would have to try a ninety-degree deflection shot, shooting at the side of an aircraft moving crossways at more than two hundred miles per hour—but he had no choice.

He had succeeded in hitting targets this way before, and he succeeded again.

As the Zero became a fireball, McGuire jumped on the six of another and roared in close. After already downing two enemy aircraft that day, it occurred to McGuire that he was probably low on ammunition and that he should make every round count. He closed to a distance that would barely be considered safe for following a big rig in your car on a modern interstate highway.

McGuire thumbed the trigger and watched pieces of metal fly off the Zero before it rolled to the side and burst into flames.

By now the injured Lightning that McGuire had sought to save had escaped, but its hunters were still hunting. They had just watched McGuire kill three of their number, and they were out for blood.

He checked his six. The Zero behind him now was practically on top of him, just as he had been on top of a Zero moments before. For a moment he was helpless prey, but a moment was all it took.

Machine-gun rounds ripped apart the Lightning's left engine. Suddenly McGuire's skull was slammed forward as bullets impacted the small slab of armor plate behind his head. Bullets filled the cockpit, destroying the instrument panel and cutting a bloody notch in his wrist.

The P-38, no longer controllable, slumped and began to fall. Seeing their prey going down in smoke, the Japanese broke off the attack. One of them would report an aerial victory that night.

Tommy McGuire found himself encased in seven tons of falling metal with the blue Pacific racing up at him.

He popped the canopy, unsnapped his harness, and jumped.

At that moment, he felt a rude jerk as his body slammed against the airplane. His parachute strap was snarled inside the cockpit, and he realized that he was going down with the plane.

Clawing desperately, he finally freed himself and pulled the ripcord—completely out of the parachute.

He was still falling like a chunk of scrap metal, and the blue Pacific was getting ever closer.

Somehow, despite his injured wrist, he managed to find and pull the severed ripcord cable and his parachute opened—barely high enough to break his fall.

Moments later, he hit the water and tried to inflate his life vest. Fortunately, at least half of it had not been punctured by the shrapnel that had ripped up the cockpit. P-38 pilots also had a small, one-man inflatable life raft attached to their parachute pack, but in McGuire's case, it had been shredded.

As McGuire bobbed in the swells, listing to one side because of his half-inflated vest, he thought about his bloody wrist and how the ferrous smell of this red liquid would soon begin to attract the sharks that abounded in these waters. Tommy was still alive, but he was having a *really* bad day. On top of all his other troubles, he had lost his boss's plane.

Minutes turned into hours, but at last, a large, dark shape appeared above his head. Stenciled on the side were the numbers 152. It was the Elco eighty-foot motor torpedo boat known as *Lakacookie*, commissioned in New Jersey as PT-152 a year earlier. Having seen McGuire duel with the Japanese fighters and watched him go down, the crew of the PT Boat had decided to look for survivors. Naturally, the boy who entered the world in New Jersey twenty-three years before was glad to see them, regardless of where their boat had been made.

By the time McGuire was rescued, the word had gone around at Dobo that he probably wouldn't be coming home. The toll against the Japanese that day had been twenty-seven dive bombers and twenty fighters. McGuire was assumed to be the only American loss until the squadron finally got word about the rescue from the navy.

His injuries landed McGuire in the 10th Evacuation Hospital at Oro

Bay, where Major Nichols found him and awarded him his Purple Heart medal. As for his actions that day in saving the crippled Lightning and downing three enemy aircraft, Nichols recommended a second Silver Star. As for his borrowing the boss's airplane, Nichols told him that it had saved lives, but not to do it again. Nichols remained in the U.S. Air Force after the war and retired in 1970 as a major general, having served as chief of staff of the Seventh Air Force during the war in Southeast Asia.

Dick Bong returned to Dobodura shortly after McGuire was shot down, having missed both Neel Kearby's big day and the big air battles over Oro Bay. He flew his next mission on October 24, escorting B-25s on a mission against Rabaul. The Fifth Air Force reported at least forty-five bombers destroyed on the ground at the Vunakanau, Rapopo, and Tobera airfields, and that the more than fifty P-38s claimed to have downed more than thirty-five Japanese aircraft. Bong's logbook notes that he shot at three but scored no hits. The two weeks in Australia may have dulled his aim.

As the weekend approached and a storm front finally blew through the area, he'd have another chance. October 29 was earmarked for another maximum-effort Fifth Air Force offensive against Rabaul as had been flown during the middle of the month. Kenney sent thirty-seven B-24s escorted by fifty-three P-38s, while other bombers worked over the Japanese positions on New Guinea's northern coast.

The 9th Fighter Squadron contributed thirteen Lightnings to the Rabaul mission, and Dick Bong's was among them. Their first contact with Japanese fighters came just after noon in the target area. Bong watched them dive from twenty-two thousand feet, slashing through the bomber formation. He and his wingman gave chase, only to discover that Zeros were on their tails as well.

Bong shook his pursuers and broke out of his dive over the water at about a thousand feet. He found himself head on with a Zero and quickly blew him out of the sky.

He looked up to see two more Zeros heading away and gave chase. He managed to destroy one, and would have downed both, but he was running low on ammunition and broke off his attack to return to Dobodura. With nineteen confirmed victories, Dick Bong was now the top-scoring USAAF ace in the South West Pacific Area by a margin of three.

CHAPTER 21

November 1943: The Pied Piper of Poplar

·SCORE·

BONG: 19

McGUIRE: 13

THE Japanese at Rabaul had taken a severe beating during October, but they were no more willing to give up than the Soviets had been at Stalingrad during the terrible campaign of the previous winter. After the October 29 attack, Japanese air strength was down to about 50 fighters and 25 bombers, but the enemy moved quickly to replace the losses. Unbeknownst to the Allies, the Japanese increased their strength in Rabaul to at least 165 fighters and 50 bombers over the next two days. Even more Japanese aircraft were now at Truk, en route to New Britain.

On November 2 the Americans launched another big attack, expecting to face a much smaller Japanese air fleet. They flew into what General Kenney later described as "the toughest fight the Fifth Air Force encountered in the whole war."

The 57 P-38s that flew the mission found themselves outnumbered two to one, but not outclassed. Though 9 P-38s were shot down, they downed more than 40 Japanese fighters and downed 12 more as probables. The gunners in the bombers, meanwhile, claimed 27 fighters, while losing 6 of their own. Dick Bong flew the mission as second in command to the fighter commander, his old friend Captain Jerry Johnson, but Bong scored no victories.

After more than two months of launching maximum-effort attacks to deplete the Japanese air assets, the Fifth Air Force was feeling the pinch itself. The missions were taking their toll on aircraft and crews, Kenney was scheduled to receive a hundred new Lightnings by year's end, but Hap Arnold could promise him only forty. Across the globe, the Allies were up to their necks in fighting the Germans, and the Allied leaders had already agreed to give that aspect of fighting World War II a priority over actions in the Pacific. The Allies had gone ashore at Salerno on the Italian mainland in September, and the going was far rougher than expected. In the strategic air war against the heartland of the Reich, Allied losses were frighteningly high. Arnold's priorities were with replacing these losses. He would give Kenney only what could be spared.

Against this backdrop, Kenney was reticent when MacArthur asked for another maximum effort, on November 5. MacArthur's reasoning was that Admiral William "Bull" Halsey's Task Force 38 was steaming into the area, and he was ready to launch air strikes of his own against Rabaul using aircraft from his five aircraft carriers. He had convinced MacArthur that it would be a good idea to have a coordinated USAAF strike. Kenney reluctantly agreed to do the best he could.

On November 5, Bong led the 9th Fighter Squadron's Red Flight as sixty-seven Lightnings escorted twenty-seven B-24 bombers back to Rabaul. The Fifth Air Force planes arrived after the carrier planes had come and gone. Task Force 38 attacked with ninety-seven aircraft, including fifty-two fighters, which shot down more than two dozen of the enemy. As the U.S. Navy planes departed, so, too, had most of the Japanese, who had gone in search of the carriers. Only about fifteen Japanese fighters were left to face the P-38s.

Bong's Red Flight was coming over the target at twenty thousand feet when he saw the Japanese Zeros below. He ordered the planes to drop their external tanks and attack. Bong led the way, jumping one Zero from behind. A short, well-placed burst and the aircraft exploded. A second Zero that Bong chased tried to outmaneuver him but failed. Bong tried twice more against two other aircraft as they ran to escape, but he scored no further kills. Nor did anyone else in the 9th Fighter Squadron. The two that Bong destroyed were the only Japanese aircraft downed by the Fifth Air Force that day.

Two days later, it was a different story as Bong led Red Flight to Rabaul yet again. This time there were plenty of targets, but Dick was the one not to score, although he engaged several and did manage to break up a gaggle of them that were ganging up on a crippled P-38. Between forty and sixty Japanese interceptors challenged the 9th Fighter Squadron, and twenty-three died trying.

Five of the Lightnings, however, went down. Among them was Dick's wingman, Lieutenant Stanley Johnson, who was shot down as he and Bong were trying to save another man targeted by Zeros. It was the second time in as many missions that Bong had lost a wingman. Two days earlier, Lieutenant George Haniotis disappeared while Bong was engaging the two Zeros he destroyed. Haniotis went down at sea, survived, and was spotted floating in his life raft by returning USAAF aircraft. But by the time air-sea rescue reached the area, he was gone.

Through the years, a footnote to Bong's story had always brought him into question for having lost two wingmen in so short a time. Was there something he did wrong?

The answer is twofold. First, it is the job of a wingman to stay with his leader, not the other way around. Second, by all accounts, Dick Bong is remembered by all who flew with him as being the antithesis of careless. Walter Markey, who had flown with Bong since the two men first arrived in Australia in September 1942, later confirmed that he'd never met anyone who had refused to fly as Bong's wingman. It was often said that few men, if any, in the 49th Fighter Group would have turned down an opportunity to fly on his wing.

THOUGH it was not known at the time, the November 7 mission to Rabaul would be Dick Bong's last of the year. Orders had been issued that provided him with thirty days' leave—and transportation to the United States. At 3:30 A.M. on November 12, he tucked his clarinet into his duffel bag and departed from Amberly Field, crossed the international date line, and arrived in San Francisco on November 14.

As he was traveling across the vast Pacific, he may have been thinking of George Haniotis, adrift down there somewhere. Dick may have been thinking about George's family, and he was certainly thinking about his own. Aside from that, the thing that appears to have been foremost on his mind was getting to Wisconsin in time for the start of hunting season on November 18. He had no idea how much things had changed. The Dick Bong who was known to a few was about to meet the Dick Bong who was known to more people than he could have imagined.

The young man who had traveled westward on that route more than a year earlier as just one more among thousands of second lieutenants, now returned as a captain and a decorated hero.

The pilot who had been just a pilot among pilots a few months before was now the highest-scoring USAAF ace in the South West Pacific—and indeed in the entire USAAF, because none of the aces in the European Theater had reached twenty-one. Since the top-scoring *American* ace was a marine, the USAAF was especially anxious to promote *their* top ace. News releases and photos of Bong were widely distributed to the media.

The shy boy from Wisconsin who had often gone unnoticed in groups was now surprised to discover that he was a media celebrity. Reporters were few in New Guinea, but as soon as he landed on American soil, they suddenly descended on poor Dick.

They also descended on the Bong farm in Wisconsin. As Carl Bong wrote later is his memoir of his brother, "Reporters of the United Press, Associated Press and the International News Service from around the country swarmed into the area to report and record Dick's every move. Some arrived early. The first ones came from the local *Superior Evening Telegram*. They came out to the house and took human interest photos of Mom, Dad and the family, depicting some of the everyday life on the farm and the preparations being made for Dick's homecoming. A phone call revealed that Dick was driving up from Milwaukee with two newsmen and was expected to be home sometime late in the evening of the sixteenth. The whole family was home and, after the chores were done and the supper dishes put away, we settled in to wait for Dick's arrival. Our driveway is about a hundred yards long and throughout the evening there was usually someone keeping an eye out for any car lights that might turn in to the house."

After several false alarms, the car in which Dick was riding turned down the driveway at a quarter after one the next morning. By this time, the air cadet band from Superior State Teachers College, Dick's alma mater, was on hand to salute him.

Before dawn on the first day of hunting season, Dick Bong got his long-anticipated opportunity to go deer hunting. Accompanied by his father, brother, three uncles, a cousin, and various others, he set out loaded for deer. With the media hovering around, it is a wonder that the Bong party managed to get seven bucks in four days—including the amazing ten-point buck that was bagged by Dick's father on the first day.

Dick Bong was thinking about little other than getting out into the cold, crisp weather with his 300 Savage and sinking his teeth into a fresh venison steak, but events were in motion about twenty miles away that would change his life.

As often happens in the fall on campuses around the United States, at Superior State Teachers College, many people were thinking about homecoming. Until the year before, homecoming had been a very big deal. There had been a football team, a bonfire, sororities, fraternities, a big dance, and a homecoming king and queen.

This year, things were different. There were fraternities but no football team. The young men had gone to war. The homecoming king would be chosen from among the young aviation cadets who happened to be home on leave. The homecoming queen would be chosen, as in 1942, by the Lambda Sigma Lambda sorority, specifically six girls: Marge Bahrman, Bev Barnett, Margi Flinn, Mary Gray, Marianne Meyers, and the 1942 queen, Marjorie Vattendahl. The "Dambda Lambdas," as they called themselves, picked a girl named Vi Pappelis, and brainstormed over who to pick to crown her as queen.

It was Margi Flinn who picked up a copy of the *Superior Evening Telegram* and suggested the most famous former student of Superior State Teachers College. But a question remained: how would the Dambda Lambdas coerce Captain Richard Ira Bong to come out to the school on November 20 and participate in the affair?

A group of girls drove to the Bong farm, missed Dick by minutes, but left a note. They then contacted Dick's sister Geraldine "Jerry" Bong, who was a student at Superior State, and asked that she plead their case. She did, and successfully.

"Color his eyes with the clearest of blue, make them squint just a bit from peering into the hot New Guinea skies," Marge Vattendahl wrote in 1946, recalling her first impression of the young flier as he appeared that night with his customary shy grin in place. "Make his blond hair short, wavy and bleached from the sun. Place a smile, an engaging grin on his face. Let him be modest but not bashful, unassuming but not confused and proud but not arrogant of a job well done. Put him in an Air Corps uniform, place the insignia of the Fifth Air Force and captain's bars on his shoulders and put nineteen decorations with room for more on his tunic."

That Marge was smitten is certainly an understatement.

The evening passed quickly, with nearly every girl in the room crowding in to get Bong to dance with her. He politely declined them all, telling them he had never learned to dance. After the dance, Marge and Margi Flinn stopped by Chef's, the local diner where young people gathered after school dances. Walking into the crowded café, Marge saw the young pilot seated in a booth with two of his sisters and his friend Pete Peterson—who was Jerry Bong's date. Marge and Margi were invited to join them, but there was little chance for conversation as everyone from college girls to young boys lined up to get the autograph of the USAAF's top ace.

On Monday, Jerry called Marge with a bombshell. Her shy brother wanted to ask Marge for a date.

That Marge was over the moon is certainly an understatement.

The young captain made a good impression on Marge's parents—how could he not? Then he took her to dinner at the local country club. Fortunately, they were given a table where Dick was not immediately harassed by autograph hounds, and for a while they were able to have a quiet dinner conversation. The club bought dinner for the local hero and his date.

The two young people saw each other several times over the ensuing week. He took her bowling, and she asked to go flying with him. It was Marge's first airplane ride. Dick rented a Piper Cub and took both Marge and his mother up for a spin over the northern Wisconsin countryside. She recalled feeling petrified by his low-level maneuvering, but all in all it was an experience she would never forget. While he was on furlough, Dick also made good on his promise to take every member of his family for a plane ride.

It was a strange incongruity. We see a smiling, baby-faced man—scarcely not a boy—laughing as he maneuvers his airplane over idyllic, picture-postcard Wisconsin farms and forests blanketed with fresh, pure, newly fallen snow. We can hardly reconcile this Norman Rockwell scene with the battle-hardened ace, his visage stern, as he maneuvers his airplane over the bloody jungles of New Guinea, pouring death and destruction into the fuselages of enemy aircraft.

Such is the nature of war. Those Americans who were there in those years, on the home front and the battlefronts of World War II, knew that the bullets were hurled and the sacrifices made so there would be a postwar world of picture-postcard moments rather than the jackboots of tyranny that the Axis had brought to nations from France to the Philippines. Today, when we look back at those times, flipping through the pages of the newspapers and magazines that carried the stories of Dick Bong's heroism, our eyes also fall on pages of advertising implicit in their promise that the sacrifices would bring the better, postwar life of which Dick and Marge dared to dream.

One night, Dick and Marge went to the movies in Duluth. During the film, the leading man referred to the leading lady—whose character is named Marge—as "Luscious," and Bong seized on this as his nickname for the girl he was falling for. In turn, Marge coined a nickname for him. When *Collier's* magazine sent a photographer to town that week to take pictures of Dick as he walked the streets of Poplar "acting normal," he was followed everywhere by a dozen or so kids. This led Marge to dub her blue-eyed boy the "Pied Piper of Poplar."

CHAPTER 22

December 1943: Vals for Christmas

•SCORE•

BONG: 21
McGUIRE: 13

D ICK Bong had unexpectedly fallen in love, just as Tommy McGuire had unexpectedly fallen in love two very long years earlier.

However, just as it was with Tommy and Marilynn, the world was at war, and Bong's life was not his own. He was a warrior, with battles to fight. Even more alien to his nature, he was an unwitting celebrity with public appearances to make. On December 10 he was summoned to Washington, D.C., where he attended a session in the House of Representatives and received a standing ovation from the floor. Alvin O'Konski, a first-term Wisconsin congressman and later a tireless booster of the young hero, took Dick under his wing and showed him off all over town. Twentieth Century-Fox filmed him for a newsreel, and he was sent up to New York City for another round of appearances. The army put him up at the Ambassador Hotel, and shuttled him over to the Waldorf-Astoria to take part in a "Report to the Nation" radio broadcast on the CBS Radio Network.

The media attention swirling around Dick Bong reverberated across the Pacific to Australia, where Tommy McGuire was still recovering from the broken ribs, injured wrist, and other bumps and bruises he had suffered on

October 17. There was a war on, and neither Bong nor McGuire was, for the moment, part of it. The Lightning pilots of the 49th and 475th fighter groups—as well as the Jug jockeys of the 348th—continued to escort bombers to Rabaul and Wewak and continued to score aerial victories against the Japanese.

When McGuire had left in October, eyes had been on him, but things were moving quickly. Neel Kearby shot three Zeros northwest of Wewak on December to bring his score to fifteen and put him two ahead of McGuire. Before he went Stateside on leave—wearing a third Oak Leaf Cluster on his Distinguished Flying Cross—Tommy Lynch had brought his own score to sixteen, three ahead of McGuire. McGuire had gone away as the top-scoring ace in the 475th, but that honor now belonged, posthumously, to Danny Roberts, the commander of the 433rd Fighter Squadron, who had scored his fifteenth on the same day in November when he was killed in a midair collision over Finschhafen.

Anxious to get back into action, McGuire finally returned to Dobodura by the end of November, adding some air time to his logbook by sitting in as copilot of the battle-worn B-25 that the 475th had commandeered as a transport to ferry its men between Australia and New Guinea—and for hauling booze from Brisbane. Once back at Dobo, McGuire's first battle was not with the enemy but with the flight surgeon whom he battled for the clean bill of health he needed before he could get back into the cockpit.

The good news finally came, and on December 12 Tommy McGuire was in a Lightning for the first time in nearly two months. He was so glad to be back in a fighter that he put the P-38 through a series of maneuvers, stalls, and aerobatics that nearly scared his wingman—a new pilot named John Tilley—out of his skin.

Beginning on December 12, the 475th Fighter Group, now under the command of Lieutenant Colonel Charles "Mac" MacDonald, divided its time between attacks in the Wewak area and supporting the Allied invasion of Cape Gloucester, on New Britain. The Allies had decided not to attempt a frontal assault on the Japanese fortress at Rabaul, but to land on Cape Gloucester, at the opposite end of the island, and to seize the Japanese airfield at Arawe. This would give the Allies an improved capability of interdicting Japanese supply lines in the area, thus isolating Rabaul without a costly direct attack.

After the Fifth Air Force had bombed the area for three days, the ground battle began on December 15 as the U.S. Army's 112th Cavalry Regiment landed—and continued with a larger landing on December 26, as the 1st Marine Division went ashore.

The initial Japanese air response to the Cape Gloucester operations was sluggish and, to use General Kenney words, "quite haphazard." Even as the numbers of Japanese aircraft sent against the Allies began to increase, the P-38s and P-47s were able to keep them at bay and to destroy a disproportionately large number of them.

Through it all, however, Tommy McGuire failed to score. When Neel Kearby scored back-to-back victories on December 22 and 23 to increase his tally to seventeen, McGuire began to feel that his time in the spotlight had come and gone.

McGuire had been the toast of New Guinea in August with seven victories in his first dozen days, but Kearby's six—and possibly a seventh—in one day in October had made him the man to beat. As happens so often in wartime, however, reversal of fortune is often just a day away, and it often comes when least expected.

On December 26, the morning after a raucous Christmas party at Dobo, elements of the 49th, 348th, and 475th fighter groups were out in strength to support the Marine Corps operation at Cape Gloucester. As Fifth Air Force B-25s came in to bomb Japanese positions ashore, and as IJNAF bombers made their way toward a counterstrike against Allied ships offshore, there were the makings of an enormous air battle. A Japanese air armada of an estimated eighty-five planes was intercepted by a Fifth Air Force fighter contingent that numbered thirty-three P-38s and forty-seven P-47s.

As McGuire's 431st Fighter Squadron made contact with the enemy, eight Lightnings climbed to meet the escorting Zeros, while eight dove to attack a large number of Aichi D3A Val dive bombers headed out to attack the Allied ships. McGuire picked up a Val, maneuvered onto its six, and opened fire, blowing it out of the sky and ending his nine-week dry spell.

Banking away from the falling fireball that would never again threaten an American ship, McGuire slid another Val into his sights and sent it plunging in flames.

As he rolled away from his second victory of the day, McGuire could see yet another dive bomber lining up to attack a U.S. Navy destroyer. He intervened, guns blazing. Just as the third bomber exploded, McGuire found a fourth in his sights, and this, too, went down. These four were part of thirty-seven Japanese dive bombers that went down that day. Meanwhile, the Fifth Air Force fighters claimed twenty-four Japanese fighters.

The Battle of Cape Gloucester was a big one for the pilots of the Fifth Air Force. After scoring four victories in twenty minutes, Tommy McGuire landed twice to refuel and rearm, and by the end of the day he had added seven hours, thirty minutes to his flight log. For his actions that day, McGuire was written up for the Distinguished Service Cross, the penultimate American decoration, and the same medal awarded to Dick Bong in July. As Bong had in July, McGuire also received his captain's bars.

McGuire had added four confirmed victories to his total—bringing his cumulative score to seventeen to match Neel Kearby, but he would share his good fortune, and end the year with just sixteen. There are varying versions of the story of how McGuire's four victories on December 26 became three. In a letter to Marilynn that she later shared with Charles Martin, he explained that there was a dispute with a P-47 pilot over who should claim one of the four. They agreed to cut cards for the claim to this victory, and as Tommy told his wife, he lost. On the other hand, according to the official daily history of the 431st Fighter Squadron, McGuire gave the one victory as a Christmas present to a P-47 pilot who had not scored.

As Tommy McGuire gave, so, too, did he receive.

Three days later, Captain McGuire was named as the operations officer, the second in command, of the 431st Fighter Squadron.

CHAPTER 23

January 1944: The Next Great Ace?

•SCORE•

BONG: 21

McGUIRE: 16

MARGE Vattendahl spent New Year's Eve in the arms of her young hero who had just returned home to Poplar after being the toast of the town in New York City.

He was now more than a hero—he was a star. Superior took the opportunity of his being home to designate January 7 as "Dick Bong Day" and to throw a party. Both the American Legion and the Concordia Lutheran Church celebrated with a luncheon, and the Veterans of Foreign Wars held the banquet. The theme painted on the banners read "Bonds, Bombs, Bullets, and Bong." They sold a lot of war bonds in Superior that day, which bought a lot of bombs and bullets. People were ready to step up to the plate for those things, but excited to step up to the plate to see and be seen with their hometown hero.

A day later, that hometown hero was off to Minneapolis to sell more bonds, and then on to California. He was feted at an enormous show in the Hollywood Bowl, where the banners read "Bing and Bong." Imagine the shy kid from Poplar sharing the bill with Bing Crosby. Just a few months earlier, it would have been unthinkable.

As Marge Vattendahl was at Superior State Teachers College finishing up the semester, her young hero was touring the Hollywood studios, shaking hands with Bob Hope, Barbara Stanwyck, and Roy Rogers.

By now the "M" word had come up in conversation a few times—both between Marge and Dick, and between Marge and others. It had even came up one night in January while Marge and Dick's sister Jerry were playing with a Ouija board.

Marriage was a subject that came up a lot during World War II as young knights bade their ladies au revoir to take up arms. It came up for Tommy and Marilynn, and they went ahead with it. Tommy Lynch, the twenty-six-year-old major who had commanded the 39th Fighter Squadron and with whom Bong had once flown, also had just tied the knot. Like Bong, he had gone home on leave, but unlike Bong, he already had a lady waiting for him. On October 23, 1943, safely home in Pennsylvania, he and his fiancée, Rosemary Fullen, were married.

As Tommy McGuire had with Marilynn, Major and Mrs. Thomas J. Lynch enjoyed a brief life together that was cut short by the call to duty. Initially Lynch, like Dick Bong, hit the war bond trail, but both Tommy and Rosemary knew as they said "I do" that his trail would eventually lead him back to the South West Pacific.

As it came up for Dick Bong to think about marriage, many things resonated, one being contrary to all others. Many things happened to Dick Bong in Wisconsin during the ten weeks he was on leave that winter. The biggest and best was certainly meeting Marge Vattendahl. Arguably the most sobering was meeting Mrs. Stanley Johnson, the young—Marge's age—wife of the equally young wingman he had lost on the November 7 mission to Rabaul. She had come to Superior from her home in Montana to visit a friend. When she heard the hoopla surrounding this hero of the 49th Fighter Group, she sought him out. Bong had to tell her the story of how the life of her own young hero had ended.

Dick Bong had a lump in his throat, and a gnawing apprehension that he shared with Marge as January came to an end and he prepared to go back to New Guinea. He told her that marriage was certainly in the cards, but not until he returned at last, and finally, from the war.

• • •

CAPTAIN Dick Bong had gone home in November as the unrivaled USAAF ace in World War II, but the young hero had spent two months touring the United States to sell war bonds rather than prowling the New Guinea skies. Even as the media at home were expending ink on Dick, the war correspondents in the Pacific were keeping their eyes peeled for the *next* great ace.

McGuire's triple on the day after Christmas made him a man to watch, but as the new year began, the correspondents had their eyes on Neel Kearby as sportscasters ogle a promising quarterback. He was certainly the USAAF's man of the hour. He was Dick Bong's first serious rival. With twin victories on both January 3 and January 9, Kearby had tied Bong by the time that General Douglas MacArthur personally awarded Kearby the Medal of Honor in his Brisbane headquarters in late January. He was the first USAAF fighter pilot to receive the nation's highest award for valor during World War II.

Both Bong and McGuire had captain's bars and a Distinguished Service Cross. Neel Kearby—*Colonel* Neel Kearby—had twenty-one victories *and* the Medal of Honor. He was, for the moment, the USAAF's next great ace. He was even photographed with John Wayne when the Hollywood star made a publicity visit to the South West Pacific. Across the globe, none of the great USAAF Eighth Air Force aces in the European Theater—such as Francis "Gabby" Gabreski, Don Gentile, Bob Johnson, or Walker "Bud" Mahurin—had yet scored twenty against the Luftwaffe, but the situation was constantly changing, and air operations were increasing rapidly in Europe.

Heroes are defined by their own heroism, but their legends are defined by those who celebrate that heroism. In the age of knighthood and chivalry, and long before, legends were molded by the poets who wrote the great epics. In later years, legends were molded by the media. Heroes are not creations of the media, but the stories by which they are remembered—or forgotten, as the case may be—are. It may not have occurred to Dick Bong and Neel Kearby that they were rivals, but the media decreed it so.

There was a "race" between these aces. How could there not be? The two highest-scoring USAAF aces were in the same theater of operations, and as Bong returned to New Guinea, they were tied at twenty-one. How could this not be a good story? It was the stuff of legend.

THE race between USAAF pilots was made all that much more suspenseful for the fact of the shadow that lingered just offstage in January 1944, that being the presence of the "ghost" of Major Gregory "Pappy" Boyington, U.S. Marine Corps. Though a great deal of media attention was expended on discussions of the hypothetical first USAAF ace to break Rickenbacker's score of 26—which had already been matched by Joe Foss of the marines—fighter pilots in the field all knew that the number to beat was now Boyington's total score of twenty-eight.

Boyington was a prime example of the classic archetype of the swashbuckling hero who breaks the rules off the battlefield while being both brave and effective in battle. In the air he was an extraordinary pilot and a skilled squadron leader with an almost uncanny knack for aerial combat. On the ground, however, he drank heavily and had an almost unnatural proclivity for fistfights. Boyington was the "bad boy" fighter pilot who became highest-scoring ace ever to fly with the U.S. Marine Corps, having scored twenty-two of his twenty-eight total victories with the corps, plus another six with the American Volunteer Group—the legendary "Flying Tigers"—in China.

When the Flying Tigers were incorporated into the USAAF at the start of World War II, Boyington chose to return to the Marine Corps. Because of his bad temper and discipline issues, it was not until January 1943 that he was finally able to get his Marine Corps commission reinstated and to have an opportunity to go overseas again. In May 1943 he became commander of Marine Fighter Squadron VMF-222 on Guadalcanal, but the unit saw little actual combat and Boyington became restless. After suffering a minor broken bone in a scuffle with some squadronmates, Boyington was sent to New Zealand for recuperation.

When he returned to Espíritu Santo in the central Solomon Islands combat zone in September 1943, Boyington lacked a squadron assignment, so he set up a squadron of his own. Utilizing the unused designation VMF-214, he assembled his unit from unassigned Vought F4U Corsair fighters and unassigned pilots like himself. Some of the aviators—though not all—were facing disciplinary action for various minor infractions, and this tended to feed the folklore of VMF-214 as a band of misfits and outcasts, which they would always insist they were not. Nevertheless, they called themselves the "Black Sheep Squadron." Major Boyington was given the nickname "Pappy" because, at thirty-one, he was almost ten years older than most of his pilots.

What followed for the ensuing twelve weeks was the stuff from which sagas are written. Indeed, it was the stuff from which a Hollywood movie and a television series *would* be made. These also were the best weeks of Boyington's career. In less than four months, the Black Sheep of VMF-214 shot down ninety-four Japanese aircraft—mostly fighters—and damaged or destroyed more than a hundred others on the ground. Boyington himself would shoot down nineteen of this total through the end of 1943, including five on one day.

As 1944 began, Boyington had twenty-five aerial victories (including the six scored with the American Volunteer Group) to his credit, one short of the twenty-six scored by Eddie Rickenbacker. There was a great deal of interest—including intense speculation by the media in the United States— in when Boyington would match or exceed the "magic twenty-six."

For Boyington it naturally became something of an obsession. This was especially underscored by the fact that VMF-214's combat tour would end in just days.

On January 3, 1944, Pappy Boyington and his Black Sheep took off on a mission to the Japanese base at Kahili on New Britain. They were intercepted by an overwhelming number of Imperial Japanese Navy fighters, but Boyington managed to shoot down three, exceeding the Rickenbacker number, previously matched only by Joe Foss. However, the day was not to be one of triumph for Boyington. He was set upon by a Zero of the 253rd Kokutai and shot down. It was long believed that the pilot of the Zero was piloted by Masajiro Kawato, an ace with nineteen victories, but recently that has been disproved.

Nobody had seen whether Boyington might have survived, and a massive search for him came up empty-handed. When he was not found, and nothing was heard through international channels regarding his having been captured, he was officially declared missing in action. Assumed to be dead, and a fallen hero at that, Boyington was posthumously awarded the Medal of Honor and the Navy Cross. However, Boyington had survived the crash, and was picked up by a Japanese submarine and taken to New Britain. The fact of his survival was never officially admitted by the Japanese and it was not known to the Americans until after the war.

J UST as the media realized that high-scoring aces made good copy, General George Kenney realized the value of media attention directed toward his own Fifth Air Force heroes. With the major emphasis by the Allies being the war against Germany, the South West Pacific was a poor stepchild when it came to earmarking resources. Kenney was constantly begging Hap Arnold for more of everything, and heading the list were Lightnings and qualified pilots. Arnold's response was always to remind Kenney that resources were finite and that the European Theater was the top priority.

However, Kenney reasoned that if media attention could be focused on the South West Pacific, it would be an area of operations that would not be forgotten. What better way to focus media attention than heroes? A rivalry between heroes!

In Bong and Kearby, Kenney had two diametric opposites. Kearby had come to the South West Pacific stating that he was going to be America's top ace in World War II. Bong was not given to pronouncements when actions spoke with more eloquence.

If the media were playing their part by creating the legends, for Kenney it was a matter of managing the protagonists. Having high-scoring aces was a double-edged sword. The more they saw action, the more they would score and the greater their public-relations value. Conversely, the more they saw action, the more they ran the risk of that action being their last—as had seemed to have been the case with Boyington. In the epics, martyred heroes carry special memories, but Kenney preferred his heroes to be alive.

He liked the public-relations value of an "Ace Race," but he feared that too heated a rivalry would breed dangerous recklessness. He worried more about the impetuous Kearby than the cool Bong.

"I told Kearby not to engage in a race with that little Norwegian lad," Kenney wrote in his memoirs. He often referred to Bong as "Norwegian," though his ancestry was Swedish. "Bong didn't care who was high man. He would never be in a race and I didn't want Kearby to press his luck and take too many chances for the sake of having his name first on the scoreboard. I told him to be satisfied from now on to dive through a Jap formation, shoot one plane down, and come on home. In that way he would live forever, but if he kept coming back to get the second one and the third one he would be asking for trouble. Kearby agreed that it was good advice but that he would like to get an even fifty before he went home."

CHAPTER 24

February 1944:
The Flying Circus

·SCORE·

BONG: 21
McGUIRE: 16

BOTH Captain Dick Bong and Major Tommy Lynch returned to the South West Pacific Area in early February to discover that operations had changed considerably since they went home on leave the previous fall. The Fifth Air Force, though still considered a lower priority than the numbered air forces fighting the Germans, was growing both in size and in tactical effectiveness. So, too, was its effectiveness in generating the headlines that George Kenney knew translated into the resources he needed to increase his tactical effectiveness. With Foss having been shipped home and Boyington believed to be dead, media attention was on the USAAF men who were still flying missions and generating good copy.

As the Fifth Air Force grew, Japanese strength and effectiveness in the air over the South West Pacific continued to decline. The Japanese aircraft industry could not keep pace with that of the United States. In 1939, the first year of World War II, the American aircraft industry produced 2,141 military aircraft compared to 4,467 produced in Japan. In 1944, Japanese production would increase to 28,180 units, but the Americans would build 96,318 warplanes.

More detrimental to Japanese effectiveness in the air than lack of aircraft was the growing shortage of good pilots. In 1942, U.S. pilots had faced some of the best-trained and best-equipped fighter pilots in the world. Now they were fighting the second string. The legendary aces Saburo Sakai, Junichi Sasai, and Hiroyoshi Nishizawa were out of the picture. Sakai was badly injured on August 8, 1942, while battling U.S. Navy Avenger torpedo bombers. Eighteen days later, on August 26, while escorting bombers over Guadalcanal, Sasai was shot down by U.S. Marine Corps major Marion Carl, himself an eighteen-victory ace. After the evacuation of Guadalcanal, Nishizawa—the man they called the "Devil"—had been out of action until May 1943, when the 251st Kokutai was sent back to Rabaul. In October, after a brief assignment to the 253rd Kokutai, Nishizawa was promoted to warrant officer and rotated back to Japan.

Another reason why Japan suffered so seriously from the lack of good pilots was that its fighter pilots typically did not use parachutes, considering defeat to be so shameful as to be the equivalent of death. Some pilots used them, but most did not. Had more of Japan's well-trained pilots carried parachutes, many would have lived to fight another day.

By February 1944, the Japanese pilots who rose to do battle with the Americans were ill equipped and poorly trained. Sakai, who had returned to flight status as an instructor after his recuperation, found it an uphill battle, as training time was so greatly truncated that vital skills could not be taught.

"All the lessons of the past battles were relived again, trying to implant the invaluable lessons, the little tricks, the advantages in these new men," he wrote in his memoirs of the situation in early 1944. "But we didn't have enough time. We couldn't watch for individual errors and take the long hours necessary to weed the faults out of a trainee. Hardly a day passed when fire engines and ambulances did not race down the runways, sirens shrieking, to dig one or more pilots out of the plane they had wrecked on a clumsy takeoff or landing. Not all the new pilots were so ill equipped to master the training planes and fighters. Many appeared as gifted in the air as the great aces in 1939 and 1940 had been. But their numbers were distressingly few, and there would be no painless interval for them to gain many hours in the air or any combat experience before they were thrown against the Americans."

For Dick Bong, the return to the South West Pacific Area meant a change of assignment, and the discovery that the 9th Fighter Squadron was no longer flying P-38s. Whether from a shortage of Lightnings or from a desire to concentrate most of them in the 475th Fighter Group, Kenney had decided to convert the 9th from P-38s to P-47s. General Paul Wurtsmith's V Fighter Command now had nineteen squadrons, and all but eight were equipped with P-47s.

Rather than assign Bong and Tommy Lynch to one of the squadrons within the all-Lightning 475th, Kenney and Wurtsmith conceived a rather unorthodox appointment for them. First, they were assigned to Wurtsmith's staff, at the V Fighter Command headquarters at Nadzab, up the river from Lae. Next they were relieved of administrative duties in order to "freelance."

It is unclear whose idea this unorthodox scheme was. Most accounts credit Kenney, but in his own book about Dick Bong, Kenney writes, "On Bong's arrival, General 'Squeeze' Wurtsmith, the head of the V Fighter Command, assigned Tommy to his staff as his operative officer, and Dick as Lynch's assistant. When they wanted to know if that meant they were out of combat, Wurtsmith said that while they were no longer assigned to a combat squadron, they could 'freelance' together as a team, either alone or attaching themselves to any squadron in the command, whenever they could be spared from their staff duties. 'Squeeze' ran the Fighter Command without too much help, so they figured they would get enough action so that they wouldn't forget how to fly."

Though unusual in modern military structure, freelancing was not without precedent in military history. Before its widespread use as a term for self-employed professionals, freelance had a similar meaning among warriors that dated back to the time of the Crusades. As Walter Clifford Meller has written, "The license and vices imported by those who had returned from the Crusades, and who had been, from long years of warfare, completely weaned from any peaceful avocations, became the rogues [in the meaning that describes soldiers of fortune, rather than villains].... The class therefore, of able, wise and valiant men such as the bannerets to enlist these freelances, was of immense value. Their institution at this unsettled period, when old feudal chains were broken and the sterner discipline of a past age decayed, was not only a necessity but a blessing to the overlord and the sovereign."

Often, in the glory days of medieval knighthood, the overlord would reward his favorite knights with special arms and armor and with special steeds. In turn, the knights would personalize these with their own colors, their own coats of arms. In the case of Lynch and Bong, their new equipment, their new steeds, were factory-fresh, latest-variant, Block 15 P-38Js. Lynch's wore the tail number 42-103987, and Bong's was 42-103993. The aircraft were among the first to reach the Southwest Pacific Area in gleaming natural metal finish, rather than having been painted in dark green camouflage, as were the earlier Lightnings in the theater, the P-38Gs, P-38Hs, and the Block 5 and Block 10 P-38Js.

One advantage of the natural metal aircraft was that they were lighter, and the unpainted surface created less drag. This meant that they were both faster and easier to maneuver. Another advantage was that the P-38J-15s also were equipped to accommodate larger external fuel tanks, so they had a longer range than the earlier Lightning variants.

During 1942 and 1943, as Japanese air attacks on Allied bases were not only probable but also routine, new American aircraft coming into the theater were painted in dark camouflage colors. It was a testament to the changing tactical situation that these measures were no longer deemed necessary.

Bong and Lynch took their special status and their new Lightnings a step farther by adding colorful trim paint. Lynch used black-and-white striping, and Bong painted his pop spinners and the tips of the twin tails bright red. In World War I, when the pilots of Baron von Richthofen's Jagdgeschwader 1 had started painting their aircraft in garish colors, they earned the appellation "Flying Circus." Those who saw Lynch and Bong, with their brighter-than-normal Lightnings, revived the term, and the pair of aces became the V Fighter Command's two-man "Flying Circus."

It should be added that the markings adopted by the two young Americans were nowhere near as gaudy as those used by Richthofen and his men a generation earlier. In fact, it was the uncustomary brightness of natural metal to those used to dull green that really set the P-38J-15s apart. Within a month or so, though, half or more of the Lightnings in New Guinea would be unpainted P-38Js.

At about this time, or perhaps as late as March, Bong did something that most pilots had done within weeks of arriving overseas, but something he had conspicuously neglected to do: he named his airplane. As he wrote home on March 13, he had a copy of Marge's high school graduation picture, which he had copied and blown up to twenty by twenty-four inches and glued to the side of his new P-38J-15. Next to it he proudly painted her name—in bright red.

Kenney wanted to keep his theater from being forgotten at home, and creating his circus of freelancers certainly fit the plan. The notion of a Flying Circus that included the man tied as the top-scoring USAAF ace in the world certainly drew the eyes of the media.

The pair of able, wise, and valiant men who the generals picked as their freelancers would not disappoint their overlords. The men were friends who had flown together before, and they quickly became an effective team, trading lead and wingman positions from mission to mission. Their first victory came on February 10. Lynch was flying lead, fifteen thousand feet over the Japanese field at Tadji, west of Wewak, when the two men observed a twin-engine Kawasaki Ki-48 bomber taking off. Diving to attack, Lynch opened fire as the aircraft climbed out over the sea. The right wing caught fire and the bomber plunged into the waves. The freelancers then eluded the Japanese fighters taking off from Tadji and slipped away.

Five days later, the Flying Circus attached themselves to a flight of 80th Fighter Squadron Lightnings escorting bombers on a raid against Kavieng on the island of New Ireland, northeast of New Britain and a short distance from Rabaul. For the fighter escort, the mission was uneventful as the bombers got in and out unchallenged by enemy interceptors.

As the American aircraft headed home, however, the Flying Circus detected a lone aircraft eastbound at twelve thousand feet, over the northern shore of New Britain. Bong, who was flying lead that day, banked left and pursued the aircraft, which turned out to be a Kawasaki Ki-61 "inline job."

Bong bored in on the Tony, whose pilot apparently was unaware that he was being hunted. By the time he figured that out, it was too late. Bong opened fire at just seventy-five yards, pouring it on until the Japanese fighter exploded, practically in his lap.

Late on the afternoon of February 27, the Fifth Air Force picked up and decoded a Japanese radio message giving the arrival time at Wewak of a transport aircraft carrying a group of staff officers from Rabaul.

As Kenney recalled, "By the time we got the information, it was almost too late for an interception, but we gave the information to Bong and Lynch, who hurriedly took off and flew wide open all the way, arriving over Wewak about two minutes before the Jap plane was scheduled to land. The inconsiderate [enemy aircraft], however, was ahead of schedule, had already landed, and was taxiing down the runway. Lynch dived to the attack but found that in his hurry to get away his gunsights had not been installed. He called to Bong to take the Jap. Bong fired one burst, the plane was enveloped in flames for a second or two, and then it blew up. No one was seen to leave it, before or after the attack. The two kids then machine-gunned a party of at least a hundred Japs who had evidently come down to greet the visitors. Subsequent frantic radio messages passing between Wewak and Tokyo indicated that the victims were a major general, a brigadier, and a whole staff of high-ranking officers."

Bong and Lynch returned to Nadzab, and were invited to report personally to Kenney at his advance headquarters. Kenney listened to their story and wanted Bong to have credit on his scorecard of victories for destroying the enemy aircraft. However, the rules of engagement in the South West Pacific stated that pilots were not given credit for aircraft destroyed on the ground. Other air forces did give credit for such kills, but even Kenney couldn't bend those rules in his theater.

"I asked Dick if he was sure that the Jap transport was actually on the ground when he hit it," Kenney recalled. "Couldn't it have been just an inch or so above the runway? Maybe the plane's wheels had touched and it had bounced back into the air temporarily? Everyone knew that some Japs were poor pilots. Lynch stood there grinning, and said that whatever Bong decided was okay with him. Dick listened seriously, as if it were a problem in mathematics, and then looked up and said simply, earnestly, and without a trace of disappointment, 'General, he was on the ground all right. He had even stopped rolling.'"

CHAPTER 25

March 1944: And Then There Were Two

•SCORE•

BONG: 22
McGUIRE: 16

BY March of 1944, watching the box scores of the great USAAF aces in the South West Pacific Area became a pastime not unlike watching the win-loss stats of a favorite baseball team. In January, as Dick Bong was blushing onstage at the Hollywood Bowl, Neel Kearby was racking up enough victories to put him in a dead heat with the kid from Poplar. However, Kearby scored naught in February, and all eyes were now on the Flying Circus. Having downed the Tony over New Britain, Bong began March with twenty-two, one ahead of Kearby.

The two Tommys, Lynch and McGuire, had been tied at sixteen, but Lynch had scored one in February, and McGuire's dry spell reached back to the day after Christmas.

On March 3 the Flying Circus left Nadzab on a late-afternoon mission to Tadji, on the northern coast of New Guinea, where Lynch had made his first kill since the creation of the Flying Circus.

Again, the hunting was good.

At 5:40 P.M., ninety minutes out of Nadzab, the two aces observed a Mitsubishi Ki-21 "Sally" bomber on final approach to the airfield at Tadji.

Lynch made a firing pass, and Bong followed up for the kill. As the Sally tumbled into the forest below, the two Lightning pilots climbed back to six thousand feet, at which time they spotted five enemy fighters straight ahead of them over the sea.

The Flying Circus attacked from behind, each Lightning opening fire on a Ki-61 Tony. Bong overtook his quarry, having done some damage but not having delivered a fatal blow.

As Bong turned, he saw the pilot bailing out of the burning Tony that Lynch had targeted. Lynch then turned to the Tony that Bong had damaged and shot him down.

The two men then made another sweep over the field at Tadji just as two more Ki-21s were on final approach. Lynch took the lead but ran out of ammunition. Bong then jumped onto the six of the same bomber and dropped him into the jungle only about a hundred yards from the bomber he had shot down earlier.

Bong's score was now twenty-four, and Lynch's stood at nineteen.

Neel Kearby was anxious now to both catch up with Bong again and to stay ahead of Lynch.

Two days later, on March 5, all three would be hunting in the airspace above Tadji and Wewak.

Bong and Lynch arrived shortly after 1:00 P.M., having taken off from Nadzab at 11:20 A.M. Lynch was flying lead and was the first to spot a trio of Ki-43 Oscars far below. He and Bong skinned their tanks and dove on the Oscars from seventeen thousand feet.

Lynch immediately locked on and nailed one of the Japanese fighters, but broke off his attack when half a dozen enemy reinforcements intervened to help their fellow pilots.

The Flying Circus ducked into a cloud to get away.

They were heading for home when they decided that one more pass couldn't hurt, so they reversed course and went back to hunt Oscars again.

Lynch scored hits on the first enemy he saw, but a large piece of metal that ripped off the Oscar damaged his left engine cowling.

Bong, meanwhile, made several firing passes at various Oscars, including several difficult sixty-degree-deflection shots, without scoring any observable hits. He then spotted one enemy fighter heading north, away from the battle. He caught up with this Oscar, opened fire at four hundred yards, and watched him crash near the Dagua airfield.

At that point Bong rejoined Lynch, and together they dueled with several Oscars for about ten minutes without appreciable damage to any of the aircraft involved.

As they headed home at about 1:40 P.M., Neel Kearby was just getting ready to go hunting with Major Sam Blair and Captain Bill Dunham. They headed toward Tadji, but were near Wewak, the scene of Kearby's October triumph, when they made contact with the enemy at about 5:20 P.M. They were probably unaware that the Flying Circus had been in this same airspace just four hours earlier.

The Jug pilots watched a lone Ki-61 landing at Dagua, but let him go. He would be on the ground before they could touch him. Moments later, though, they spotted three enemy twin-engined bombers—possibly Mitsubishi G3M Nells—on final approach to Dagua and attacked.

Diving fast and furiously, each American lined up an enemy aircraft and opened fire. Both Kearby and Dunham scored simultaneously, and Blair a few seconds later.

In their hurry to attack, the Americans apparently had neither noticed—nor looked for—between nine and fifteen Japanese fighters following the three bombers into Dagua.

The three Ki-43 Oscars in the lead immediately attacked the Americans.

Kearby rolled out to the right to shake the Oscar that had picked up his six. Dunham came in from the opposite direction for a fast firing pass at the Oscar on Kearby's tail but was quickly out of firing position.

Blair discovered several enemy on his tail and dove into a cloud to escape.

The fight was a fast one. The Japanese fighters had been low on fuel and were anxious to land.

Dunham and Blair linked up as the enemy broke off their attack, and the two men went in search of Kearby.

They circled for as long as their own fuel situation would permit, then headed for home, expecting to find that Kearby had beaten them back. He had not.

They waited. The whole 348th Fighter Group waited for its commanding officer, who now had twenty-two confirmed victories, but he never returned. He would officially remain listed as missing in action until after the war.

Though it would not be known for several years, Neel Kearby had managed to bail out of his aircraft before it crashed. Some native people living in the New Guinea rain forest had seen him come down, and they later showed an Australian search party where he had been buried.

It was never made clear to the Australians how Kearby died, whether he landed hard in his parachute or was hung up in the trees and shot by the Japanese. The remains of his Jug, *Fiery Ginger IV*, named for his red-haired wife, Virginia, were later found near the village of Pibu.

Like Kearby and his companions, Bong and Lynch had each downed an enemy aircraft on March 5, although Bong's was disallowed and listed as a probable because his gun camera had failed. He had been on the other side of a cloud from Lynch and thus it had not been witnessed.

For Tommy Lynch, these were the best of times. With the Flying Circus he had advanced his score to eighteen, and had just earned promotion to lieutenant colonel. It was definitely something to write home to Rosemary about.

Three days later, on March 8, the Flying Circus was back up in the vicinity of Hollandia, on the northern coast of New Guinea. They made a pass over Tadji, which had recently been attacked by Fifth Air Force bombers, but encountered no Japanese fighters. Looking for targets of opportunity, they spotted some coastal supply ships headed toward Hollandia and decided to go down to wavetop level and make a strafing pass or two.

The first pass was good, one of the luggers caught fire, so they made another.

This time Lynch's Lightning was hit by ground fire from one of the ships.

The nose of the P-38 was damaged and the right engine was belching smoke as Lynch pulled up from twenty to twenty-five hundred feet and headed south. He radioed Bong. How bad was his engine burning? Bong replied with reassurance.

Lynch began to lose altitude, and Bong shouted at him to bail out. As Bong watched, Lynch struggled to get free, and started to come out the left side of the cockpit.

Suddenly the forward section of the Lightning fell away and Lynch fell with it. Bong could see Lynch and his parachute pack, but he did not see the parachute open.

Dick Bong circled the crash site for a long time, looking for signs of life, but saw none.

Now a party of one, the Flying Circus was no more.

In less than a week, General Kenney had lost two of his best pilots, and two of his most celebrated aces. Now he was worried about Dick Bong.

"I was afraid that seeing Tommy go might affect his nerve," Kenney wrote. "So I ordered him to Brisbane to ferry a new airplane back to his squadron and sent a message to the depot commander there that if the airplane was ready to fly before another couple of weeks I would demote him at least two grades."

Bong was deeply affected by the death of a friend, a death he had witnessed, but he had not and would not lose his nerve. He didn't leave on his Brisbane errand until the third week of March, and he flew several uneventful patrols before he left.

As he departed for Brisbane, Bong's P-38J Lightning, tail number 42-103993, which he had named *Marge*, was temporarily assigned to Lieutenant Tom Malone, who flew it on weather reconnaissance missions into the New Guinea interior. *Marge* must not have liked having another man's hands on its controls, for on March 24 it began behaving badly. Nearly an hour into the mission, Malone was experiencing extreme turbulence at thirty thousand feet when things began to go wrong mechanically. First the oil cooler in the left engine malfunctioned, next the radio failed, and then the electrical system in the left engine failed.

As Malone turned back to Nadzab, he tried to feather the left prop but couldn't. He began losing altitude until he was flying in dense cloud cover at an altitude lower than the tops of the nearby mountains—which were invisible because he was in the clouds.

At this point, Malone decided to bail out. Luckily for him, he was found by a U.S. Army patrol.

Marge is still up there on the side of some New Guinea peak, badly damaged by the crash and probable fire, and overgrown by more than half a century of jungle growth, probably lost for all time.

The Flying Circus had lasted just three weeks, and now both of the brightly painted, natural metal Lightnings that were its namesake lay rusting away in anonymity.

O NCE an eye-catching rarity in the South West Pacific, the natural metal Block 15 P-38J Lightnings would begin to be a more common sight during March 1944. The 475th Fighter Group, Kenney's all-Lightning group, was next. Early in the month, as the Flying Circus was gaining its notoriety, the 475th's operations officer, Major Oliver McAfee, called a meeting of the operations officers of the group's three squadrons to tell them that the arrival of fifteen P-38J-15s was imminent.

That was the good news. The bad news for two of the three men present was that all of the new planes would go to a single squadron. The reason was that the new variant would require specialized spare parts, and spreading the aircraft among all three squadrons would introduce maintenance problems.

The three ops officers decided to flip coins for the faster, longer-range Lightnings, and Tommy McGuire won them for the 431st Fighter Squadron, nicknamed "Hades." The 432nd and 433rd, nicknamed "Clover" and "Possum," respectively, would have to wait. Three months earlier, McGuire had cut cards for the credit to a Val dive bomber shot down, and he had lost. He felt as though he deserved to win this round.

On March 11, three days after Tommy Lynch was killed, McGuire and fourteen other 431st pilots flew down to Dobodura to claim their shiny new birds and fly them up to Nadzab.

Sergeant George Jeschke painted the name *Pudgy III* on the side of Tommy's new Lightning, and Tommy took her off on her first mission on March 14. No enemy aircraft was encountered that day, and the first mission for *Pudgy III* was notable only in McGuire's discovery that the check valves between the fuel tanks on all the P-38J-15s had been installed backward in Burbank. Fortunately, they were all switched before this minor mistake became a fatal one.

The longer range of the P-38J-15s allowed the 431st Fighter Squadron to fly more missions deep inside Japanese airspace, but the aerial combat that had been so intense for the Flying Circus that month eluded McGuire's squadron. Tommy McGuire's quest for his elusive seventeenth victory continued to go unanswered in a succession of routine patrols.

While Bong, Lynch, and Kearby were occupying the headlines at home, Tommy McGuire's name actually entered the *Congressional Record* in March. Though Tommy wouldn't hear about it for another four months, Thomas B. McGuire Sr. had forwarded some clippings about his son's 1943 exploits to his old friend John Parnell Thomas, a former mayor of Allendale, New Jersey, who had represented the Seventh Congressional District of New Jersey in Congress since 1937. Thomas read Tommy's accomplishments into the record, identifying him as a New Jersey resident—which he had not been since he was a child. Tom Sr. was, however, a New Jersey resident, and he was Thomas's friend, and that, apparently, was all that mattered. Though Tommy was officially listed now as a San Antonio resident because Marilynn lived there, his true hometown was actually Nadzab, New Guinea. He had no other home that he would have recognized.

The downside of Allied air supremacy over New Guinea was that there were now fewer instances of aerial combat, and fewer opportunities for eager aces to run up their scores. Another downside to the lack of action was that new men arriving in the squadron would not have the chance to hone their skills as fighter pilots, skills that would be vitally important when they did find themselves in the kinds of serious dogfights that both Bong and McGuire had experienced during their respective first weeks in the South West Pacific.

With this in mind, McGuire used his downtime to begin formulating his thoughts about air combat into an informal manual of fighter tactics. He expanded the scope of his work by incorporating the perspectives of other aces in the 431st. Eventually he shared his treatise with Major Verl Jett, successor to Franklin Nichols as the commander of the 431st, who in turn shared it with Colonel Mac MacDonald, the commander of the 475th and an ace in his own right, who was impressed with McGuire's ideas and with his initiative. Like McGuire, MacDonald just yearned for an opportunity for the Satan's Angels to put the theory into practice.

CHAPTER 26

April 1944: Cases for the Ace of Aces

•SCORE•

BONG: 24
McGUIRE: 16

D ICK Bong's sojourn in Australia was a success.

It was a success for Bong because he was able to do some scrounging for things such as bedsheets—a highly prized luxury in the forward areas of the South West Pacific—and soft drinks that helped make life livable in his tent at Nadzab.

The Australia trip was a success for General Kenney, who was able to confirm that his young "Norwegian" ace was still fit to fly after the "trauma" of Tommy Lynch's death. In fact, Bong manifested a cool detachment that seemed to shield him from the reality of such a loss.

"It turned out that I needn't have worried about Bong's morale," Kenney later admitted. "I came back to Brisbane after he had been there about ten days, eating a lot of good food, drinking gallons of fresh milk, and sleeping at least ten hours out of every twenty-four. He had begun to get bored with going out to the depot each day and being told that his airplane was not yet ready. For the past couple of days he had been working with a sergeant out there, designing and building an attachment to carry a couple of cases of Coca-Cola on each wing when he ferried the airplane back to New Guinea.

He then collected his four cases of Coke and loaded them ready to go as soon as the airplane was pronounced ready to go."

Meanwhile, the Allied leaders in the South West Pacific Area and the SOPAC were executing their next big strategic moves. For more than a month, Allied planes had been attacking Tadji, and Allied aces had been earning victories in the skies above it. Now General MacArthur and Admiral Halsey planned for the bold move of going behind enemy lines to capture it for use as a forward operating base. Such an audacious move would not have been possible without the Allied air supremacy that had been paid for with the last blood of men such as Neel Kearby and Tommy Lynch.

Initially, the plan had been to secure an advance airfield in the Hansa Bay area, but with growing naval superiority it became possible to think of going even farther, and to capture Tadji and Hollandia. As forward bases, these locations were also much closer to the Philippines, which was *the* major strategic goal for MacArthur. When he was ordered to abandon his valiant, surrounded force in the Philippines in 1942, the had told the world "I shall return." That promise had been in the forefront of his thinking ever since.

The spring of 1944 also marked the beginning of the "island-hopping campaign" for which MacArthur is remembered, and which was practiced throughout the Pacific Theater. The idea behind this strategy was to use Allied naval and air superiority to isolate Japanese stongpoints on Pacific islands. The Japanese had expended a great deal of effort turning their bases at such locations as Truk, Rabaul, and others into impregnable fortresses. They were so well fortified that attacking and capturing them would be hopelessly costly. However, the weakness of such bases was that without naval superiority, the Japanese could not keep them supplied, and without air superiority, they were worthless in terms of launching attacks against the Allies.

Originally, the Allies had planned to invade and capture Rabaul, but there was no longer a point in wasting time, effort, and lives. Once the Japanese lost their upper hand in naval power and airpower, their fortresses were isolated and inconsequential to the Allies, so they were simply bypassed or "hopped," and left to wither on the vine.

The opening actions in the Hollandia operations began in late March while Dick Bong was in Australia, but he returned in time to take part in a major air assault on Hollandia on April 3. The Fifth Air Force launched a massive strike force of more than three hundred aircraft, including B-24 heavy bombers, B-25 medium bombers, and A-20 attack bombers, escorted by P-38s.

No longer with a squadron assignment and no longer with an assigned aircraft since *Marge* had been lost, Bong borrowed a Lightning and was attached to the 432nd "Clover" Fighter Squadron of the 475th. As the armada approached Hollandia, the Japanese interceptors were out in force.

As the 432nd skinned their tanks, two Lightnings each promptly engaged a Ki-43, and both of these Oscars quickly went down in flames. The air battle had begun.

Dick Bong opened fire twice on an Oscar himself, but the Japanese pilot outmaneuvered him and escaped. Bong also maneuvered, and got on the Oscar's six for a quick burst that included a few hits.

Again the Oscar escaped, this time into the gunsights of other P-38s. And yet again, the skillful Japanese pilot maneuvered himself out of the line of fire, but this time Bong was waiting.

He lined the Oscar up for a close shot from behind and sent it tumbling down in flames.

April 3 was a big day for Dick Bong and for the 475th Fighter Group. Of an estimated Japanese force of sixty fighters, the official USAAF total was twenty-six shot down. The Americans lost just a single Lightning. Lieutenant Joseph Forster of the 432nd Fighter Squadron had the best score that day, claiming the first three of his eventual nine confirmed victories.

Bong's single victory, however, put him just one short of matching Eddie Rickenbacker's World War I total of twenty-six. When Joe Foss had reached the magic number of twenty-six, the Marine Corps had withdrawn him from action to preserve him as a live hero rather than risking him in further action. The rumor was that Bong would be sent home when he topped both Rickenbacker and Foss with twenty-seven.

"Guess you know that I have twenty-five confirmed Nips now," he wrote in a letter to his mother that night. "Actually have twenty-eight, but three of them are not confirmed. Oh well, this war isn't over yet. They tell me that if I get twenty-seven confirmed they will send me home so fast I won't know what hit me. Good idea, I think."

In the same letter, he also wrote that he was getting a letter nearly every day from Marge, and added, "I think I'm going to ask that girl to marry me, what do you think of that? Good idea, I think."

In a letter to Marge, he mentioned his twenty-fifth victory, but not marriage plans, as he wondered, "I'm so near the top, do you think I'll make it?"

The question was largely rhetorical, of course, because Dick Bong was on a roll.

The question was answered on April 12, as the Fifth Air Force sent nearly two hundred bombers, escorted by more than sixty P-38s, to blast Japanese positions along the coast from Hollandia to Wewak. This day, Bong was flying with the 80th "Headhunters" Fighter Squadron, which had been temporarily attached to the 475th Fighter Group. Still without an assigned aircraft, he had borrowed *Down Beat*, the P-38J-15 normally flown by Lieutenant Bill Caldwell.

As he had on April 3 and 12, Bong was flying last in the squadron formation, in the "tail-end Charlie" position. Interceptor pilots often would strike at the rear, hoping that the straggler was easy prey. Bong flew in this slot intending to turn such an enterprising predator into prey himself.

As the Headhunters arrived over Hollandia at about 11:30 A.M., they were intercepted by IJAAF Ki-43 Oscars and Ki-61 Tonys, attacking from above and below.

Captain Cornelius Smith was the first Headhunter to score, and Bong went after a second Oscar nearby.

The Oscar attempted to dive through a cloud to escape, but Bong chased him, guns blazing. Beneath the clouds, Lieutenant James Ince confirmed that Dick Bong's twenty-sixth victim careened into Tannemerah Bay offshore from Hollandia.

Climbing back into the raging air battle, Bong picked up a two-ship Japanese element racing away from the fray. He blasted the wingman until he began to see smoke, then attacked the leader, who made no attempt to turn on him. Both Oscars were smoking when they entered the cloud and Bong banked back toward the battle.

This time Bong spotted an Oscar on a Lightning's tail and opened fire. Riddled with lead, the engine on the enemy fighter seized and it dropped, plunging into Tannemerah Bay.

In his fourth engagement that day, Bong dove on an Oscar below him. The Japanese pilot slipped out of the noose, but Bong continued his pursuit until he was very close at wavetop altitude. Dick opened fire, chewing up the right wing of the Oscar and degrading its stability. Suddenly the Japanese plane banked hard, clipped its wingtip on a wavetop, and went out of control, crashing onto a shallow coral reef.

Climbing back into the fray again, Dick's fifth and final engagement came as he attacked an Oscar just as the Japanese pilot outmaneuvered another P-38. This one managed to wriggle out of Dick's grasp and made a fast firing pass before he escaped.

Bong returned to Nadzab that night knowing that he had both tied and exceeded Rickenbacker's magic twenty-six. He came home claiming three victories to bring his total to twenty-eight, but to his dismay, only the first two had been witnessed, and his gun camera had failed to record the third. He was sure that he had twenty-eight, but even with twenty-seven, he exceeded all other USAAF aces to date.

Two other American pilots in the battle that day—Captain Jay "Cock Robin" Robbins and Lieutenant Burnell Adams—also scored doubles, but Dick Bong returned to Nadzab as the star of the USAAF. In his letter to Marge less than two weeks before, he wondered whether he would make it. Now he had.

GENERAL George Kenney immediately promoted Bong to major—and grounded him from flying in combat. There was a lot to celebrate at Fifth Air Force headquarters, and Kenney wanted to celebrate with his favorite ace safe and sound. After what had happened with Kearby and Lynch, he did't want to take any chances.

One of Kenney's "boys" was the top scorer in the USAAF—at least for now. In Europe, Bob Johnson, flying a P-47 with the 56th Fighter Group of the Eighth Air Force, was close, and he would make it to twenty-seven on May 8, but a Fifth Air Force pilot got there *first*.

Eddie Rickenbacker had been America's Ace of Aces in World War I, and within hours, the media back home were crowning a new Ace of Aces. The former Ace of Aces was just as pleased as anyone, however.

USAAF public affairs played on this and even stage-managed a radio conversation between Bong and Rickenbacker. A live hookup was done between Bong at Port Moresby and Rickenbacker in the United States, with arrangements made by George Folser of NBC Radio. Nervous that the shy Bong wouldn't know what to say, they had drafted a script for the two men to read. If it sounded awkward, it was.

Rickenbacker had earlier sent a congratulatory telegram, telling Bong, "Just received the good news that you are the first one to break my record in World War I by bringing down twenty-seven planes in combat, as well as your promotion, so justly deserved. I hasten to offer my sincere congratulations with the hope that you will double or triple this number. But in trying, use the same calculating techniques that have brought you results to date, for we will need your kind back home after this war is over. My promise of a case of Scotch still holds. So be on the lookout for it."

When the news of the Scotch hit the front pages in the papers back on the home front, however, a fuss was raised by various temperance organizations who felt it inappropriate for soldiers to celebrate with liquor. On April 15, the United Press wire service reported that O. J. Christgau, the state superintendent of the Iowa Anti-Saloon League, articulated the point of view of many such organizations when he wired Rickenbacker asking whether he had been "incorrectly quoted" in the reports about the offer of the whiskey.

"If incorrectly quoted," Christgau crowed, "I urge you to repudiate the statement immediately. If correctly quoted, I urge you to consider the far-reaching implications of your press endorsement of whiskey for American fliers. The teen-age alcohol program [problem?] is serious enough without the First World War ace flier glorifying whiskey by publicly offering a prize to the idolized flying hero of the present World War. What good would a case of Scotch have done you while you were on that life raft? Thousands of preachers who referred to your providential survival will be deeply disappointed if you have been correctly quoted."

Indeed, apparently there were hundreds, if not thousands, of preachers on the case, echoing Christgau in letters and telegrams to U.S. Army headquarters and to General MacArthur in the field. Though MacArthur himself had earlier added a case of champagne to Rickenbacker's offer, two days after Christgau's scalding remarks, he reversed himself, ordering that Bong should *not* receive alcoholic beverages as a "reward" for knocking down twenty-seven Japanese planes. MacArthur issuing a statement that he did not consider "liquor or spirituous wines as appropriate recognition of Bong's deeds," adding that he had "the highest admiration for Major Bong's skill and gallantry."

In Washington, the USAAF public affairs people entered damage control mode, reporting that Bong himself had turned down the whiskey and had asked for Coca-Cola instead.

General Arnold sent two cases of Coca-Cola, accompanied by this message: "I understand you prefer this type of refreshment to others. You thoroughly deserve to have the kind you want. The Army Air Forces are proud of you and your splendid record. Congratulations!"

In fact, Bong was not much of a drinker, but neither was he a teetotaler. His brother Carl, writing of Dick after the war, noted that when the gang gathered at the Gravel Pit Tavern in Poplar after a hunting trip, Dick would often have a glass of dry sherry.

In the case of the Rickenbacker "prize," Bong had actually wanted the Scotch, mainly because he had promised bottles to friends. Ralph Wandrey, one of Bong's squadronmates from the 49th Fighter Group, later told Marge, "Dick had said that if he broke the record, I would get a bottle of Scotch. Instead, I had to settle for a bottle of Coke!"

In the meantime, the media attention that descended on Dick Bong and his family was more oppressive even than the disappointment about the whiskey. Newspaper, radio, and wire service reporters had descended on both Port Moresby and Poplar, working angles and angling for interviews. Major Norman Myers, a Vermont native, was the public affairs officer who managed Dick's "press availability," even helping to arrange a poker game at Port Moresby in which the young ace sat in with a group of newsmen.

One of these card players, Frank Kluckhohn of the *New York Times*, apparently lost a few dollars, as he noted after the game that "like Babe Ruth in his baseball heyday, or Bobbie Jones at golf, Major Bong has an amazing eye and fast reflexes. He knows instinctively how to measure risks and, incidently, is a master craftsman at his job of flying."

The journalists discovered that the same qualities that made Bong good at poker also "incidently" made him a good fighter pilot. Of course, beneath the hyperbole spun about Bong in the media that spring, there are occasional insightful portraits of him. They may or may not tell us what the quiet kid from Poplar was really like, but they at least relate the impression one got from seeing him up close. We can thank Kluckhohn for one of these.

"This lad is naturally modest to the point almost of shyness while having deep confidence in his ability to do his job," wrote Kluckhohn in a piece he wired to the *New York Times* on April 18. "Most youngsters his age would be bubbling over if they were in his position. But the twenty-three-year-old ace takes it in his stride. He has an inherent sense of balance and proportion on the ground, as well as in the air, which this correspondent believes is so well rooted nothing will upset it. He has a touch of iciness in his makeup of truly Arctic proportions. He keeps his mouth clamped because it is his nature to do so, but when he opens it is to make not only a pertinent remark, but usually a witty one."

Not all of the remarks were witty, but usually they were pertinent. The night after the poker game, the boisterous discourse between reporters and pilots in the tent where Bong had gone to bed reached the point where he told them to "get the hell out."

The media attention was definitely intrusive, but what bothered Dick the most, though, was Kenney's grounding order.

"I've heard that you are having trouble with the reporters back there and I'm certainly having my troubles with them," Bong wrote his mother on April 19. "I broke the record and by so doing procured for myself a lot of trouble, and besides that they have grounded me from combat flying. I suppose that doesn't make you mad, but it certainly doesn't make me happy. I suppose Marge is catching hell, too. I feel kind of sorry for her in this position. I wasn't thinking far enough ahead or I would not have put her picture on my airplane and she could have lived in peace. I didn't figure on breaking the record, but they got in front of me so I had to shoot them down. Oh well, live and learn, I guess."

With the reporters came the news photographers, who snapped pictures and asked him to pose with the Lightning named *Marge* that everyone had been talking about. When it was ascertained that this was not possible because she was lying in her jungle grave, the Fifth Air Force public affairs people arranged to have the markings from the lost real *Marge* replicated on another airplane so Dick could be photographed with her.

Because it made good copy, the story circulated in the media that Marge Vattendahl, because her portrait was on *Marge*, was the "most sought-after, and the most *shot at* girl in the South West Pacific Area." In fact, Dick had scored only four of his total victories in 42-103993, and had flown relatively few combat missions in the aircraft after attaching her portrait. He was never in combat with the faux *Marge* that was created in April as a backdrop for pictures, and he had scored his historic victories twenty-six and twenty-seven while flying *Down Beat*, not *Marge*. Of course, the press wasn't about to let the facts interfere with a colorful story.

If Marge was not actually the most sought-after girl in the South West Pacific, she did soon find herself the most sought-after girl in Superior. As soon as the press figured out who the woman on the airplane was, they swarmed over her as though she were a movie star.

"I was called out of classes because some reporter wanted to know this and that," she recalled in her memoirs. "Shots were taken of me in the class room as I was fulfilling my practice teaching requirements at East High School and at [Superior State Teachers College] and...at our campus hangout, the Coffee Shop."

The latter establishment was run by two sisters who had a sign on the wall that read, "We serve pies like mother used to make—before she took up welding." Many mothers were working in the nearby Lake Superior shipyards.

Dick Bong spent the remainder of April dodging the reporters at Nadzab, and each morning watching the other Lightnings take off—without him—to fly their missions to Wewak and Hollandia. The actual Allied landings at Hollandia, and the subsequent battle for the city, Operations Reckless and Persecution, took place between April 21 and 27, as the U.S. Army's 24th and the 41st infantry divisions, under Lieutenant General Robert Eichelberger, went ashore and wrested control of the area from the exhausted Japanese defenders.

Eventually the Scotch did arrive, unheralded, at Nadzab. Kenney added a case of champagne himself, but that did little to make up for the grounding order, which Kenney adamantly declined to rescind.

Eventually the grounding order would finally be rescinded. Kenney knew this and so did Bong. In the meantime, though, Kenney had a plan.

Before Bong would again pilot a Lightning in Pacific skies, he would return to the United States to sell bonds and then to attend gunnery school!

Gunnery school?

It seems counterintuitive that the USAAF's Ace of Aces should be reassigned to gunnery school, but in retrospect, there was a method to this apparent madness. Bong was a natural when it came to shooting. All those deer seasons in the Wisconsin woods had honed a natural skill. Yet he had learned the art of fighter plane gunnery when such training was in its infancy.

In the back of Kenney's mind, he knew that to combine extraordinary natural talent with unrivaled experience, then filter it through state-of-the-art training, could yield spectacular results.

Kenney told Bong that he wanted him back. He wanted him to return to the South West Pacific and use his spectacular combination of skill, experience, and training to teach others. The next generation of fighter pilots would then enter combat far better equipped to be *great* fighter pilots than were the men who had been compelled to learn on the job in the early days.

In Bong's last meeting with Kenney before Bong shouldered his duffel bag for his trip home, the general also promised him that he would pull out the stops to confirm Dick's twenty-eighth victory. He had shown the general on an aerial photograph exactly where that plane had gone down. Bong told him that it was an Oscar, that he had hit the left wing, the pilot, and the engine, and that the plane had not burned.

"When we had secured the Hollandia area [a few weeks later] I got a diver to go down where Bong had said the airplane went in," Kenney recalled. "The diver located it almost instantly and we pulled it up. It was an Oscar, the left wing had eleven bullet holes in it, the pilot had been hit in the head and neck, two cylinders in the engine were knocked out, and there was no sign of fire. I put out an order giving Bong official credit for the victory."

With that, Bong would be tied with the "late" Pappy Boyington as the top-scoring American ace—at least so far—in World War II.

CHAPTER 27

May 1944: Modesty Equal to Merit

•SCORE•

BONG: 28
McGUIRE: 16

A s Dick Bong made his much-heralded departure from the South West Pacific Area during the first week of May, the buzz around the New Guinea fighter fields—and among the reporters who still hung out at Port Moresby cruising for copy—turned to speculation over who would now be the top-scoring USAAF ace remaining in the area. The two top contenders were the "two Macs," Colonel Charles MacDonald, commander of the 475th Fighter Group, and Tommy McGuire, the operations officer at the 431st Fighter Squadron. Though neither man had yet reached twenty victories, most of the other pilots still flying were in single digits.

While Bong had been freelancing his way from one of the guys to Ace of Aces, McGuire was hard at work at his staff job. Kenney's having freed Bong and Lynch from administrative duties with the Hades Squadron had given them the freedom and the opportunity to spend their time flying fighters rather than flying a desk. Bong's most fruitful period of aerial combat since the summer of 1943 coincided with a four-month dry spell for McGuire, as his duties as ops officer kept him behind a clipboard, more often working up schedules for others to fly than flying himself. Naturally, he began to wonder whether his skill as a fighter pilot was rusting away.

As though almost on cue, McGuire's career as operations officer ended on almost exactly the same day that Dick Bong finally got the orders rotating him out of the South West Pacific.

On April 28, Colonel MacDonald had ordered McGuire to come to his command tent.

What could he want?

MacDonald told him that Major Verl Jett, commander of the 431st Fighter Squadron and a seven-victory ace, was on his way back to the States after thirty-two months overseas, and that McGuire was to be the new squadron commander, effective May 2. McGuire's nearest rival was giving him an unprecedented opportunity. More than enhancing his own tally, MacDonald, the group commander, saw great merit in putting one of his most eager and competent pilots in a position where he could benefit the Satan's Angels as a whole.

The 431st had a new boss, who was coincidentally also its highest-scoring ace. Within two weeks it also would have a new home. With the capture of Hollandia, the Fifth Air Force was pulling up stakes and moving north. By the middle of the month, the whole 475th Fighter Group, as well as 9th Fighter Squadron of the 49th Fighter Group, would relocate to Hollandia. So, too, would several medium-bomber outfits. Kenney also had wanted to move heavy-bomber units into Hollandia, but the length of the runway made it suitable for smaller aircraft only.

With an Allied foothold on New Guinea's northern shore, the center of gravity within the South West Pacific was moving both north and west, pushing the enemy back—and soon to be tightening that proverbial noose on the Philippines, to which Douglas MacArthur had promised he would return.

Though Admiral Nimitz and the U.S. Navy brass had proposed that the Allies bypass and blockade the Philippines, rather than attempting to recapture them, MacArthur would not hear of it. He took it personally. He felt that he had made a personal commitment to the Philippine people and the Americans in the islands that he would return, and there was no question that this should be done. Besides, he did not want to see twelve million

Filipinos starving under a blockade. With Nimitz present, MacArthur had made his case for recapturing the Philippines directly to President Roosevelt at the high-level strategic planning conference in Hawaii in January 1944—and he won.

The 475th opened up shop at the former Japanese air base near Hollandia on May 15, even as U.S. troops were still hunting enemy snipers around the perimeter. Tommy McGuire's squadron flew their first mission from the new location the next day. Targets would now include islands such as Biak and Noemfoor, to the west. In fact, MacArthur already had his eyes on these islands to be captured rather than "hopped," and Kenney was eyeing Biak as a future forward operating base as soon as it could be captured from the Japanese.

The ground echelon wouldn't catch up with the Satan's Angels flight crews for several weeks, but this didn't stop the pilots from going into action. The day after the official relocation, Tommy McGuire led a flight of 431st Lightnings on an escort mission, riding herd on a group of B-24 bombers flying against an IJAAF air base on Noemfoor. The P-38s were at fifteen thousand feet when they spotted four Ki-43 Oscars ten thousand feet below. They dove to attack, each of the Americans picking an enemy fighter.

It was as though all of those months since Tommy had last scored in December hadn't happened. The skill that he feared he lost, was there. He bore in on the Oscar and sent the aircraft tumbling earthward in flames after just a short burst.

Two days later, on May 18, McGuire led nine Lightnings, escorting B-24s to a strike against a Japanese air base at Manokwari, at the western end of New Guinea. Nearing the target, they observed eight Japanese fighters, which fled rather than face the Americans.

Tommy picked one that was climbing up and away from the others and gave chase. It was a Nakajima Ki-44, a derivative of the Ki-43 with improved speed and climbing characteristics. Code-named "Tojo" by the Allies, the fast-climbing Ki-44 was known to the IJAAF as Shoki, or Queller of Demons. On May 18, however, this Ki-44 was neither quelling demons nor outclimbing Tommy McGuire.

Two bursts from the guns of *Pudgy III* and the engine of the Nakajima was aflame. As McGuire banked to rejoin his flight, he noticed the enemy pilot bailing out. This struck him as unusual, as Japanese fighter pilots were not usually known to use parachutes.

The next day, as one downed Japanese army flier was waking up to fly another day, Tommy McGuire got some good news and some bad news.

The good news was that his promotion to major—appropriate for his role as a squadron commander—became official.

The bad news was that the malaise he had started feeling was diagnosed by the flight surgeon as a case of dengue fever. Dengue fever is an acute febrile disease transmitted to humans by mosquitoes; the symptoms include fever, nausea, severe headache, and rashes, as well as muscle and joint pain so severe that dengue fever is known as the "bone-crusher disease."

A s Tommy McGuire was suffering through nearly two weeks of feeling his bones being crushed, Dick Bong was half a world away enduring another, albeit familiar, form, of torture. America's new Ace of Aces had reached Washington, D.C. on May 9, where he met with USAAF Commanding General Hap Arnold for a photo op and the promise of a three-week furlough at home.

Bong's first press conference came two days later, with Secretary of War Henry Stimson at his side in the secretary's conference room at the Pentagon. When asked why General Kenney had sent him home, Bong quipped, "because he didn't want me to get killed."

Much to the chagrin of the handler whom Arnold had assigned to babysit Bong, he told the media in a self-deprecating way that most of his victories had been scored while flying straight on from the front or the rear of his opponents, and that there were pilots better than he was at deflection shots.

One of the reporters, putting the two and two of Bong's being sent home to gunnery school with his difficulty with deflection shots, queried whether USAAF gunnery training might not leave "a lot to be desired."

The USAAF public affairs man—whom, as the reporters noted, outranked Bong by "a couple of steps"—interrupted the answer to suggest that this was not what Major Bong intended to imply.

"Oh," Bong replied in a manner that was described as lackadaisical, "I guess that's as good as anything."

On May 12, Bong was the guest at a Capitol Hill luncheon hosted by Wisconsin's Republican senator Robert "Young Bob" LaFollette Jr., the son and heir of the colorful Senator Robert "Fighting Bob" LaFollette. Also present were a future U.S. vice president, Senator Alben Barkley, and future presidential hopeful Senator Robert Taft. Much to his relief, Bong was not required to make a speech, and most of the talking was done by men who were much more accustomed to that activity. The old lions of Washington politics did give the twenty-three-year-old pilot a more than polite round of applause.

More on Dick's mind that day was a chance meeting earlier, when he ran into Eddie Rickenbacker in a hallway at the Pentagon. It was the first time that the two men had been in the same building since that day back in November 1942 when Bong, as a novice flier, had told America's World War I Ace of Aces that the enemy was pretty thick in the skies over the South West Pacific Area, and where Rickenbacker made his infamous promise of the case of Scotch. Of course, nobody could know back then that it would be this pink-cheeked farmboy who would be posing for photographs with the great Rick at the Pentagon just eighteen months later.

The two Aces of Aces had a chance to speak briefly about the nuances of aerial combat and to compare the SPAD XIII to the P-38J-15. However, history longs to have had the chance to push them into a room, offer them a Coca-Cola (or a Scotch or a dry sherry), close the door, and leave them alone for a couple of hours of *real* conversation. Alas, Young Bob was waiting, as were more reporters.

By all accounts, Dick Bong had developed a dislike for reporters that was deeper and stronger than mere annoyance. If ever there was anyone who could correctly be called an unwilling celebrity, it was Bong.

On Saturday, May 13, Dick Bong was at last released from Washington duty, and he headed west to see his mother for Mother's Day. That morning, a *New York Times* editorial wrote of him, "In Poplar and away from Poplar, Major Bong has a strong tendency, somewhat uncommon in our time, to keep his mouth shut. Likewise he can keep his face shut and unreadable. So he is gifted at poker and the chips don't fall where they may but on his side. He is copiously embroidered with decorations, but, as Richard Henry Lee would put it, his modesty is equal to his merit.... Good luck to him wherever he goes. He's a fine lad and his name sounds like a bell."

Dick met his mother in Chicago. Dora Bong, along with the mothers of European Theater aces Bob Johnson and Don Gentile, had been invited to the Windy City by radio station WLS to take part in a patriotic Mother's Day broadcast.

Marge Vattendahl had traveled to Chicago with Dora, checking into the hotel under the name Margaret Olson to avoid the press of the press. Delayed by bad weather, Dick reached the hotel on Sunday morning. When he was unable to reach Marge on the house phone, the young major corraled the hotel's house detective to check her room.

"His immediate thought was that I had been kidnapped by reporters for an exclusive story," she wrote later. "I was sound asleep. Never quite lived that down! Well, I'm a sound sleeper!"

CHAPTER 28

June 1944: "And the Angels Sing"

•SCORE•

BONG: 28
McGUIRE: 18

O N the first day of June, Major Richard Ira Bong and Marjorie Ann Vattendahl took a drive. The unwilling celebrity parked the car on a short, winding road not far from his home, fumbled with a locked glove compartment, and took out a pink velvet ring case. America's Ace of Aces put a diamond ring on the finger of that other unwilling celebrity and made it official.

"What words could I possibly use now to describe the feelings of two young people in love?" Marge wrote half a century later of that cool evening beneath the promising new foliage of the Wisconsin spring. 'And the Angels Sing'? But perhaps young people today can still understand the emotions that we felt then."

For Dick and Marge, his second furlough back in northwestern Wisconsin would have a special meaning, but many people in Poplar and Superior remember those weeks as the time when America's Ace of Aces buzzed the towns in a P-38. People who lived there had never seen a Lightning in their airspace before.

There were pictures in the local paper of him making a low-level pass over the Walter Butler Shipyard, a mode of visiting that he probably preferred to visits he made to Great Lakes shipyards, stalked by reporters, at ground level.

If Bong managed to avoid the reporters that day, his mother was not so lucky at another point during the year. If they could not get Dick, Butler nabbed Dora Bong. As a celebrity mother, she was invited to swing the champagne bottle to help launch the USS *Grainger*, a deep-ocean cargo ship that Butler built. It was all in the service of publicity for the war effort.

Dora's younger son Carl "Bud" Bong, a senior at Poplar High School, was certainly proud to have Dick as the toast of the town. This would have gone double on June 3, when the heroic young major stood on the stage at Poplar High School to hand out the diplomas to Carl and his fellow graduates.

With the ring on Marge's finger, and the Class of 1944 scattering into the wind, Dick Bong's furlough in Poplar came to an end. The P-38 was seen in Superior skies for the last time, watched until it disappeared into the distant horizon.

The war bond tour took Dick Bong to New Jersey and then to Washington, D.C., for a June 8 meeting with Bob Johnson. The two men shared war stories, horror stories about the media attention, and asked each other whether they would be going overseas again. Each told the other that they were through. Only Johnson was right.

"We had a great visit with General Arnold," Johnson later recalled of their session with the USAAF chief. "The general asked many questions about our combat with the enemy. Part of his interest was to find out if our own aircraft were adequate compared to the enemy aircraft, and part of his interest was envy that he could not participate as we had."

The two men went their separate ways, with Bong heading west across the southern tier of the United States, from Florida through Louisiana and Texas, and back to Luke Field in Arizona, where he long ago earned his wings as part of Class 42A. He visited the Lockheed plant in Burbank, California, and on July 7 he settled in at Foster Field in Matagorda County, on the Texas Gulf Coast.

. . .

IN Superior, 1,400 air miles from Matagorda County, Marge Vattendahl counted the days until she would see her flier again. It would in fact be just days, as Dick would be back in Wisconsin for a brief visit at the end of the month.

In San Antonio, only about 140 air miles from Matagorda County, Marilynn McGuire counted the days until she would see *her* flier again. She had no idea how many days it would be. It had already been seventeen months. There had been some talk that he might be home around the first weeks of 1944, but that had not materialized.

Marilynn had watched as aces such as Bong and Johnson came home and wondered why Tommy could not be among this elite. She was pleased for him when she heard that he had been promoted to major, but knew that the command responsibilities would inevitably get in the way of his coming home soon.

CHAPTER 29

June 1944: A Stranger Comes to Hollandia

•SCORE•

BONG: 28
McGUIRE: 18

$\mathbf{A}$s Marilynn waited, the man she loved, the man known to his troops as "Major Mac," had kicked the bone crusher and was back in the skies over western New Guinea.

By now, the bones being crushed were those of the Japanese war machine. The U.S. Army's 41st Infantry Division landed at Biak and was pressing forward to capture the Japanese airfields on the island. Wakde, on the northern coast west of Hollandia, had been captured during late May, and Fifth Air Force bombers were pressing the attack farther and farther west.

Meanwhile, the Americans landed at Owi, a small, uninhabited island near Biak. Because it was flat and relatively treeless, Kenney decided that it would be an ideal place to build a refueling field for planes flying long distances to the west and north.

By this time, George Kenney had a new job. As Tommy McGuire had been kicked upstairs, so, too, had his boss's boss—and his boss. On June 15, the Fifth Air Force and the Thirteenth Air Force were operationally merged under the umbrella of a new organization called the Far East Air Forces (FEAF), with Kenney as its commander. Whitey Whitehead, meanwhile, was promoted to major general and moved up to command the Fifth, under Kenney.

On June 16, the target for the day was the Japanese base near Sorong on Jefman Island, near the distant western end of New Guinea. Lightnings drawn from all three 475th Fighter Group squadrons, as well as of the 35th Fighter Squadron, were tasked with escorting the B-25s sent to attack Jefman. Colonel MacDonald was supposed to have been leading the Lightnings, but when he had to turn back because of an electrical problem, Tommy McGuire assumed command in *Pudgy III*.

As the Americans came over the Jefman airfield, a number of Japanese fighters were taking off. Closest to the Lightnings was a lone Mitsubishi Ki-51, a fixed-landing-gear reconnaissance aircraft. Code-named Sonia, it was clumsy and slow, and never designed for air-to-air combat. Its presence in the airspace over the field as IJAAF interceptors rose to do battle with the Lightning was purely an accident of being in the wrong place at the wrong time.

As Major Mac led the P-38s down to meet the Ki-43 Oscar fighters, he opened fire at the Sonia, easily hitting it as he flashed past. A second Lightning pilot finished off the burning Ki-51, and the Americans hurtled toward the enemy fighters.

The fourteen climbing Oscars were hoping to make a quick and deadly pass against the B-25s before they could be interrupted by the Lightnings, but they were disappointed.

McGuire and his wingman, a new man named Ricky Provincio, went after a pair of Oscars. McGuire opened up on one of them and watched it disintegrate into a ball of fire. The dying Oscar's wing was damaged, and the aircraft broke left. So, too, did Ricky Provincio. Leading it like an expert, he fired and watched the Oscar suddenly explode, marking his first victory.

Another Sonia drifted into Tommy McGuire's gunsight, and he opened fire, sending it spiraling into the ocean below.

For Tommy McGuire, the Oscar and the Sonia made June 16 his first multiple victory day since December. One other pilot also got a double that day, and the total score for the 431st was nine. The following day, when Tommy McGuire led the 431st over Jefman again, no Japanese fighters were able to get into the air to challenge them.

. . .

WHILE waiting for the airfields on Biak, Noemfoor, and Wakde to be made ready for them, the 475th was flying extremely long-distance missions out of Hollandia, missions that pushed the limits of the Lightning's range capabilities. Just as Colonel MacDonald and his men were discussing the technical issues associated with this predicament, the answer arrived in the form of a mysterious stranger.

On June 26, he walked into MacDonald's command hut unannounced, a tall, slender, balding man in an unmarked khaki uniform. He said that he was looking for MacDonald and that he had come to Hollandia to compare range, firepower, and the general characteristics of the Lightning with those of single-engine fighters.

Without giving much attention to the stranger, MacDonald asked him what his name was and whether he was a pilot.

The man acknowledged that yes, he was a pilot, but MacDonald did a double take when the tall man identified himself.

"Charles Lindbergh? Not *the* Charles Lindbergh?"

It was. It was the Lone Eagle himself.

As had been the case with Dick Bong and Tommy McGuire, Lindbergh had once been a boyhood hero of Mac MacDonald. Throughout the 2.37 million people who wore the USAAF uniform that afternoon were thousands upon thousands of men who had been boys when Lindbergh flew the Atlantic in 1927, and who had become pilots in part because of him.

In the wake of Pearl Harbor, Lindbergh abandoned his isolationism in favor of supporting a nation that had been attacked. He had approached both Hap Arnold and Secretary of War Stimson to offer his services to the war effort, but his offer was declined. Having flown with the Air Corps in the early 1920s, Lindbergh had been promoted to the rank of colonel after his famous 1927 flight, though he was no longer on active duty. He offered to go back on active duty with this rank and to do what he could for his country. His offer was turned down. His prewar pronouncements made him a political pariah.

Lindbergh found a place in private industry as a consultant, first with Ford, which was building a vast factory at Willow Run, Michigan, to bring auto industry mass production techniques to the building of Consolidated B-24 bombers. He later worked with the Chance Vought Division of United Aircraft Company, the builder of the F4U Corsair, a fighter that entered widespread service with the U.S. Navy and Marine Corps in 1942 and 1943. It was with Chance Vought that Lindbergh had come to the Pacific Theater as a civilian technical representative in the spring of 1944. He visited several Marine Corsair units—including VMF-222, with whom he flew combat missions. He worked out the technical method for greatly increasing the aircraft's bomb load.

Lindbergh had heard about the capabilities of the P-38 Lightning, with which he'd had no firsthand experience, and decided that he would call on the 475th Fighter Group. He was traveling under U.S. Navy orders, but when he showed them to a USAAF colonel at Nadzab, he authorized Lindbergh to hitch a ride to Hollandia in a C-47 that was going that way.

By all accounts, the two pilots hit it off straightaway, discussing their mutual passion: flight. In the course of their conversation, Lindbergh told MacDonald what he'd heard about the Lightning, and said that he'd like to fly one. MacDonald said he'd arrange for him to join a routine patrol, a "four-plane antiboredom flight," the next day.

Lindbergh went back out on the flight line after his cordial chat with MacDonald, and was on hand when McGuire returned from his patrol that afternoon. Reportedly the Lone Eagle was unimpressed by the loop that McGuire did over the field before he brought *Pudgy III* in for a perfect landing. When told that the young pilot who had just flown the maneuver was the leading USAAF in the Pacific Theater, Lindbergh reportedly said that he would not live to be an old pilot doing stunts like that.

Tommy McGuire did not meet his boyhood hero until later in the day when MacDonald summoned him to the command tent. The commanding officer told Tommy that he would fly as the Lone Eagle's wingman. Tommy was intrigued by the prospect. Several people whispered that the "elderly" Lindbergh might be too old to fly a Lightning on a patrol, but McGuire was looking forward to it.

"I'd like to see how the old boy does," he said.

McGuire was a few weeks shy of turning twenty-four. Lindbergh was a venerable forty-two. By wartime standards, he was indeed an "old boy."

As McGuire led the briefing at dawn the following day, Lindbergh paid close attention, listening carefully as any new man would be expected to do. The other two planes in the "antiboredom patrol" would be flown by MacDonald himself, with Lieutenant Norris Clark as his wingman. In case they ran into trouble, Lindbergh would be surrounded by the two "Macs," the top-scoring aces in the 475th.

Lindbergh quickly mastered the Lightning as the four aircraft headed toward Jefman Island. As anticipated, no enemy fighters were observed, so MacDonald ordered a strafing attack against four barges that were anchored tightly against a steep section of coastline. Lindbergh flew the mission as skillfully as the others and was delighted to be seeing some action.

Tommy Lynch's demise notwithstanding, strafing barges and luggers was still considered relatively safe and easy. The odds of being hit by the guns on the barges were remote, although obviously not nonexistent.

Over the next few days, Lindbergh continued to fly with the 475th on bombing and barge strafing sorties against Noemfoor and Jefman.

"Lindbergh was indefatigable," Charles MacDonald later observed. "He flew more missions than was normally expected of a regular combat pilot. He dive-bombed enemy positions, sank barges, and patrolled our landing forces on Noemfoor Island. He was shot at by almost every antiaircraft gun the Nips had in western New Guinea."

McGuire and the other pilots who flew with Lindbergh and got to know him came to like him. He was quiet and not boastful, letting his actions speak for him, and when speaking pilot to pilot, nothing speaks more eloquently than the kind of skills that Lindbergh possessed in the cockpit. They—and he—were well aware of his civilian status, but they called him "Colonel" out of respect. He was a pilot, and in the air, true hierarchy flows from skill and respect for that skill. Lindbergh had plenty of both.

Every man in the 475th knew about his America First dalliance, but every one of them still remembered where he had been back in May 1927.

"I can't believe it," McGuire admitted to his crew chief, Sergeant Frank Kish, and later related by Kish to Charles Martin. "I'm going to be flying with a man I've admired all my life."

CHAPTER 30

July 1944: The Lone Eagle on His Wing

•SCORE•

BONG: 28
McGUIRE: 20

As July began, the idea of Charles Lindbergh flying with the 475th Fighter Group was no longer a novelty, although many of the pilots found it anything but routine. He usually flew in the number three slot in a four-ship flight, the leader of the second element behind the flight leader. He often flew in Tommy McGuire's Hades Red Flight, and one can only imagine what went through Tommy's mind to have the Lone Eagle under his command.

Writing home, he downplayed Lindbergh's presence, knowing that his America First connection still made him a controversial figure. In a letter to his father in New Jersey later in July, Tommy wrote with the utmost understatement, "Charles A. Lindbergh was over here and I went on a flight with him. Take it easy on that though, it's a touchy subject as you know."

The 475th flew top cover for the American amphibious landings at Noemfoor on July 2. The following day, as the Satan's Angels escorted a flotilla of B-24 heavies to Jefman, Lindbergh was an element leader in Hades White Flight, the four-ship flight led by Colonel Mac MacDonald in his Lightning named *Putt Putt Maru*.

After the B-24s exited the target area unchallenged by enemy fighters, the four Lightnings peeled off to attack surface shipping in the area.

The July 3 mission proved routine and uneventful in most respects—until the return flight. One by one, the pilots began reporting that his fuel situation was critical, and MacDonald decided that they should land at the small strip on Owi to refuel. Lindbergh's wingman was especially concerned about his fuel situation, but Lindbergh made a number of engine and propeller pitch setting suggestions that seemed to help.

When they finally landed at Owi, nearly everyone was running on fumes, but Lindbergh's wingman had 70 gallons and Lindbergh still had an astonishing 260 gallons left in his tanks. Why, MacDonald wondered out loud, had the Lone Eagle used so little? He had seen Lindbergh fly just as far as everyone else. In fact, Lindbergh had made a few extra passes at some of the targets.

He explained to MacDonald that he had raised his manifold pressure, while lowering his engine's revolutions per minute. Lindbergh also discussed fuel mixture settings and other tricks. He went on to say that it was a procedure that he had pioneered when working as a consultant for Pan American Airways. They had wanted to develop techniques for extending the range of their Clipper airliners on long, over-water routes, and Lindbergh gave them the answer.

When the Hades White Flight made it back to Hollandia, MacDonald asked Lindbergh to share the technique with the whole 475th Fighter Group. They were astonished. How could this be? Everything that Lindbergh said made sense, and he had obviously been proven right. Nobody questioned the ocean-flying credentials of the first man to fly the Atlantic alone.

With Lindbergh's help, the men would soon learn the procedures for conserving fuel, and they were able to extend their range and have more time over their targets. Doing as the Lone Eagle showed them, the 475th pilots were soon flying missions far deeper into enemy airspace than ever before—far deeper, in fact, than the Japanese had anticipated.

It was on Independence Day, the day after the fuel consumption epiphany, when General George Kenney learned that the Lone Eagle was in his theater. The commander of the newly formed FEAF was entertaining some reporters on the Fourth of July when he was asked whether he knew that

Charles Lindbergh was in New Guinea. He admitted that he didn't, and immediately sent someone to locate the Lone Eagle. He then summoned Lindbergh to accompany him on a visit to General MacArthur in Brisbane.

Scott Berg, in his biography of Lindbergh, relates that the summons came directly from MacArthur on July 10, while in his biography Kenney tells that he contacted Lindbergh directly on or shortly after July 4. In his account, Kenney seemed to be unaware that Lindbergh had already been flying combat missions.

As Kenney recalled, "I could imagine how his unauthorized appearance in our theater might be looked upon by some of the GHQ crowd, so I said, 'Let's go pay General MacArthur a call and get a legal status for you before we do anything else.'"

In any case, Lindbergh and Kenney reached Australia on or about July 12 and met with MacArthur. According to Kenney, the senior commander was the "soul of cordiality."

In his recollection, Kenney takes credit for the idea of using Lindbergh's techniques for long-distance flying. He relates that he told MacArthur that he had "an important job that would keep [Lindbergh] busy every minute that he could spare. If anyone could fly a little monoplane all the way from New York to Paris and have gas left over, he ought to be able to teach my P-38 pilots how to get more range out of their airplanes. If he could do that, it would mean that we could make longer jumps and get to the Philippines that much quicker. So I wanted to take him under my wing, issue the necessary orders, and put him to work. Lindbergh nodded with that charming kid grin of his that is one of his best assets."

At that point, Kenney recalls taking Lindbergh to his office, where he "got Lindbergh fixed up with enough pieces of paper to legalize his status and then we talked about the job. He was quite enthusiastic about its possibilities and thought that with a little training he could increase our operating radius of action nearly 50 percent. We were now operating the P-38s to a distance of about four hundred miles from our airdromes. If Lindbergh was right, we could stretch it to six hundred."

In fact, the self-effacing Lindbergh probably allowed Kenney to believe that he had the idea first.

"I told him that I didn't want him to get into combat," Kenney recalled, still unaware that Lindbergh had already been in combat. Kenney hadn't asked and Lindbergh hadn't volunteered the information. The Lone Eagle probably just smiled his "charming kid grin" as Kenney continued.

"He was actually a civilian, with a lot of headline possibilities," Kenney fussed. "Those headlines would not be good, if he should get shot down, and they would be still worse if by any chance the Japs should capture him. He thought that it would be hard to check on how well the pilots were absorbing his teachings if he couldn't go along to watch them and, besides, he wanted to observe the P-38 in combat to get the answers in regard to the comparison of single-engined versus two-engined fighters. I said that the Nip aircraft were not flying over New Guinea any longer, except for an occasional night bomber, so I'd let him go along with the fighter escort to the bombers and strafers making attacks anywhere except on Halmahera. Up there, a fight would be a certainty. I reiterated I didn't want him to get into combat."

In his own diary, Lindbergh wrote, "MacArthur said it would be a gift from heaven if [teaching the pilots a technique to substantially increase their range] could be done, and asked me if I were in a position to go back up to New Guinea to instruct the squadrons in the methods of fuel economy which would make such a radius possible."

Of course he would.

With that, Lindbergh returned to the 475th Fighter Group to take up where he had left off. MacArthur had ordered Kenney to put Lindbergh on observer's status, noting that it "would not make it legal for you to do any shooting. But if you are on observer's status, no one back in the States will know whether you use your guns or not."

Soon the observer was able to help the Satan's Angels extend the combat radius of their Lightnings not merely to six hundred miles, but to eight hundred miles. There were complaints about the ten-hour missions and how stiff the pilots were when they staggered out of their cockpits, but nobody complained about coming home with plenty of reserve fuel.

On July 10, while Lindbergh was en route to Brisbane, the 475th Fighter Group had departed Hollandia for the long-awaited relocation to the island of Biak, where they shared space with the 49th Fighter Group. Having once operated P-38s, the Forty-niners had converted briefly to P-47s but were now using P-38s again. The first operations out of Biak took place on July 14, involving the fighters escorting bombers to the Japanese airfields on the Vogel-kop Peninsula and Halmahera Island, the largest of the Maluku Islands.

On Biak, the men of Satan's Angels gradually settled into their new home at the Mokmer airstrip, and to getting their tents or huts, and their personal space situated as they had been accustomed at their previous "homes" in Nadzab and Hollandia. This done, when not flying, they often had time on their hands. On July 24, a group of pilots were sitting around talking after supper when Lindbergh suggested that they look at some caves that were nearby, west of Mokmer.

A few of the men crowded into a jeep and drove as far as they could. During the Japanese defense of the island, these caves had been Japanese strongholds that were neutralized by U.S. Army troops as they had battled for control of the island a few weeks earlier.

Inside the cave, the stench of the flesh of humans and their food supplies rotting for weeks in the tropical heat was indescribable. The buzzing of flies rivaled the decibel level of an Allison engine as heard through earphones in a closed cockpit. Returning to their jeep, the men passed what Lindbergh described in his diary as about a dozen Japanese troops "lying sprawled about in the gruesome positions which only mangled bodies can take."

For some reason, Lindbergh's interest in the macabre scenes within the caves persisted, and two days later he returned with Tommy McGuire. Having been greeted at the entrance of a cave by the corpse of a Japanese machine gunner—still tied to his weapon with a rope to prevent him from retreating—they penetrated into the darkness. Again, the aroma was overpowering, the gases of putrefaction so thick that they could hardly breathe—but did not want to. During these episodes, Lindbergh noted having been especially disturbed by a group of Japanese bodies in a shell crater, on top of which the Americans had dumped garbage.

On the morning after his cave excursion with Lindbergh, Major Mac was leading his flight up to the island of Halmahera, where, to quote Kenney, "a fight would be a certainty."

It was a bizarre scene straight out of a movie. At about noon, as the Fifth Air Force B-24s began their bomb run against the airfield at Lolobata, the pilots in the escorting 431st Fighter Squadron Lightnings could look off to the north and watch a violent eruption of the 4,380-foot volcano Dukono.

Several IJAAF Ki-43s flew into the scene as the smoke from the conflagration at Lolobata mixed with volcanic ash. McGuire and his flight went after the Oscars, but the enemy retreated. It quickly became apparent to McGuire that the Japanese wanted to be chased. They wanted the Lightnings to come in low over a concentration of Japanese antiaircraft guns. The Japanese were playing a game, but McGuire was determined to demonstrate that it was a game two could play.

Ordering his flight to remain at higher altitude, McGuire and *Pudgy III* went in alone after a piece of bait.

He made a fast pass at the Oscar, banked hard, and was gone before the antiaircraft gunners could get him in their kill box.

The fast pass was enough. The Ki-43 was burning, and it was too low for its pilot to regain control before the plane cartwheeled into the ground to add its own smoke to the billowing clouds over Lolobata.

Following Major Mac's example, two other Hades Squadron pilots removed Oscars from the IJAAF inventory over Halmahera that day.

Charles Lindbergh had not been on the Lolobata mission, but he flew as often as any man officially assigned to a combat role within the 475th. Occasionally he flew with McGuire's Hades Red Flight, but more often he went out as an element leader in Colonel MacDonald's Hades White Flight. On July 28 he was flying in this position as MacDonald led two flights of Lightnings from the 433rd Possum Fighter Squadron on a dawn patrol over the islands of Amboina (now Ambon) and Ceram (now known as Seram or Serang), smaller islands in the Maluku group near Halmahera.

The mission was to escort some B-25s from the 345th Bombardment Group who were targeting a Japanese airfield at Amboina. They had seen no enemy air activity when there was suddenly a radio call from another patrol, Lightnings from the 9th Fighter Squadron of the 49th Fighter Group. They were mixing it up with some Japanese aircraft and were getting low on ammunition. MacDonald ordered his formation to follow him into action.

The enemy aircraft involved were a pair of Ki-51 Sonias, the same type of aircraft that McGuire had encountered on June 16. Slow aircraft with fixed landing gear, the Sonias were not known for their maneuverability, but they had managed to stymie the Lightnings, whose speed was a disadvantage against a slower-moving aircraft if the latter was handled by an expert pilot. Part of that skill is to play the faster aircraft and resist the overpowering tendency to run for it—in which case the Lightning's speed advantage comes into play and the game ends quickly.

In this case, the pilots were Sergeant Saneyoshi Yokogi and Captain Saburo Shimada, the commander of the 73rd Chutai. One was an expert, the other not. They had been returning from a search mission when they were pounced upon by the Forty-niners.

Yokogi was neither as skilled nor as lucky as his boss. He got nicked by a Lightning cannon shell, he got scared, he tried to run, and he died.

Meanwhile, against Shimada's skilled maneuvering and cool head, the Forty-niners had shot all their ammo without hitting him.

Then MacDonald's men arrived.

With Captain Danny Miller on his wing and Lindbergh close behind, MacDonald entered the fray, the guns of *Putt Putt Maru* blazing. Both MacDonald and Miller made ineffectual firing passes, unable to draw a bead on the jinking Sonia.

Shimada turned and twisted, adroitly outmaneuvering the big P-38s. He turned and twisted, but found himself face to face with a Lightning heading straight for him at incredible speed.

Inside the P-38, Charles Lindbergh saw the Ki-51 coming at him. He instinctively thumbed the trigger, and soon saw tracers coming at him as well.

Before Shimada could turn, the big, fiery balls of the tracers hurtled toward him.

As Shimada closed on him, the thought of a head-on collision entered Lindbergh's mind.

In seconds, it was over. Lindbergh's rounds found their mark.

The Lone Eagle turned his Lightning as hard as possible to get out of the way and felt the gut-wrenching concussion of compressed air as the Sonia missed him by five feet.

As he banked away, "Colonel" Lindbergh and the other Americans could see Shimada plunge into the ocean.

CHAPTER 31

August 1944: Just Doing
His Job

•SCORE•

BONG: 28
McGUIRE: 21

MARILYNN McGuire came home from her job at the telephone company and literally ripped open the letter. It was her only link to the husband she had not seen in eighteen months.

She wrote to Tommy constantly, as did he to her. He wrote to her about conditions at his "homes" at Nadzab, Hollandia, and Mokmer. He assured her that despite the lovely sunsets and palm trees, the South West Pacific Area was "damned sure" not a tropical paradise. His experience with dengue fever, and everyone's experience with a range of aggravations from dysentery to insects, certainly underscored that fact, but he spared Marilynn the details. Like many of the men in the South West Pacific, McGuire had lost a great deal of weight and had been suffering off and on from malaria, but he spared Marilynn the details.

He did mention that Lindbergh had been in Hollandia. Though the official line was to downplay Charles Lindbergh's presence, the media knew he was there, and Marilynn had already read about it in the papers. Tommy sent her a snapshot of him and told her that he seemed like "a hell of a fine man."

Tommy wrote often of his own aerial victories, and their increasing number. He didn't spare the details. He told her that when Dick Bong left, he had a chance to become the top-scoring ace in the South West Pacific.

This troubled her.

It was not that she wasn't proud of his accomplishments, it was that a warrior's lady knows—warriors' ladies have always known—that victories come only in battles, and that in the battles that Tommy fought, there always was a loser.

The knight's battles have always been unlike many of those fought by the infantryman, the archer, or the artilleryman. The knight's battles are never anonymous; they are always face to face. He almost never knows the true identity of his opponent, but he almost always sees him. In medieval times, and in the skies of the world wars, the knights often saw the face of their opponents and thought, "It's him or me."

Marilynn knew this and told Tommy to take it easy. She wanted him to think beyond this race to be the top-scoring ace, this Race of Aces that was mentioned in the newspapers.

She wrote often, telling him to preserve himself for her, to resist this dangerous temptation, the obsession with being America's leading ace—and to please come home soon.

"Darling, I am not trying to beat anyone's record," Tommy wrote back in a letter that Marilynn saved for more than half a century and later shared with Charles Martin. "I'm just doing my job, if I should happen to break it that's swell but I'm not out for a record. About getting home I can't give you a definite answer because I don't know, but I have a hunch that October might see me home."

October?

That was two months away. It had now been eighteen months since she had last seen Tommy, so what were two compared to that eternity?

Home?

It was an odd concept for Tommy McGuire. For Tommy's dad and his chum Congressman John Parnell Thomas, home was New Jersey—although the only home Tommy had really known for most of his life had been Sebring. Now, with Polly gone, he had no home there any longer. If home is where the heart is, then it was with Marilynn, but the only home they had known was the Alamo Plaza in Baton Rouge, and now she was in San Antonio.

Home for Tommy McGuire was, of course, where he hung his well-worn signature five-hundred-mission cap. These days that was at Mokmer Airfield on an island he had never heard of when last he laid his eyes on Marilynn.

At Mokmer, Tommy gained a new roommate in early August. It was that "hell of a fine man."

The first few days of the month had been a time of upheaval for the Satan's Angels, and for both Colonel Charles MacDonald and "Colonel" Charles Lindbergh.

It all began on Tuesday, August 1, when heavy cloud cover blanketed the usual targets around Ceram, essentially grounding the 475th Fighter Group. MacDonald decided that the Angels should exploit Lindbergh's range-boosting techniques to the max and go where they had never gone before.

The place was the Palau Island group about five hundred miles east of the Philippines, and nearly that far north of Biak.

Consisting of four main islands—Angaur, Babeldaob, Koror, and Peleliu—and a myriad of smaller ones, Palau had been sold by Spain to Germany after the Spanish-American War, and occupied by Japan after the First World War. In the grand strategy of the Pacific Theater, General MacArthur intended to capture Peleliu and Angaur because of the Japanese airfields there. When it came time for his return to the Philippines, he did not want Japanese air bases on his right flank.

Preparatory to the joint U.S. Army and Marine Corps landings in the Palaus in September, MacArthur had ordered Kenney to soften them up with Fifth Air Force bombers based in New Guinea. To the displeasure of the bomber crews, these missions were flown without fighter escort—officially because the distance was considered too great. The August 1 mission that MacDonald planned would be a first.

MacDonald's flight, which included Major Meryl Smith as well as Lindbergh—but not Tommy McGuire—reached the Palau archipelago and had began to strafe enemy ships at sea when they were jumped by a group of IJNAF Zeros. MacDonald and Smith counterattacked and knocked down three of the Zeros. In the melee, another Zero managed to get onto Smith's six and open fire.

Lindbergh, being the closest American to Smith, intervened but was outmaneuvered. The Zero abandoned Smith as Lindbergh overshot him and locked onto Lindbergh's six.

The Lone Eagle tried to get away, but the Zero remained on his tail. It was the moment when one's life passes before one. He recalled later that his thoughts were with Anne and their four children, aged two to thirteen. The oldest, Jon, would turn fourteen in two weeks.

"My body is braced and tense. There is an eternity of time. The world was never clearer," he said of the moment, before qualifying the resignation with the encouraging. "But there is no sputtering of an engine, no fragments flying off a wing, no shattering of glass on the instrument board in front of me."

Seeing what was happening, both MacDonald and Smith raced to Lindbergh's aid. In the 475th Fighter Group's own official history, it is said that they downed the Zero on Lindbergh's tail and tore through several others to save the iconic aviator's life.

That done, it was Lindbergh's fuel management tricks that got them all home to Mokmer after one of the longest operational P-38 missions to date.

It was a milestone mission in many ways. They dodged the weather going back, but MacDonald ran into a storm of epic proportions as soon as *Putt Putt Maru* touched down. He may have been an ace four times over and a highly regarded group commander, but to General Paul Wurtsmith at V Fighter Command, Mac MacDonald was a subordinate who had screwed up big time.

There are varying accounts of which of MacDonald's gaffes that Tuesday had infuriated Wurtsmith the most, but there were plenty to choose from. Nearly losing Lindbergh was a big one. MacArthur's orders to Kenney, and Kenney's orders to Wurtsmith were to keep him safely away from flying bullets. Had the Zero pilot been a slightly better shot, the headlines would have caused other heads to roll.

Another blunder that was high on Wurtsmith's list, and arguably even higher than Lindbergh on Kenney's list, was MacDonald's choice of targets. Kenney's bomber crews had asked for fighter escort up there and the fighter pilots declined, insisting that the Palau archipelago was beyond range. Now, MacDonald had been flying up there with fighters. If the Palau archipelago was close enough for a fighter sweep, why, then, couldn't the fighters accompany the bombers? From the point of view of the bomber crews, the refusal of the fighter pilots to escort them had been exposed as hollow, and either laziness or cowardice.

In any case, MacDonald was bounced out of the theater on sixty days of administrative leave—both as a form of punishment, and to have him out of the way until the fuss blew over.

Until that time, Lindbergh had been bunking with MacDonald in his hut, but with him gone, the Lone Eagle needed a place to crash, and Tommy McGuire invited him to share his hovel. The two men became friends—as much as men in combat can allow themselves to be friends.

They shared the ups and the downs of the occasional air raid, and shared things that they had in common. They had both lived in New Jersey, and by coincidence, they both had learned to fly in Georgia. Both men also had the experience of bailing out of a fatally crippled airplane.

They talked at length about their families. When Bill O'Brien, McGuire's operations officer in the 431st Fighter Squadron, was lost on a mission to Ceram, Lindbergh shared his feelings about losing young Charles to kidnapping and murder, a horror that remained in his nightmares even after more than a decade had passed.

Anne Morrow Lindbergh later wrote that the camaraderie that her husband found among the fellow pilots on Biak that summer, especially with McGuire, made him happier than he had been in the company of others since their son's death in 1932.

Some of the things that Lindbergh and McGuire did in their spare time were more age-appropriate for a twenty-two-year-old than for a man of Lindbergh's age and stature. When complaints about the monotony of the mess hall fare reached a crescendo, it was Lindbergh who suggested that they go fishing—with dynamite.

Anyone who has dived on the coral reefs that surround Pacific islands has seen the bewildering numbers and varieties of fish that congregate there. For people who live on those islands, many of those species are an important part of the variety in their diet. Having ascertained from the locals which fish were indeed desirable, Lindbergh and McGuire rowed out past the reef in a rubber boat with some dynamite borrowed from the Corps of Engineers who built the roads and runways for the USAAF. Once perfected, the process was repeated often and with excellent results.

The fish fries at the Lindbergh-McGuire hut became the stuff of legend around the 475th, but as with most legends in the real world, the Lindbergh-McGuire partnership was short-lived as the two men went their separate ways. By the middle of August, both had left Biak. Lindbergh was en route Stateside by way of Kwajalein, where he would log more time in F4U Corsairs before heading home for good in mid-September.

Tommy McGuire, still recovering from the weight loss and other residual effects of dengue fever, and racked by recurrent bouts of malaria, bade farewell to his friend, the "hell of a fine man," and was sent off to Brisbane for R&R and to gain weight. Always skinny as a rail, Tommy had sunk to below 120 pounds.

Going to Brisbane for R&R was a prized reward for the pilots in the South West Pacific, a chance to sleep in a real bed, eat real food, drink real beer and, yes, be in the company of real women. The pilots who were able to avail themselves of this realized that there were many in the U.S. Army and Marine Corps, such as the infantry, who did not get a chance to leave the mud and mosquitoes, the perpetual sticky itchiness of living in the tropics. Being in Australia in the cool midwinter of August was almost like being back home—but *only* almost.

Members of the 431st Fighter Squadron who had gone to Australia in the past recalled that their squadron commander, the twenty-four-year-old "old man" with the black mustache, had hovered around them protectively, a constant conscience of moderation. He had not wanted to see his men get in trouble as they partied the nights away. On the August trip, however, McGuire went his separate way and they hardly saw him.

As Tommy flew down to Brisbane, the thought of going home, all the way to San Antonio, must have weighed on his mind. Dick Bong had gone home twice since he was assigned to the South West Pacific, and Mac MacDonald was on his way home now, but still the Pacific was a wide distance in 1944, a distance that took at least several days by air. There was really no practical way for Marilynn to get there. As for Tommy getting home, he probably could have pulled some strings, given his being a major and the top-scoring USAAF ace. However, in the back of his mind he feared that he might never get back to the South West Pacific and to the race to get ahead of Dick Bong to be America's top ace of all time.

CHAPTER 32

September 1944: Very Little and Very Safe

•SCORE•

BONG: 28
McGUIRE: 21

THE air war over New Guinea was essentially over. So, too, in the SOPAC. The air supremacy for which Americans had fought and died for more than two long, hard years had been achieved. Every account of the air war in the South West Pacific notes how quickly and dramatically things had changed during the summer of 1944.

At the same time, the U.S. Navy's growing armada of aircraft carriers had achieved the same over much of the vast Pacific Ocean. In no action was this more graphically illustrated than in the "Great Marianas Turkey Shoot," the great air battle on June 19 during the American naval victory in the First Battle of the Philippine Sea. In this fight, U.S. Navy carrier-based Grumman F6F Hellcat fighters downed more than four hundred Japanese aircraft in a few hours. Only twenty-nine American planes went down, and half of the pilots were rescued. It had been a blow among blows for the Japanese, and one from which the once-powerful IJNAF would never recover.

By now, the strategic focus in the Pacific was on General MacArthur's return to the Philippines. Having gotten President Roosevelt's personal endorsement for such a strategy in January, MacArthur's plan thus far had been capturing the stepping-stones—the islands with airfields—that he would need to conduct a campaign in the Philippines. American combat aircraft were already fighting the Japanese in the skies over the Philippines, but they were carrier-based U.S. Navy aircraft. To get his USAAF Far East Air Forces into action, MacArthur needed islands with airfields.

The strategy called for Palau and Morotai to be captured by mid-September, with a mammoth American landing on the major Philippine island of Leyte in December. However, the improving tactical situation presented him with an opportunity to land in Leyte in October, and MacArthur chose to take that opportunity.

Aside from MacArthur, for whom the return to the Philippines had taken on an importance that bordered on obsession, no one looked forward to the coming campaign more than the fighter pilots, whose own obsession was aerial combat. As Allied air supremacy was achieved over New Guinea, the Japanese withdrew their aircraft, husbanding them for protection of their assets in occupied Borneo and for future battles, especially the Philippines campaign that they knew was coming.

The FEAF continued to fly increasing numbers of bombing missions, but the bombers went virtually unchallenged by Japanese interceptors. For the American aces and would-be aces, life was now a matter of routine patrols through empty skies. As George Kenney observed, there would be few further opportunities for aerial combat "until we got to the Philippines....There simply were no more fights in the theater within the range of a P-38 anymore."

As September came, day after day of uneventful missions ran into evenings of the men sitting around the camp at Mokmer talking about how they wished they were home. There was a guy from San Antonio in the group, and he and Tommy McGuire began reminiscing.

When it was available, the nights that followed boring days also were filled with recreational boozing. One night, someone had a case of Coca-Cola and someone else showed up with a couple of bottles of dark, syrupy Australian rum. As Tommy later wrote to Marilynn, it was "vile stuff but potent." The following morning found McGuire and his tentmates up at 6:00 A.M., woken by a noisy bird in the tree above. Nursing hangovers and cursing the bird, they tried unsuccessfully to shoot it down with their M1911 .45-caliber sidearms.

McGuire yearned for San Antonio and he yearned for Marilynn, but he had become chained to an obsession, and a contest that he was determined to see through to the end.

DICK stayed until September but none of us got much of a chance to see him for he was in constant motion," Marge Vattendahl wrote in her memoirs. "He explained that he was to become an instructor when he returned overseas and this was said, I think, to allay our fears that he was returning to active combat. An instructor? Sure!"

Indeed, Dick Bong was headed back to the South West Pacific Area—officially to be based at Nadzab as an "noncombatant" instructor. His job—officially—was to teach new pilots to become aces. General Kenney had given him permission to fly with combat patrols, but he specifically instructed his Ace of Aces to fire only in "self-defense."

As Dick wrote home on September 18, "I don't know about the combat flying, but if I do any it will be very little and very safe."

As the word reached Mokmer that Dick Bong was back in the theater, Tommy McGuire cursed the lack of opportunity he'd had to increase his score to compete with the Ace of Aces while Bong was Stateside. Because of the dearth of opportunities and the curse of the dengue fever, McGuire had scored just once in more than three months.

To add insult to injury, he had lost his airplane. While McGuire had been in Brisbane, Major George Dewey, a staff officer at the 475th Fighter Group headquarters, had borrowed and wrecked *Pudgy III*. He had totaled her, and there was nothing to be done until new aircraft worked their way from Burbank through the supply chain to Mokmer. McGuire finally got his new Lightning, which was naturally named *Pudgy IV*.

After McGuire returned from Australia, he was still battling the effects of malaria and not gaining weight. Late September found him hospitalized again with a high fever. Even when he managed to get out of the hospital, flight surgeons grounded him. Chained to his obsession, he reached out to General Kenney himself to get back into the air.

"I'm still behind," McGuire told the FEAF commander. "By the time those fool docs let me fly again there is no telling how many that guy Bong will knock down. General, how about letting me go?"

Kenney told him to take it easy until he had recuperated.

"There was no need for him to worry as I had put Bong on a gunnery instructing job and hadn't assigned him to a combat outfit," Kenney pointed out. "He was disappointed because I wouldn't overrule the doctors but seemed a little more cheerful as he said he guessed he'd go back to his squadron and see what had been going on since he went to the hospital."

As we know from hindsight, and as many predicted at the time, the inactivity in the South West Pacific skies during September 1944 was merely the lull before a very intense storm.

CHAPTER 33

October 1944: Shooting Gallery Skies

•SCORE•

BONG: 28
McGUIRE: 21

I have a hunch that October might see me home."
The words that Tommy wrote to Marilynn during the summer had kept her going. In October, the words came back to haunt her, as he seemed to have forgotten them. Now he wrote her of the ceremony on September 23 in which he finally received medals for which he had been written up months before.

Perhaps her heart soared when she read of four Distinguished Service Crosses and two Silver Stars. Probably her heart fell when he wrote that he had spoken to General Wurtsmith after the ceremony, "and he said I should get out around the last of Dec., so looks like a Very Happy New Year, Mrs. McGuire."

What happened to *October*?

Home for Christmas?

Marilynn could not know.

Another Christmas without Tommy?

Almost certainly.

Very Happy New Year?

Mrs. McGuire hoped so and longed for it.

Marilynn was aware of Tommy's growing fame. More and more she was reading about her once-anonymous husband in the papers. Because he was officially listed as having San Antonio as a "hometown," U.S. Army press releases targeted the media in that city. Marilynn's family and her friends at work pointed out Tommy's name in the pages of the *San Antonio Express* and the *San Antonio News*.

Meanwhile, like Marjorie Vattendahl, Marilynn McGuire was learning the hard side of fame by association. Reporters had started to come snooping, looking for tidbits about how it felt to be the wife of the second-highest-scoring ace. What did Marilynn think of the "Ace Race"? As with Marge, the thought excited her, but more than that, it frightened her.

A CROSS the globe, the two aces themselves, and their warrior comrades, were gearing up for the action that had largely eluded them through the summer. Both men also were saddling up new warhorses from among the newest Lightning variant, the Block 1 P-38L. This Lightning, more powerful than the P-38J-15, was powered by Allison V1710-111 engines rated at 1,475 horsepower, with a war emergency rating of 1,600 horsepower at 28,700 feet. As with the latest-model P-38J-25 (most of the Lightnings used by the 475th were earlier P-38J-15s), the P-38L-1 had power-boosted ailerons that made it easier for pilots to maneuver at high airspeed.

McGuire now traded his recently acquired *Pudgy IV* for a new P-38L-1, which George Jeschke painted in even brighter colors, naming her *Pudgy V*. Dick Bong, officially no longer in combat, also received a P-38L-1, but unlike his earlier P-38J-15, to which he had pasted Marge's portrait, he did not personalize the new Lightning. It might be surmised that his not naming his later Lightning was a deliberate choice, although in a letter he wrote home in late November, he said it was only because he hadn't been able to get a portrait of Marge enlarged yet. He never got around to it.

The application of Lindbergh's fuel management techniques to the P-38L, and the neutralization of Japanese airpower in western New Guinea, coincided with new strategic possibilities. As part of the overall strategy for recapturing the Philippines and defeating the Japanese war machine, General Kenney had long had his eye on the formerly Dutch-owned oil refinery complex at Balikpapan on the island of Borneo. Since its capture in February 1942, Balikpapan had been one of the largest sources of aviation feel for the Japanese war machine. Kenney longed to attack it, but for more than two years it had been outside the practical range of his bombers, and certainly beyond the range of escorting fighters. Now, with the completion of long runways at Sansapor at the northwestern tip of New Guinea, which had been captured by U.S. forces in August, Kenney had a place from which to launch air assaults on the source of the lifeblood of Japanese airpower.

The first two raids by B-24s in this campaign came on September 30 and October 3, followed by a maximum effort by 106 B-24s against Balikpapan on October 10. For this mission, the heavy bombers were escorted by three dozen fighters: P-47s of the 40th and 41st fighter squadrons of the 35th Fighter Group, and P-38s from the 9th Flying Knights Fighter Squadron of the 49th Fighter Group—Dick Bong's former squadron. A fighter escort was seen as vital to the success of the mission, as the IJNAF had concentrated substantial numbers of interceptor units there to protect the vital facilities. Japanese airpower may have long since dried up in New Guinea, but at Balikpapan, the situation was as it had been over New Guinea a year or so before.

Seeing that things could be shaping up for a really big air battle on October 10, Dick Bong, a "noncombatant instructor," approached Colonel George Walker, commander of the Forty-niners, to lobby him for a slot with his old outfit on the mission. Walker queried his boss, General Wurtsmith, who signed off on the idea, and Bong was slated for element leader within Walker's own Flying Knights Red Flight on the mission that day.

At 10:45 A.M., as the flight was at fourteen thousand feet and within sight of Borneo, Bong broke radio silence to tell Walker that he had spotted a lone aircraft far below. In turn, Walker gave Bong the lead and ordered the flight to execute a 180-degree turn to investigate.

Ten minutes later, as the Americans approached head on, Bong accelerated and maneuvered onto the enemy's tail. It was a Nakajima J1N Gekko (Moonlight), a twin-engine, two-seat aircraft code-named "Irving" by the Allies. Though originally designed as a reconnaissance aircraft, the Japanese later modified the Gekkos as night fighters, retrofitting them with twin

20mm cannons in the nose to augment a rear-mounted machine gun manned by the second crewman.

With Bong suddenly on his tail, the Gekko pilot could not bring his cannons to bear, and he made a turn to the right. Bong followed.

Lieutenant Warren Curton, Walker's wingman, said later that the machine gunner in the backseat took to his parachute as soon as he saw Bong approaching. What was it about the sight of a P-38 that made someone voluntarily jump and fall for two miles into a shark-infested ocean rather than stand and fight?

Bong gave the enemy aircraft a short burst. The extinguished Moonlight immediately burst into flames and spiraled downward.

Red Flight reversed course and headed on toward Balikpapan, where a large number of Mitsubishi A6M Zeros and Nakajima Ki-43 Oscars were climbing to intercept the B-24s. This time, Walker led the diving attack. The Oscar he targeted gave him the slip. It was a good example of a very good Japanese pilot turning the P-38's superior speed against it by allowing the larger aircraft to overshoot.

The Japanese pilot who outmaneuvered Walker next slid in behind Curton and opened fire. The man in the Oscar had outflown Walker and Curton, but he had not planned on having Dick Bong witness his little sleight of hand.

Bong had seen what the Oscar's pilot was about to do before he did it, and hit him just as he hit Curton. The Japanese pilot died very quickly, and the boy from Wisconsin now had thirty victories to his credit, placing him two ahead of Boyington as the top-scoring American ace of World War II.

Moments later, another enemy fighter tried to get out of Walker's sights only to wander directly into Curton's, and the young wingman had his own second victory.

The 9th Fighter Squadron contingent exited the target area at about eleven-fifteen and headed home, having downed six enemy aircraft. The total score for all the American fighters that day was thirty-five, with the gunners in the bombers claiming nearly fifty, although many were later discounted. Only one American fighter was lost, along with four of the bombers. Meanwhile, the Pandasari Refinery at Balikpapan was heavily damaged, and oil tank farms all over the area were turned into that many massive torches.

When he learned that his famous gunnery instructor had come back from Balikpapan with two more victories, General Kenney asked to see Bong's after-action report. In it he noticed that he turned in that the first enemy aircraft had been destroyed at an altitude of fifteen hundred feet and the second at eighteen thousand feet.

"Dick, I want to talk to you about those two Japs that you shot down in self defense," Kenney said, ordering Bong to his office. It must have reminded both men of that day so long ago in San Francisco when Kenney reprimanded the young pilot for pushing the limits. "How high were you flying when you saw that first Jap plane and how high was he?"

"Well, General," Bong explained, "I was with the rest of the fighter cover at about eighteen thousand feet when I saw this Nip plane headed west toward Balikpapan. He was pretty low, all right. I guess at about one thousand five hundred or maybe two thousand feet, but I figured he had seen our bombers and was going back to warn the rest of his gang and I'd better stop him. I don't believe he even saw me coming."

"That doesn't sound much like self-defense to me," Kenney said. "How about the second one?"

"Oh, that really *was* self-defense," Bong maintained. "Honest, when I climbed back to join the rest of our fighters, the fight was on and this bird tried to make a pass at me. I had to shoot him down or he might have gotten me."

Bong then changed the subject, telling Kenney that the gunnery course he took in Texas had really helped him with ammunition management. Kenney had sent Bong home to learn gunnery in order to teach gunnery. Now Kenney himself was learning. He was learning that his excellent young fighter pilot had, by his experiences in Texas, become extraordinary. Bong later related that if he had known in December 1942 what he knew in October 1944, his score would have been at least seventy-five by then, not merely thirty.

"All the outfit did much better today than ever before," Bong said with a smile. "They didn't fire anywhere near as much ammunition as they generally do and they got a lot of Nips."

"How many rounds did you fire and how far away did you start shooting?" Kenney queried.

"Each time I pushed the gun barrels into the Nip's cockpit and pulled the trigger. I only fired two bursts, one for each Jap."

As Kenney later asked himself rhetorically, how mad could he get at a pilot who had just shot down two enemy aircraft and brought his own plane back without a scratch on it?

On the evening of October 10, Kenney sent a telegram to General Arnold, telling the USAAF commanding general:

"During the strike on Balikpapan by five heavy-bomber groups on October 10, Major Richard Bong in a P-38 accompanied the escorting fighters to observe the results of the gunnery instruction he had been giving since his return from the United States. While conducting his observations, he was forced in self-defense to shoot down two Nip aircraft. While regrettable, this brings his official score to thirty enemy aircraft destroyed in aerial combat. Have cautioned Bong to be more careful in the future."

"Congratulations to Major Bong on his continued mastery of the manly art of self-defense," Arnold replied with a figurative wink. "Feel sure your warning will have desired effect."

Bong's status as an "instructor" would soon be going through a change. According to Kenney, his Ace of Aces soon convinced him that the best way to "teach" gunnery was by flying on combat patrols rather that teaching the subject as abstract and theoretical. In Texas there were no enemy aircraft on which to demonstrate techniques. In the South West Pacific Area there were.

In a subsequent communication to Arnold, Kenney recalled what he described as the "more or less facetious radiograms" that the men had exchanged. He went on to explain that "along about the first of October Bong informed me that all fighter replacements now coming in had taken the same [gunnery] course that he had attended [in Texas] and that there was nothing that he could teach them. He then asked to be attached to the various units at the front to bring such of those pilots who had not taken the course up to date."

Many people have suggested that Kenney had all along planned to use Bong's "instructor" status as a deliberate smoke screen to cover an undisclosed scheme for Bong to resume freelancing. There was an assumption by everyone from Marge Vattendahl to Bong's fellow pilots that there was a wink-and-nod understanding to this effect between the general and the ace. Certainly this would seem to be the case when one reads between the lines in the conversations Kenney chose to retell in his memoirs.

However, Kenney probably had gone into the plan back in April with the intention of *really* using his retrained Ace of Aces only as an instructor. This is suggested by the fact that Kenney would continue to curb his activities from time to time. Kenney ordered Bong to fly no more missions to Balikpapan, but he would be more ambiguous about Bong staying out of later operations in the Philippines. Apparently Kenney couldn't help taking pride in the continued successes of his young ace, and the temptation to give in to the momentum probably overcame his earlier intentions.

News of Bong's return to combat quickly circulated in the media, and made the papers in Wisconsin.

"Sure enough," Marge Vattendahl later wrote. She, like many others, believed that Dick's being an instructor was merely a charade. "Shortly after his return overseas, an article appeared about 'Instructor Bong' taking his 'pupils' up for hands-on-training and what should appear in the blue but a few enemy planes? The instructor showed them how it was done and added a few more miniature flags on his P-38. My response to that was to write him a potent letter."

Marge wanted her man safe and had told him so.

She was probably relieved when he replied that he had been "grounded all over again....I did some test work, tried it, and that was the result. Looks like I'm grounded for good this time. That ought to make you happy."

If only she knew. What he described as being "grounded" was merely Kenney's having forbidden him to fly another mission to Balikpapan.

However, while Dick Bong would fly no more escort missions to Balikpapan, Tommy McGuire did.

Word of Bong's two additional scores had circulated through all the USAAF fighter fields in the South West Pacific by nightfall on October 10. Until Bong had returned from the States, McGuire had been the top-scoring ace in the theater, but he had been trapped in a situation where his score was capped by lack of targets, and there was nothing he could do about it. For the pilots of the 475th Fighter Group, who had seen precious little action for months, the battle over Balikpapan was reminiscent of the good old days when the skies were filled with potential targets.

Although the effects of the conglomeration of tropical sicknesses that had dogged him were finally fading, the news about Bong was like a body blow for McGuire. Determined to break out of the doldrums, McGuire decided that he would do what was necessary to get into the shooting gallery skies over Balikpapan.

Unbeknownst to Colonel MacDonald, his boss at the 475th Fighter Group, Tommy McGuire went AWOL. He figured that MacDonald, only just back from his own exile in the States for bending the rules, wouldn't mind if Tommy bent the rules a little. McGuire probably was right, although he was about to bend the rules to the breaking point. The 475th wasn't assigned to fly the Balikpapan missions, but the 9th Fighter Squadron was, so McGuire talked his way into being attached to the 9th for the next big mission.

On October 13, McGuire flew *Pudgy V* up to the American staging base at Morotai. The next morning he flew as wingman to his old friend Major Jerry Johnson as one of 60 fighter pilots escorting 101 B-24s.

Reaching Balikpapan airspace, the American armada was set upon by 50 Japanese interceptors of various types. McGuire stayed on Johnson's wing for two passes and was rewarded for his patience as an Oscar slid into his sights. He thumbed the trigger, and the Japanese plane began to burn. Its pilot was climbing out as *Pudgy V* flashed past.

Seeing another Oscar beneath him at fifteen thousand feet, McGuire dove on him. Smoke began quickly pouring out of the Japanese plane and it began spinning and falling.

Next, McGuire set his sights on an aircraft he identified as the type the Americans code-named "Hamp," the A6M3 variant of the Mitsubishi A6M Zero. When first encountered by the Allies, the A6M3 was given a separate code name because its distinctive clipped wings made it appear like a different airplane. Different or not, the A6M3's tail disintegrated just like any other when subjected to a hail of fire from *Pudgy V.*

As the flaming Hamp crashed, McGuire went after a Ki-44 like a man obsessed. It dived and picked up speed, and McGuire chased it down for eleven thousand vertical feet.

The Ki-44, the aircraft Americans called "Tojo" and the Japanese called "Queller of Demons," was fast, but the P-38L Lightning was faster.

McGuire hit the Japanese plane with two bursts and saw it crash into Macassar Strait. As on May 18, the man quelling demons was not the pilot of a Ki-44, but the boy named Tommy McGuire.

Of the four aircraft he shot down on October 14, all but the second were witnessed by others. Unseen and unrecorded by fouled gun cameras, it went uncredited. Officially, though, McGuire had now come within six victories of matching Dick Bong.

Like Bong, McGuire came home from a Balikpapan mission to a reprimand. MacDonald was unaware until McGuire returned that he had been flying with the rival 49th Fighter Group. Being AWOL was one thing, but what really fried MacDonald was that McGuire's three confirmed kills for the date would be credited to the Forty-niners and *not* to Satan's Angels.

The mission, however, was a success. The Pandasari Refinery was damaged further, and a neighboring refinery appeared to have been destroyed. Kenney would later report that "on the 14th we just about finished Balikpapan off for the rest of the war.... We stopped worrying that the Nips would get any aviation fuel out of that place for many months to come."

In fact, the Japanese did eventually get the Balikpapan refineries back on line, but considerable damage had been done, and the flow of fuel was never the same.

Another maximum effort, with more than 120 bombers, was put on the schedule for October 18, but it was canceled after takeoff because of bad weather, and not rescheduled. Other events soon overtook the stage, rendering Balikpapan a mere sideshow.

O N October 20, all eyes turned north as Douglas MacArthur finally made good on his promise to return to the Philippines. In the largest amphibious operation yet undertaken by American and Allied forces in the Pacific Theater, the four divisions of the U.S. Sixth Army, under Lieutenant General Walter Krueger, landed on the eastern coast of Leyte.

Then home to a population of 900,000 people, 2,205-square-mile Leyte was a strategically important island, as it was centrally located in the heart of the Philippine archipelago. Because of its location, Leyte was seen as an important staging base and an important operating base from which Kenney's FEAF would cover American operations in the island of Luzon, the largest and most populous in the Philippines, and the location of Manila, the capital and largest city.

The Japanese offered little initial resistance to the Leyte landings, and at 1:30 P.M. on the first day, General MacArthur made a dramatic entrance, wading ashore through the surf with Philippine president Sergio Osmena at his side, and announcing through a radio broadcast to the Philippines that he had returned.

Everyone on both sides understood that the capture of Leyte—which was a process still incomplete in November 1944—marked only a foothold. For MacArthur to truly make good on his promise to "return" to the Philippines, American troops would have to invade and liberate Luzon and the city of Manila.

Manila, which had been MacArthur's home and headquarters before December 1941, was now the home and headquarters of General Tomoyuki Yamashita, the commander whose forces had beat the British at "invincible" Singapore in 1942.

Despite a lackluster defense against the initial Leyte landings, the Japanese quickly stiffened their resistance. Yamashita had been brought in to see that Japan did not relinquish it without a fight—a really big fight.

The initial objectives of the Leyte operation were the cities of Dulag and Tacloban, the latter being the regional capital as well as home to a major airfield. Tacloban had already been earmarked as a major operating base for George Kenney's FEAF aircraft.

Securing Tacloban happened more quickly than expected as the Japanese simply abandoned the all-important airfield. Kenney personally accompanied Major General Verne Mudge of the 1st Cavalry Division to the field on October 21. Aside from a few snipers, the Japanese offered no resistance. Indeed, the Japanese who had been based at Tacloban left in such a hurry that when Kenney and Mudge inspected the officers' quarters, they found personal effects, samurai swords, pistols, and uniforms still in closets.

Also notable in its absence had been a serious effort by Japanese aircraft to disrupt the American landings. During the first several days, only a few aircraft came overhead, but among them were the first experiences that most of the Americans had with kamikaze—suicide—attacks.

At sea, it was a different story. As MacArthur was taking up residence in the government buildings in Tacloban, and as Kenney was prodding the engineers to hurry with filling bomb craters and laying metal runway matting at the Tacloban airfield, momentous events were taking place offshore. The U.S. Navy was sailing into what naval historians regard as the largest naval battle of World War II and probably of all time.

Known as the Battle of Leyte Gulf, or the Second Battle of the Philippine Sea, it was actually a series of four major interrelated actions that unfolded in the ocean east of the Philippines between October 23 and 26, pitting the last major concentration of Imperial Japanese Navy seapower against the U.S. Third Fleet, under Admiral Bull Halsey, and the Seventh Fleet, under Admiral Thomas Kinkaid. When it was over, the Japanese had lost the majority of their surviving large warships, and were never again able to challenge the U.S. Navy in a significant surface action.

JUST before noon on October 27, the first thirty-four P-38s of the 49th Fighter Group roared in from the staging base at Morotai and landed at Tacloban. Greeted by cheering Americans and Filipinos, they arrived not a moment too soon. Having just fought an immense battle, the U.S. Navy's carrier force was retiring for refueling and reequipping, so the USAAF fighters would take up the baton of American airpower over the Philippines.

Kenney had been lunching with MacArthur when Colonel George Walker led the first of the incoming Lightnings overhead, and the two men immediately ordered a jeep to take them out to the Tacloban airfield.

They arrived in time to see the last of the P-38s touch down. Many of the pilots were out of the cockpit when MacArthur greeted them happily, shaking hands and telling them, "You don't know how glad I am to see you."

The last Lightning taxied in; its pilot emerged and went about securing his aircraft rather than making his way over to the knot of people clustering around the supreme commander.

Kenney squinted at the man and recognized him. It was Major Richard Ira Bong. The gunnery instructor whom Kenney had ordered to avoid combat had just flown into the most forward front lines of USAAF operations in the Pacific Theater.

"Who told you to come up here?" Kenney demanded, having ordered Bong to join him and MacArthur.

"Oh, I had permission from General Whitehead," Bong replied casually.

"Did he tell you that you could fly combat after you got here?" Kenney queried.

"No," Bong smiled meekly. "But can I?"

As Kenney recalled, everyone laughed, including him. The FEAF commander then told the young pilot he repeatedly referred to as a "cherub" that the tactical situation was such that anyone who "knew anything about a P-38 and had one to fly" could fly combat missions. In the eyes of Kenney—and MacArthur as well—Bong's status as an "instructor" was now officially over.

Did Kenney not know ahead of time that Bong would be coming to Tacloban, and with the first wave of Forty-niners? Was he feigning surprise for the benefit of MacArthur? Was the foregoing conversation merely created for dramatic effect by Kenney for his postwar memoirs?

We'll never really know.

Whether Kenney had truly intended Bong to be a noncombatant, or whether the whole thing was just a charade, it no longer mattered. Though his status was still listed as "gunnery instructor," Bong was now officially back in action.

Moments later, the Forty-niners got their baptism of fire on the ground at their new home when a pair of Japanese aircraft roared over Tacloban. American antiaircraft gunners succeeded in chasing the enemy away, and four hours later, the Forty-niners launched their first mission, strafing enemy positions ahead of U.S. Army ground operations. Bong was flying with Jerry Johnson and Lieutenant Colonel Bob Morrissey in Captive Green Flight when they received word that enemy aircraft were in the vicinity of Tacloban airfield. George Walker had taken off with the flight, but had aborted early because of engine trouble, leaving just the trio.

As the three Americans returned to base, they crossed paths with a pair of IJAAF Ki-43 Oscars. Bong and Johnson each made a pass at the lead plane, and Johnson took it out. As Morrissey shot down the second Oscar, Bong observed a third enemy aircraft at ten o'clock and went after him.

As was his style, Bong went in close, guns blazing. According to his later after-action report, he observed "hits all over the airplane." The Oscar burst into flames just before it plunged into Leyte Gulf.

Bong banked away from his first victory on his first day over the Philippines, but he saw yet another Oscar and went after it. Seeing the Lightning coming, the enemy fighter made a mad dash for a cloud bank to escape. Bong would report having achieved a number of hits before losing the Oscar in the cumulus.

The day had been a good one for the Forty-niners. In addition to Bong's single confirmed kill, Morrissey scored and Johnson had shot down two.

The following day began with George Walker leading Captive Yellow Flight, which consisted of himself, along with Johnson, Morrissey, and Bong, attacking Japanese shipping at Ormoc on Leyte's western coast.

Captive Yellow returned to Tacloban at about 4:00 P.M., only to be scrambled again to intercept an enemy fighter that was observed coming over the base. Walker let Bong take the lead, and he caught up with the Oscar west of Leyte about fifteen minutes later.

Bong positioned himself on the enemy's six and opened fire. The pilot attempted to escape from the hail of bullets but Bong stayed with him until the aircraft started to burn. Jerry Johnson witnessed the crash as Bong rejoined Walker.

About half an hour later, they spotted another lone Oscar, this one carrying a bomb. As he was closing in to attack the Oscar, Bong saw the pilot release the bomb, probably to make the plane easier to maneuver in the coming fight with the American Lightning. However, the bomb crashed into the Oscar's tail, knocking it off.

The Americans had only moments to relish the irony. As they climbed toward ten thousand feet, they spotted a gaggle of seventeen Oscars beneath them. They were heading toward Biliran Strait, off the northern shore of Leyte.

Bong, with Walker flying on his wing, began following the enemy fighters, who didn't immediately observe the Americans. Suddenly Bong noticed the top Oscar begin to waggle his wings, a clear indication that the Japanese had now spotted the Americans.

Bong went after this Oscar immediately, watching the slugs from his machine guns chew it up. It was a classic, high-speed, twisting and turning dogfight straight out of a twenty-first-century Hollywood special-effects console.

Bong next took a few shots at another Japanese fighter, but was hit in the radiator of his left engine. When he returned to Tacloban, Bong's crew chief discovered that the round that punctured the Lightning's engine was not a 12.7mm Japanese slug but an American .50-caliber round. Since no Americans had been shooting at Dick, he had apparently been flying so fast and maneuvering so much that he had overtaken and collided with one of his own bullets!

That evening, Kenney sent a telegram to Arnold explaining that "In accordance with my instructions, Major Richard Bong is trying to be careful, but the Nips won't do their part. On the twenty-seventh, five hours after arriving at Tacloban, Bong was again forced to defend himself and number thirty-one resulted. On the twenty-eighth, while looking for suitable localities for airdromes in the vicinity of Tacloban, he was assaulted by two more Nips, who became numbers thirty-two and thirty-three. Unless he was bothered again today, this is his latest score."

Was Arnold aware by this time that Bong's status was *not* as a noncombatant instructor?

Almost certainly. Like Kenney, he, too, was proud of and excited by the Ace of Aces and his successes.

With his tongue firmly placed within his cheek, Arnold replied that "Major Bong's excuses in matter of shooting down three more Nips noted with happy skepticism by this headquarters. In Judge Advocate's opinion, he is liable under Articles of War [for] willful or negligent damage to enemy equipment or personnel."

CHAPTER 34

November 1944: The Race for Glory

•SCORE•

BONG: 33
McGUIRE: 24

FEW men in the South West Pacific Area were watching the growing notoriety swirling around Dick Bong's rising score more closely than Tommy McGuire. He paced the ground at Mokmer like a caged Thoroughbred, chomping at his bit for a chance to have the opportunities that Bong had enjoyed during the last ten days of October. What bothered McGuire most was that he was pacing at Mokmer, while Bong was at Tacloban, living large in a target-rich environment.

It wasn't supposed to have been that way, and Tommy McGuire knew it. The plan had been for the 475th Fighter Group to have moved north at the same time as the 49th—with McGuire's 431st Hades Fighter Squadron leading the way—but in wartime things often don't work out according to plan. While Tacloban was able to start receiving the 49th sooner than expected, the 475th was scheduled to go into Dulag, about ten miles to the south, but it remained a muddy mess longer than expected. Indeed, several aircraft trying to use Dulag as an emergency landing site had wrecked.

It wasn't supposed to have been this way. On October 16, Tommy McGuire and his fellow pilots had watched the 431st Fighter Squadron

Second Lieutenant Richard Ira Bong earned his USAAF
wings as part of Class 42A in January 1942.
(National Archives)

Second Lieutenant Thomas Buchanan McGuire, Jr. earned
his USAAF wings as part of Class 42B in February 1942.
(National Archives)

A formation flight of Lockheed P-38 Lightnings. The company produced 9,925 of the "Fork-Tailed Devils" between 1938 and 1945. *(Lockheed)*

The P-38 Lightning was armed with a 20 mm cannon with armor-piercing, high-explosive and tracer rounds, plus four Colt-Browning .50 caliber machine guns, each with 500 rounds. *(Lockheed)*

Dick Bong in the cockpit of his P-38F, possibly at Dobodura in 1943.
(US Air Force)

Dick Bong and a fellow pilot discuss a mission while standing on
the wing of his Lightning in Port Moresby, April 1944.
(National Archives)

Dick Bong poses with his famous P-38J that he christened *Marge*. He scored only four of his aerial victories in this aircraft. *(US Air Force)*

Looking calm and businesslike, Dick Bong reads from a prepared script for a radio audience in April 1944. This is perhaps his famous scripted radio "conversation" with Eddie Rickenbacker that was set up by George Folser of NBC Radio. *(National Archives)*

Taken shortly after Dick Bong's April 12, 1944, mission, in which he topped Eddie Rickenbacker's World War I score of 26, this photograph shows his P-38J marked with 27 victory flags. He had actually scored three on April 12 to bring his score to 28, but the last one was not confirmed for several weeks. *(National Archives)*

The Lone Eagle and the ace. Charles Lindbergh and Tommy McGuire at the 475th Fighter Group base at Hollandia, New Guinea, in June 1944. *(US Air Force)*

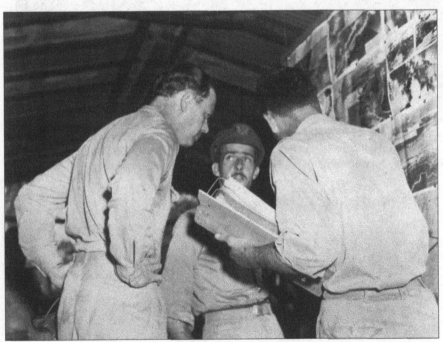

Major Tommy McGuire, commander of the 431st Fighter Squadron, on the flight line at Hollandia discussing an upcoming mission with Charles Lindbergh. *(US Air Force)*

On December 12, 1944, generals and warriors alike gathered at Tacloban as General Douglas MacArthur awarded Major Dick Bong the Medal of Honor for "conspicuous gallantry and intrepidity in action above and beyond the call of duty" in actions over Borneo and Leyte between October 10 and November 15. *(US Air Force)*

A classic photograph of Major Tommy McGuire, a seasoned squadron commander wearing his famous signature 500-hour cap and his Colt side arm. *(US Air Force)*

On March 9, 1945, Marge Vattendahl Bong made her first flight in a P-38 over Southern California. "I thought I'd be scared to death but I wasn't at all," she said. "I loved it. But, of course, that was because I was with my husband." *(Lockheed)*

ground echelon board the USS *Cushman* and set sail for Leyte. As they disembarked eleven days later, the 431st air crews were still pacing the Biak dirt, eight hundred miles behind.

Having only one fighter group on Leyte when two had been promised set back MacArthur's plan, so Kenney decided to make room at Tacloban for at least one squadron of the 475th as soon as possible. However, this move was dependent on getting the facilities enlarged, but this took time.

Finally, word came down that the 475th could send its first contingent of twenty Lightnings up to Leyte. The first squadron to go would be McGuire's 431st. Among the men who would be coming into Leyte to take up residence with the 431st would be McGuire's old friend from Alaska Major Jack Rittmayer. He had been serving in a staff job with the Fifth Air Force, and had requested a temporary reassignment so he could get some combat experience.

On November 1, Tommy McGuire led the Hades Squadron north across the equator to their new home. His arrival could not have been scripted better by Hollywood. In fact, if the story had been written by Hollywood, it would have been rejected as unbelievable.

As the Lightnings were on final approach, they received word of an enemy aircraft in the area. McGuire's ears perked up, and he abandoned his landing pattern to go hunting.

It was not a long hunting trip. Moments later, and almost directly over the Tacloban airfield, McGuire found himself facing down a Nakajima Ki-44, the "Queller of Demons."

It was not a long gun battle. Moments later, the ill-fated queller was quelled and spiraling into the ground not far from the base perimeter.

Tommy McGuire circled the field, saw no other enemy aircraft, and deftly made a perfect landing.

"This is the kind of place I like," he said to the men who crowded around *Pudgy V* as he opened the canopy and climbed out. "You have to shoot 'em down so you can land on your own airdrome."

McGuire's showy entrance on the first of November marked the first time since Nadzab the year before that he and Bong were pitching their tents at the same base. The stage was set for the climactic resumption of the "Race of Aces."

The media that had once written of a Race of Aces between Dick Bong and Neel Kearby was now filling the headlines with stories of Bong and McGuire. In *Stars and Stripes*, the weekly newspaper distributed to American service personnel worldwide, there was even a box score similar to that with which we begin the chapters in this book.

They always seemed to be eight victories apart. That had been the spread during the summer when Bong was home selling bonds and McGuire was flying with Lindbergh, and it was the spread at the beginning of November. The spread was as much a part of the mystique as the score, and an obvious source of frustration for McGuire. The only consolation McGuire could take was that when he first arrived in the South West Pacific, Bong's score had stood at sixteen. At least McGuire had cut the lead by half.

Both men knew that the world was watching them, just as both knew that the media were bent on sensationalizing their race into a heated rivalry. Reporters seized upon the race and painted them as contrasting characters in a classic heroic saga. Bong was portrayed as the bashful, rosy-cheeked farmboy from the Midwest. McGuire was the wise-cracking, fast-talking kid from New Jersey with the black mustache. Had the pair been created by central casting, they could not have presented mythmakers with a more appropriate contrast.

In his letters to Marilynn, McGuire often spoke of his desire to replace Bong as America's Ace of Aces, but his tone was never one of animosity. He was angry that Bong's status as a "gunnery instructor" permitted him to go where the pickings were the most promising, while McGuire shouldered the responsibility of being a squadron commander. But there never was evidence that McGuire personally disliked Bong.

If serious enmity was suggested, it was a media fabrication. As George Kenney put it, "No one could help liking Bong, even his closest rival for the position of top ace, Tommy McGuire, and no one could help liking McGuire, least of all Dick Bong."

War correspondents who had followed the Americans into Leyte sought the sound bites behind the *Stars and Stripes* box scores. When an Associated Press wire service reporter buttonholed McGuire about the race at Tacloban in early November, the motive was certainly the quest for a flame-fanning quip.

"Dick Bong and I are friends, and have been since we were in the 9th

Fighter Squadron together," Tommy told the journalist in a tone more diplomatic than he had used in his personal correspondence. "We are not about to get involved in some silly competition which might put our lives at risk. It isn't worth it. We're here to win the war, not some mythical title."

Inside he may have been a Thoroughbred pawing the ground, but on the outside, McGuire still could be as smooth as a show horse.

Among the USAAF aces in the European Theater, no one was anywhere near being in a position to compete with Bong and McGuire. Bob Johnson had gone home with twenty-seven, and Gabby Gabreski had reached twenty-eight when he crash-landed his damaged P-47 in Germany on July 20 and became a prisoner of war. The others, and there were hundreds, were still in the low twenties or below. Perhaps it was the sheer number of American aces in combat in Europe that kept individual scores lower.

In November 1944, however, the big competition for Bong and McGuire in their race to be America's leading ace was not from within the USAAF, but from the U.S. Navy's rising star. At the time of the Leyte invasion on October 20, Commander David McCampbell had been an ace with a respectable twenty-one victories, compared to McGuire's twenty-four and Bong's thirty at the time. Then, on October 24, at the height of the series of actions known as the Second Battle of the Philippine Sea, he shot down *nine* Japanese aircraft in a single day to bring his score to thirty.

The thirty-four-year-old Annapolis graduate was no stranger to large single-day scores. As commander of Carrier Air Group VF-15—later known as the "Fabled Fifteen"—aboard the USS *Essex*, McCampbell had scored his first aerial victory on June 11 during the American assault on Saipan, but he truly entered the history books just eight days later. During the "Great Marianas Turkey Shoot" on June 19, he had led the fighters flying to intercept a vast Japanese bomber armada headed to attack the U.S. Fifth Fleet, and personally shot down seven of the more than four hundred enemy aircraft shot down on that pivotal day in the Pacific air war. McCampbell had quickly increased his score, including a two-day run in September, during which he added seven more to his tally.

On November 7, Dave McCampbell had another multiple victory day in his F6F-5N Hellcat named *Minsi III*, downing two more to bring his score to thirty-two, only one behind Dick Bong.

The race was definitely on, and what better place for the race than Leyte's target-rich environment.

It was target-rich for a reason. The Imperial Japanese Army and its IJAAF were taking Leyte much more seriously than their lackluster defense against the initial October landings would seem to have indicated. Not only would the other American pilots now find the aerial combat they craved, they also would be treated to the peril and aggravation of Japanese air attacks against their bases—something they had not experienced for months.

Yamashita responded to the Leyte invasion by making a concerted effort to reinforce the Japanese troops on the island who had been pushed back during October. This would mean landing more men and matériel on Leyte's western coast, specifically at Ormoc Bay. However, Kenney's bombers would be overhead to see that attempts to reinforce the Ormoc area would not be made without a cost. It was over Ormoc that November's aerial battlefield would develop.

At dawn on November 10, three days after Dave McCampbell made the Race of Aces more interesting, Dick Bong was airborne over Leyte with the 49th Fighter Group, headed west toward Ormoc, tagging along with the 9th Fighter Squadron's Captive White Flight and escorting fighter-bombers.

At that same moment, Tommy McGuire also was airborne, flying a borrowed Lightning because *Pudgy V* had been badly shot up a week earlier when the 475th Fighter Group had attacked a huge Japanese convoy on a road near Ormoc Bay.

It was a target of opportunity that they happened upon while on patrol, but as targets of opportunities go, it was huge. There were tanks and trucks strung out along eight miles of road. The Americans had faced no aerial opposition, but ground fire had been fierce, and McGuire had taken a light flesh wound in that fleshiest of places, and had found it nearly impossible to sit for a week. In exchange for a bullet wound in his behind, McGuire and his men had routed and decimated an entire Imperial Japanese division with their ground attack operation.

He wrote to Marilynn that he'd gotten wounded, but that "a small piece of adhesive tape fixed me up." He added that he had told her about it only because he feared that one of the reporters lurking about Tacloban would report it and Marilynn would read in the papers that McGuire had been wounded in action. He ended his missive by promising that "things look damn good" for his being home by New Year's Day. In fact, there was no indication of that.

Finally able to sit, McGuire was on patrol again on November 10. As Bong and the Forty-niners were reaching Ormoc, McGuire spotted a lone Ki-43 Oscar near Tacloban and went after him.

Using the superior speed of the P-38L, he ran up behind the enemy aircraft, opening fire at very close range. Because he was flying an unfamiliar Lightning, and was not as aware of the calibration of the gunsight as he would have been in *Pudgy V*, he wanted to get in very tight.

It worked, but there was a disadvantage to attacking from a short distance. One minute, McGuire was thumbing the trigger; the next, he was flying through a vast, spherical debris field as the Japanese fighter disintegrated in a mass of fire and scrap metal.

One fragment of the former Oscar smashed through the Lightning's canopy, striking McGuire a glancing blow on the head.

Everything went black.

As McGuire was plunging into darkness, Dick Bong was plunging into combat with an Oscar of his own.

At 8:30 A.M., the five aircraft in Captive White Flight encountered an equal number of IJAAF Oscars, seven thousand feet over the approaches to Ormoc.

Bong picked one, hit him with a short burst, and watched him escape into a nearby cloud.

He banked away from the retreating plane, drew a bead on another Oscar, cut loose with a forty-degree deflection shot, and watched this Japanese become a falling fireball. His improved skill with deflection shots was paying off.

A third Oscar came into Bong's line of fire, but like the first, he disappeared into a cloud.

Only just a year earlier, the Americans had found the Japanese pilots much more aggressive and willing to fight. Now the results of the precipitous decline in the quality of Japanese flight training were manifesting themselves. The enemy pilots were only too willing to turn and run rather than stand and fight.

The turn-and-run tactics increased at the same time that Japan was desperately embracing kamikaze tactics. It is a great paradox that the Japanese air services, which once were home to some of the world's most skilled knights of the air, now contained *both* skittish pilots willing to do anything to escape distress and other pilots who deliberately committed suicide.

Tommy McGuire, struck on the head by the remnants of an Oscar pilot who had not had the chance to run and hide, regained consciousness before his borrowed Lightning fell out of control, and brought it home—minus most of the canopy, but otherwise intact. McGuire returned to find himself still eight behind Dick Bong.

November 10 had marked the first time that both Bong and McGuire scored on the same day. Less than a month later, it would happen again.

The media seized the moment. Bong had pulled two ahead of McCampbell, and McGuire had at last matched Eddie Rickenbacker's magic twenty-six.

Back home in New Jersey, Tom McGuire Sr. celebrated. In San Antonio, Marilynn McGuire wondered how close this brought her husband to the point where the USAAF would decide he was more valuable selling war bonds than chasing Oscars into the ground.

Having attached himself to his old outfit, the 9th Fighter Squadron, on November 10, "gunnery instructor" Dick Bong moved to the 7th Fighter Squadron the following day. With Jerry Johnson in the lead, Bong flew with the Pinky Special Flight. Their day began as an escort mission to Homonhon, the small island at the entrance to Leyte Gulf that is famous only as the place where Magellan had first landed in the Philippines in 1521 after his crossing of the Pacific. However, Pinky Special soon was vectored to Ormoc, where Japanese fighters had been observed.

Arriving in Ormoc airspace at 12:30 P.M., the Pinky Special Lightnings counted seven A6M Zeros at thirteen thousand feet. The Americans skinned their external fuel tanks and attacked immediately.

In his after-action report, Dick Bong noted that he fired at three enemy aircraft and "got two of them smoking."

Between Zeros, Bong watched Jerry Johnson turn one of the enemy fighters into a fireball. It was to be the first of two for him that day.

Though, according to his report, Bong saw neither of his own pair of

Zeros crash, others did, and Bong reported that he had observed the place "where four planes [his and Johnson's kills] crashed into the water."

Tommy McGuire saw no action on November 11, but he and *Pudgy V* were airborne over Ormoc the next day. Shot up in the November 3 strafing attack, *Pudgy V* had been repaired, and McGuire was glad to be back in a familiar cockpit. McGuire was flying with Jack Rittmayer and the elderly Robert "Pappy" Cline, so nicknamed because at age twenty-nine he was the oldest man in the 431st Fighter Squadron. Also in the flight was Colonel William Hudnell, the deputy chief of staff for personnel, logistics, and administration at Kenney's Far East Air Forces headquarters, who was on an inspection trip.

If the visiting staff officer was looking for action when he tagged along on a patrol with the USAAF's penultimate ace, he was not disappointed. The four Lightnings met and tangled with five IJNAF fighters. The enemy aircraft were not the familiar Oscars or Zeros, but rather Mitsubishi J2M inline engine fighters. Known to the Japanese as Raiden, meaning "Thunderbolt," the J2M was code-named "Jack" by the Allies. It was a rare sighting, because relatively few J2Ms were built and fewer were deployed overseas. A handful were assigned to kokutai on Saipan and in the Philippines, but most were deployed in Japan's home islands to intercept American B-29 bombers.

In the hands of a skilled pilot, the Raiden could be a potent weapon, and on November 12, this was the case. The Japanese fighters were quickly on the offensive, with one locking onto Rittmayer's six o'clock, and another lining up behind Hudnell, an air combat novice.

Had Tommy McGuire not been present, Hudnell would not have gone on to his long postwar U.S. Air Force career as a general. As it was, McGuire shot the Jack off Hudnell's tail, and then Hudnell shot down one himself.

McGuire also shot down the Jack that had threatened Rittmayer, but the surviving J2Ms escaped. When the four Lightnings banked toward home, Hudnell had scored his first, Pappy Cline his second, and Tommy McGuire's score now stood at twenty-eight—still eight behind Bong.

On November 19, a week after the showdown with the seven Jacks, the engineers finally declared the airfield at Dulag to be habitable, and the 475th Fighter Group officially relocated from the crowded facilities at Tacloban. Many of the 475th aircraft and air crews had been cooling their heels in

Biak for the preceding month because there simply had not been room for them. Now, at last, this was over.

It was a milestone day for George Kenney because it permitted him to expand and nearly double his fighter assets in the Philippines. This was certainly important, and it looked good on paper, but things were not altogether opulent at Tacloban and Dulag. MacArthur and Kenney may have been bunking in the governor's compound, but out at the airfields, conditions in the tents where the men lived were still every bit as spartan as they had been in New Guinea. Meanwhile, several major storms lashed the coast of Leyte during the latter part of 1944, forcing evacuation of the aircraft to more sheltered, if more poorly equipped, alternate fields. On top of that, the Americans were facing the worst threat of enemy air attacks since Dobodura. Japanese bombers sneaked in both day and night, forcing 49th and 475th fighter groups to keep aircraft on constant alert to protect the bases.

ALSO on Kenney's mind in mid-November was to celebrate his young hero, the "Norwegian boy" who was the USAAF's highest-scoring ace. Despite his instructor status, Bong had downed eight enemy aircraft since his return from the States, and Kenney figured that it would be good for Bong and good publicity for the Far East Air Forces if he received an appropriate decoration.

"Dick already had every other American decoration for valor and I had given him nothing since he had returned to the theater in September," Kenney later reflected. "I had been saving those victories for this very purpose. Now I figured that eight Jap aircraft destroyed in a little more than a month, especially when Bong was supposed to shoot only in 'self defense,' warranted some real recognition."

Kenney went to call on MacArthur.

"General," he said as soon as he entered MacArthur's office, "I want a Medal of Honor for Dick Bong."

"I've been wondering when you were going to bring this matter up," MacArthur said with a smile, barely glancing at the citation that Kenney had prepared. "It's long overdue."

The citation that MacArthur sent back up the chain of command to the

Pentagon read, "For conspicuous gallantry and intrepidity in action above and beyond the call of duty in the Southwest Pacific Area from October 10 to November 15, 1944. Though assigned to duty as gunnery instructor and neither required nor expected to perform combat duty, Major Bong voluntarily and at his own urgent request engaged in repeated combat missions, including unusually hazardous sorties over Balikpapan, Borneo, and in the Leyte area of the Philippines. His aggressiveness and daring resulted in his shooting down eight enemy airplanes during this period."

As Kenney celebrated his hero, his thoughts also turned to protecting him. In retrospect, we see that Kenney's urges to save Dick Bong as a live hero moved in fits and starts. Again and again, occasionally using his instructor status, Kenney grounded Bong, and then reversed course and allowed him to fly. He had sent him home in the spring after he matched and exceeded Rickenbacker's score, but he had arranged for his return to the South West Pacific and had allowed him back to combat. He grounded Bong after his double victory on November 11, but he would relax that order a couple of weeks later.

It was as though Kenney couldn't really make up his mind. It was as though he were as tempted by the lure of "just one more" as was Dick himself. Kenney unofficially encouraged Bong to fly in combat with more enthusiasm than he officially discouraged combat for his Ace of Aces.

Bong had articulated a desire to build his score to fifty, as had Neel Kearby and many other pilots who were in far less a position to imagine such a number than was Bong. At the end of November, though, the number forty was widely seen as the upper limit to which Kenney would allow Bong to expand his score.

"Dick wanted to make it an even fifty and I sympathized with him," Kenney wrote later, admitting that he was unsure of how to approach the situation. "I didn't think there was a Jap in the whole empire who could get Bong's airplane in his gunsights, but ever since Neel Kearby and Tommy Lynch had been lost, General Arnold kept sending me radio messages and letters asking me to take Dick out of combat before it was too late. General MacArthur had mentioned several times that he would hate to see Major Bong listed among those shot down. He knew Bong, had followed his string of victories, and liked the kid....After all, he had repaid Uncle Sam many times for what it had cost to make a fighter pilot out of him. Why not send him home and let him marry the girl and be a live hero?"

"Maybe if I shoot down forty Nips I can get sent home again to stay," Dick speculated in a November 24 letter to his mother. "Hope so, anyway. And listen, just in case you are worrying or think I'm crazy for flying combat, why I can tell you that I'm not sticking my neck out at all because I'm just as anxious to get home as you are to have me home."

His reassurances aside, there was still plenty to worry about in the Philippines.

Four days later, on November 28, there was an air raid warning. Japanese aircraft were incoming. Pilots who were on alert scrambled for their aircraft, or as typically happened, for the nearest Lightning that was fueled and ready to fly.

Captain John Davis, the assistant operations officer for the 49th Fighter Group, dashed onto the field and scrambled into the nearest aircraft, which happened to be a Block 1 P-38L that was painted with the tail number 44-23964 and thirty-six miniature Japanese flags.

Moments later, Davis was airborne out of Tacloban and ready to fight. Suddenly one engine burst into flames. Davis was too low to do anything but feel himself falling to his death.

Many people witnessed the crash, and recognized the Lightning with the thirty-six flags. The rumor quickly spread that Dick Bong had gone down.

CHAPTER 35

December 1944:
Medals of Honor

•SCORE•

BONG: 36

McGUIRE: 28

DICK Bong, very much alive after all, found himself without an airplane, and George Kenney pondered how close he had come to finding himself without an Ace of Aces. If Kenney had been ambivalent about setting a limit of forty for Bong before, he was much less so now. Bong had mentioned that number as a theoretical ceiling in his letter home in late November, so it had evidently been on Kenney's mind, and had been a point of discussion. However, by his own recollection, Kenney did not issue specific orders to that effect until later in December.

With his 49th Fighter Group Lightning now a debris field of smoldering wreckage, Bong moved on, hanging out his gunnery instructor shingle with the 475th Fighter Group at Dulag. This move put him and Tommy McGuire once again at the same base and in the same group. In fact, it had been McGuire himself who invited Bong to come south and fly with him in the 431st Fighter Squadron.

McGuire even invited Bong to come live in the makeshift "bungalow" he shared with Pappy Cline and Fred Champlin. The two top-scoring aces in the USAAF would not only be sharing the same hovel at the same base, but soon, they'd be going into combat in the same flight.

Bong's status apparently allowed him to make the move on his own initiative and not under orders from Kenney. Indeed, Kenney recalls having first seen Bong at Dulag sometime after the first week of December, and being surprised to discover that he had transferred himself.

As Dick Bong unpacked his gear in Dulag, Tommy McGuire sat down on December 4 to celebrate his second wedding anniversary by writing another letter promising his bride that he would be home by the first of the year.

Meanwhile, Bong was thinking about his own wedding, and rereading letters from Marge that were taking many weeks to reach him. He noted in a letter on December 8 that he had received no mail in six weeks. He, too, hoped to be home by the first of the year. Marge would be graduating from Superior State Teachers College in late January, and he said that he wanted to be home for that more than he wanted to go home with fifty flags painted on a Lightning.

A IR operations in the Philippines during the first two weeks of December took place against the backdrop of the largest military operation in the islands since October. Scheduled for December 15, this was the American invasion of the 4,081-square-mile island of Mindoro. Seventh-largest of the Philippine islands, Mindoro is two thirds of the distance from Leyte to Manila. If Leyte had been MacArthur's initial foothold in the Philippines, Mindoro was an important stepping-stone on the road to Manila.

As with Leyte, Mindoro was considered important for its potential airfields, which for the operations in Luzon would supplement and eventually replace those on Leyte such as Tacloban and Dulag. The plan of attack in Mindoro called for landings near the southwestern corner of the island at Mangarin Bay, the best harbor in Mindoro and a good potential staging base for the Luzon invasion fleet. Nearby San José offered a good base for USAAF aircraft.

Meanwhile, MacArthur intended to wrap up the Leyte campaign. For more than a month the FEAF had been attacking the Japanese forces around Ormoc Bay, isolating them by destroying the ships attempting to resupply them. The next phase was to land American troops in the vicinity in early December as a hammer to push the Japanese against the anvil of the American forces that had landed in eastern Leyte in October and in northern Leyte in November.

It was expected that the Japanese would vigorously oppose the American landings at Ormoc and Mindoro with both kamikaze and conventional bombing attacks, so in the weeks leading up to the mid-December D-days, Kenney's FEAF was tasked with destroying Japanese air assets throughout the region. This would involve both attacks by bombers against airfields, and fighter sweeps aimed at hunting and killing Japanese aircraft. The latter task was tailor-made for men such as Bong and McGuire, and they would eagerly rise to the occasion.

The fact of December 7 being the third anniversary of Pearl Harbor was lost on no one as the U.S. Army's 77th Infantry Division landed at Albuera, less than four miles south of Ormoc City. The division's three regiments went ashore unopposed by Imperial Japanese Army units, but Japanese air attacks targeted American ships in Ormoc Bay. As had been the case since October, the fierce attacks included kamikaze suicide attacks.

Overhead, the USAAF was out in force to intercept the enemy. Among the Far East Air Forces units flying that day was Daddy Green Flight of the 431st Fighter Squadron, which was spearheaded by the dream team of American aces. Tommy McGuire led as Daddy Green One, while Dick Bong led the second element as Daddy Green Three. Their wingmen were Jack Rittmayer and Floyd Fulkerson.

At 2:50 P.M., just twenty minutes after wheels-up at Dulag, Bong spotted a twin-engined Mitsubishi Ki-21 Sally bomber below them and heading toward the American ships in Ormoc Bay.

Without alerting other members of the flight, a decision for which he was subsequently criticized, Bong dived on the Sally, finally shooting it down after a fifteen-minute chase.

A lot of men in the 431st would later grumble about Bong's having ditched the rest of Daddy Green Flight to go after the Sally. There were those in both fighter groups who had long interpreted Bong's "special" status— either as freelancer or instructor—as a license to concentrate only on his own score. The incident with the Sally was seen by many as just a symptom of Bong's ego getting in the way of his operating as part of a team. On the other hand, he may have saved lives by immediately taking out a potential kamikaze.

After Bong nailed the Ki-21, the flight re-formed and continued its patrol. At three-forty, Rittmayer observed and dived on a Nakajima B5N torpedo bomber that also may have been in the midst of a kamikaze attack. Shortly after Rittmayer sent the B5N spiraling into Ormoc Bay, Daddy Green Flight saw five Nakajima Ki-44 Tojos headed toward them and toward the U.S. ships in the bay.

It seemed that by the way they flew straight in, defying the antiaircraft fire, that the Ki-44s were on a low-level suicide mission, so Bong ordered the flight to ignore the black puffs of the American antiaircraft shells bursting in the air and go after the Japanese aircraft.

It was Tommy McGuire's turn. He slashed into the enemy formation, taking a thirty-degree deflection shot at one, which immediately crashed into the bay. He banked away, lined a second Tojo up in his sights, and cut loose. It, too, tumbled out of the sky, harmlessly missing the American ships.

Meanwhile, Fulkerson also had hit a Tojo low to the water and it exploded spectacularly, dropping into the waves in fragments.

Dick Bong made a wide turn and pointed his Lightning head on at the Ki-44 flying at the rear of the flight. He opened fire, observing a number of hits on the plane's Ha-109 radial engine before it disintegrated.

As the Tojo tumbled into the water Bong banked away and came face-to-face with the last surviving enemy aircraft. He took a shot, but the Ki-44 had already been dealt a deathblow by Jack Rittmayer, and Bong watched it fall.

At four-thirty, Daddy Green Flight resumed its patrol and was ordered to fly cover for one of two U.S. Navy destroyers that were mortally wounded by kamikazes that day.

The four Americans finally returned to Dulag at seven-twenty, with Bong's score at thirty-eight and McGuire still eight behind at thirty. As Bong wrote in a letter dated the following day, there was a poker game on the night that the two aces each scored their doubles—or shortly before—that lives in infamy. Dick admitted to losing $1,500, but noted that McGuire lost $2,500. Prior to this auspicious day, their luck at cards had apparently matched their luck in battle.

As Kenney recalled it, he was unaware that his two top-scoring aces had flown together and scored together on the Pearl Harbor anniversary until after the fact. When he heard about it, he went to McGuire's quarters to ask whether it was true that Bong was flying in McGuire's squadron, and found both men there.

"You see, General, that 49th gang up at Tacloban didn't want Dick going along with them anymore, as he was stealing too many Nips from them, so he came down here to see if we would let him fly with the 475th," McGuire explained, according to Kenney, as Bong grinned and nodded his agreement. "We figured we were good enough so we could take care of our own interests along that line, so we said it would be okay. This morning he saw me getting ready to take off for a look at the Jap fields over on Mindanao and suggested that he go along. I had a hunch I shouldn't have let him come with me, but I had to be polite, so I gave in.... We spotted a couple of Oscars just ahead of us, near Pamubulon Island, flying low just over the treetops. They were on my side and I figured maybe Dick hadn't seen them so I barely whispered over the radio to my wingman to follow me and I dive to take one of the Nips. One nice burst, and down he goes. I turn to knock off the other Oscar but this eavesdropping Bong had heard me talking to my wingman and had located the Nip. Before I could get in position, I saw him blow up and Bong pulls up alongside of me waggling his wings and grinning at me, like the highway robber he is."

McGuire's wisecracking account of the day's action, filtered through the prism of Kenney's memory, is more or less accurate in its sequence, although one can imagine that Bong and McGuire were far less haphazard in their mission planning. The notion that Bong relocated to Dulag because the Forty-niners felt that he was "stealing" Japanese aircraft from them was obviously a joke.

A few days later, the news that Bong's Medal of Honor had been approved became official, and Kenney decided to arrange for the presentation to be made in the company of the 49th Fighter Group pilots.

Recognizing the public relations value, Kenney asked MacArthur to award the medal to the young Ace of Aces in a public ceremony at Tacloban. Previously, as with Neel Kearby, MacArthur had awarded Medals of Honor at private ceremonies in his office. He told Kenney that he did not want to break precedent with a public presentation. In pitching his case, Kenney told MacArthur that the 49th Fighter Group at Tacloban had been one of MacArthur's favorite fighter units, and reminded him that he had personally visited the men on previous occasions. Finally MacArthur relented, and the show was set for the following day, December 12.

One thing that can be said with certainty about MacArthur is that he understood public relations as well as anyone. A tireless self-promoter in his own right, he certainly understood the PR value of their Ace of Aces as well as Kenney did. Dick Bong was big news. He was such big news that nearly every one of his victories now garnered a paragraph or two in the *New York Times.*

Another part of MacArthur's willingness to assent to Kenney's persistence was probably the fact that MacArthur was in a very good mood that week. The War Department had just authorized five-star rank for active-duty generals and admirals for the first time in history, and MacArthur was slated to become the second five-star general in the U.S. Army on December 18. In all, only four generals (George Marshall, MacArthur, Hap Arnold, and Dwight Eisenhower) and three admirals (William Leahy, Ernest King, and Chester Nimitz) would receive five-star rank during World War II, and only one of each in the years thereafter.

Bong traveled back from his new home with the 475th at Dulag to Tacloban, the home of the Forty-niners, his old outfit and the fighter group most favored—according to Kenney's recollection—by MacArthur. General Don Hutchinson, the overall FEAF commander of the units at Tacloban and Dulag, was there, along with Lieutenant Colonel George Walker, commander of the 49th. So, too, were men with whom Bong had often flown, such as Jerry Johnson and Bob Morrissey.

If MacArthur and Bong were to play starring roles in the event, Kenney was its master of ceremonies. It was his show, staged for maximum public relations value. A light rain was falling as photographers and newsreel cameramen were brought in to preserve the scene for posterity and to get in onto front pages and theater screens in the States as soon as possible.

"We lined up eight P-38s in a half circle, with the crews standing in front of them," Kenney said, describing the scene in later years. "Out in front of his guard of honor, consisting of twelve fighter pilots, all of whom had a dozen or more victories to their credit, stood Bong, speechless with stage fright and shaking like a leaf. In a sky full of Jap airplanes, all shooting in his direction, Dick would be as cool as a cucumber, but there in front of everybody, with the great MacArthur ready to decorate him with the highest award his country could give him, Bong was terrified. The two advanced toward each other and Dick got his next shock when he saw the general beat him to the salute. I had forgotten to tell him that it was MacArthur's custom to salute the man he was decorating. Bong hurriedly recovered and returned the greeting."

A speech had been written for MacArthur, and released to the media ahead of time, which read, "Of all military attributes, the one that arouses the greatest admiration is courage. The Congress of the United States has reserved to itself the honor of decorating those among all who stand out as the bravest of the brave. It is this high and noble category, Major Bong, that you now enter as I pin upon your breast the Medal of Honor. Wear it as the symbol of the invincible courage you have displayed in mortal combat. My dear boy, may a merciful God continue to protect you—that is the prayer of your commander in chief."

For whatever reason, the theater commander simply canned the speech and spoke extemporaneously. Stepping forward and placing both hands on Bong's shoulders, he spoke just one sentence: "Major Richard Ira Bong, who has ruled the air from New Guinea to the Philippines, I now induct you into the society of the bravest of the brave, the wearers of the Congressional Medal of Honor of the United States."

With solemn attention to detail, MacArthur then pinned the starry blue ribbon on Bong's uniform shirt, shook his hand, returned his salute, and departed.

"Say, when do we eat?" Bong said, walking toward the command post with Johnson and Morrissey. "I'm hungry. I had to hurry up from Dulag this morning and didn't get any breakfast except a cup of coffee and a little cheese sandwich."

All that was available was some bread and a can of tuna. Putting his Medal of Honor into his pocket, the newest inductee into the society of the bravest of the brave made a sandwich, which he enjoyed.

The show at Tacloban, which was the talk of the Leyte airfields that day, made Tommy McGuire more determined than ever to pour himself into the Race of Aces. The following morning, December 13, he led his flight on a fighter sweep deliberately designed to entice the Japanese into a fight. His plan was for four Lightnings to head out over Cebu, an island nearly as large as Leyte and about fifty miles to the west. Here they would slowly overfly a known IJNAF base in a loose, disorganized way, giving the impression of inexperienced novices and thus easy prey.

With Captain Danny Miller, operations officer for the 475th, leading the second element, McGuire took his charade to Cebu, passing over a field where more than two dozen Japanese aircraft were parked. Having passed out of sight, McGuire led his flight up to eighteen thousand feet, where they re-formed into a tight, professional formation and headed back to the Japanese base.

The enemy had indeed done as McGuire had surmised: they were taking off and rising to stalk a clumsy prey.

Their mistake.

As the Japanese pilots scanned the horizon for the sloppy Americans, they did not initially see the four Lightnings hurtling down toward them at tremendous speed—with g-forces so great that Danny Miller thought he was going to pass out.

The pilot of one Mitsubishi J2M in particular did not see *Pudgy V* until McGuire took a sixty-degree deflection shot at four hundred yards.

After that, he saw nothing—unless, of course, he survived among the burning wreckage falling into the Cebu rain forest.

McGuire had closed the spread to seven.

TWO days later, November 15, was D-day for the Mindoro operation. The western sky was still in darkness as Tommy McGuire led Daddy Special Flight out of Dulag with wheels-up at 6:30 A.M. As on December 7, the dream team was in action, with Dick Bong leading the second element.

As USAAF strength in the Philippines grew, American fighters were ranging farther and farther from their foothold on Leyte. The four Lightnings headed west, past Ormoc Bay and across the channel separating Leyte from Cebu, then past Cebu to Negros, a 5,048-square-mile island larger than Mindoro and more than twice the size of Leyte, and where the Japanese had airfields that had yet to be bothered too much by the Americans.

The Americans were patrolling the Negros skies at seven thousand feet, looking for trouble, when Floyd Fulkerson, flying on Bong's wing, spotted a lone Ki-43 Oscar far below.

Bong nosed over and headed down, his airspeed increasing as he dove. He squeezed off a burst with 60 to 90 degrees of deflection and hit the right wing of the Japanese fighter.

Overshooting the Oscar, Bong jerked his Lightning to the left, came around 360 degrees, and attacked again. Opening fire at about a thousand feet, he watched the Oscar turn, trying to wriggle out of the way of the Lightning.

Bong lined up on the enemy's six o'clock and gave him a short burst.

This time as Bong overshot the Oscar, the enemy fighter was tumbling into the ocean below.

The skies were now empty of aircraft with the rising suns on their wings. That lone Oscar was the sole enemy aircraft encountered by Daddy Special on December 15, and Tommy McGuire would have to content himself with going home empty-handed. The flight was on the ground at five minutes to nine.

Once again, the spread in the Ace Race stood at eight.

About half an hour after the two aces returned to their quarters, a visitor came by the bungalow. General George Kenney sat down with Bong, McGuire, and some of the other pilots for a congratulatory chat. Colonel MacDonald also dropped in, and McGuire suggested that the general stay for lunch. At that time, the bill of fare at forward airfields such as Dulag typically consisted of pretty austere rations, so Kenney was surprised at what was served that day.

"Tommy said they had a cold turkey that was only half gone and if I'd stay for lunch, he'd see that I'd get my share of it," the general recalled. "I accepted the invitation and stayed for lunch. How they happened to have a turkey was really none of my business. I knew they hadn't gotten any Army issue of rations that even resembled a turkey or I would have seen one at my own mess, but I resolved to have someone conduct some judicious inquiries and in case some neighboring Filipino complained about one of his turkeys being liberated, to pay him for it and then forget the whole thing. As long as I was eating some of the plunder I really was an accessory and should accept some responsibility in the matter."

McGuire wrote to Marilynn of Kenney's visit, bragging that "I think I'm the first squadron commander who has ever had the [commanding general] of the FEAF come and visit him for three hours."

Both Kenney and McGuire recall that the visit lasted for several hours. Kenney specifically recalls that it took place on December 15, and when Bong's score stood at thirty-nine. It is amazing, and a testament to the importance that Kenney attached to his two great aces, that he would set aside three hours of his time on the Mindoro D-day to enjoy a leisurely lunch. It is also amazing that neither Bong nor McGuire flew an afternoon mission on so important a day for the FEAF.

During that three-hour lunch, Kenney may or may not have specifically mentioned the oft-discussed notion to ground Bong after forty victories, but if he did, Bong didn't take him seriously. Kenney had grounded him before, only to create a loophole through which Bong could pass—with the same needle-threading skill as he flew his P-38 down Market Street back in 1942.

For Tommy McGuire, it was a different matter. Though their personal relationship was amicable, he was anxious to see Kenney take Bong out of the air.

Bong seemed curiously ambivalent, perhaps assuming that the eight-point spread would remain. In a letter to his mother on December 17, he mentioned his having scored number thirty-nine two days earlier, and told her that "one or two Nips doesn't make any difference anymore."

Or possibly he was just trying to downplay the Race of Aces or the dangers of aerial combat that no doubt caused Dora Bong to lay awake at night.

Dick did go on to tell her that McGuire *did* consider the score and the spread to make a difference. According to Bong's assessment, McGuire was "doing his darnedest to pass me or gain on me, anyway, but since I am living with him at the present, why he has a hard time of it because I fly when he does and we break even. Sure is good hunting up here and it is the best place we have ever been, because we are much safer than we ever have been before."

Having assured his mother that he was "safe," Dick went on to mention Christmas, and asked his family to drink a toast "that we never spend another apart like this."

He added a line to say that his last letter from Marge was dated back on October 23, and went to suit up for an afternoon fighter sweep over the Mindoro Island beachhead.

Daddy Special Flight of the 431st Fighter Squadron took off from Dulag ten minutes before three o'clock on the afternoon of December 17. If one were looking for anniversaries, one could note that it had been exactly forty-one years since the first powered flights, by the Wright Brothers. Orville Wright was still alive in 1944, and marveling at how far aviation technology had come in those four decades.

Daddy Special Flight was the dream team again. McGuire was in the lead, and Bong was at number three. Their wingmen were Fulkerson and Rittmayer.

Climbing to nine thousand feet out of Dulag, it took the four Lightnings an hour and a quarter to reach Mindoro airspace. Bong contacted the air controller who was responsible for vectoring fighters to situations where they were needed. The controller identified a landing beach where U.S. Army units were being strafed by Japanese aircraft, but some American fighters that were at a lower altitude than Daddy Special Flight intervened to say that they could get there faster.

At about this time, Bong spotted two Ki-43 Oscars at twelve o'clock high, skinned his auxiliary fuel tanks, and began to climb with Rittmeyer on his wing.

The two Japanese fighters made a 180-degree turn and scooted northward, away from the Americans. As Bong and Rittmeyer climbed to fourteen thousand feet and closed in, the two fighters split, with the one in the lead beginning to dive, probably to pick up escape speed.

Bong gave chase, knowing that an Oscar could not outrun a P-38L in a dive. He chased the Oscar back down to nine thousand feet, lined up on his six, and thumbed the trigger.

According to Bong's typically terse after-action report, the Oscar "disintegrated and caught fire and dived straight down and crashed about twenty miles north of San José."

Meanwhile, Rittmeyer had finished off the second of the two Oscars.

In so doing, he broke an important rule of fighter operations that requires a wingman to remain with, and cover, his element leader, and not go off on an independent hunting expedition.

Given that Bong's victory that day marked his number forty, this fact overshadowed all else as Daddy Special Flight touched down at Dulag at six-thirty that evening.

It was now that George Kenney finally sent word to Dick Bong that he was to fly up to Tacloban and meet with him personally.

"He was going home," Kenney affirmed. "There would be no more combat and that was that, so I didn't want any more arguments. Forty was a nice, even number and he was to quit talking about fifty or any other number. I wanted him to go home while he was still in one piece, marry Marjorie, and start thinking about raising a lot of towheaded Swedes like himself."

Face-to-face, Kenney told his Ace of Aces that his career as a combat pilot was over. He probably used the line about the little "towheaded Swedes."

"Okay, General," Bong replied after listening to Kenney's lecture about going home and tasting his mother's home cooking. "I'll quit arguing and go home whenever you say, but I'd like to make one more trip to Mindoro and check over a couple of guys in the 7th Squadron of that 49th Group that need a little more gunnery instruction."

Kenney interpreted this as meaning that Bong wanted to say good-bye to his old gang, although what he probably really had in mind were numbers forty-one and forty-two for good measure.

"As a matter of fact, I think it is a good idea," Kenney told him. "I am going over there on an inspection trip myself tomorrow and I'll need some fighter escort on the way, as we will pass over a couple of hundred miles of Jap-held territory. I'd rather have you than a squadron of any other fighter pilots, so borrow a P-38 from someplace and come along. I'll let you know when I'm ready. In the meantime better get your stuff together and packed for that trip home."

As Bong shepherded his boss's C-47 on a milk-run overflight of airfield construction around San José, they could see the miracle of American logistics in action. The engineers had moved quickly. They went ashore on D-day, and the advance echelons of several FEAF units would soon be operating out of San José. Dick Bong would not be one of them. Though he would not actually be leaving the South West Pacific Area until December 29, there would be no number forty-one for Dick Bong, nor a number forty-two.

For Tommy McGuire, the horizon was wide open now. There would be the opportunities for combat that were now denied to Dick Bong. However, there would be no reunion with Marilynn by "the end of the year," as Tommy had speculated in his letters.

Once again, McGuire was the highest-scoring USAAF ace still in combat. With thirty, he was seven ahead of Jerry Johnson, who was now his nearest rival still flying with the FEAF.

WITHIN days of the American landings on Mindoro, the FEAF was flying bomber and fighter missions out of the airfields around San José. One of the first fighter units to take up residence there was the 348th Fighter Group, Neel Kearby's old P-47 outfit. With San José as an emergency landing site, P-38Ls could reach Luzon from Leyte, so units such as the 49th and 475th fighter groups would not relocate to Mindoro for several weeks.

If the strategic direction for American airpower in the Philippines during the first half of December had been conducted with the Mindoro operation in mind, air operations during the second half of the month were refocused on the continued destruction of Japanese air assets on Negros, and the campaign against the Japanese on Luzon. Ironically, one of the most important targets on Luzon was a huge air base north of Manila that had been built by the United States.

Located about sixty miles north of Manila, Clark Field originated in 1903 as the U.S. Army's Fort Stotsenburg, shortly after the United States captured the Philippines from Spain in the Spanish-American War. The base became Clark Field in 1919, named for Major Harold Clark, an early U.S. Army aviator. By 1941 it was the key USAAF base in the Far East and one of the largest American bases in the Commonwealth of the Philippines. Clark was attacked by the Japanese simultaneously with the attack on Pearl Harbor in December 1941, and captured by them a few weeks later. The Japanese turned Clark into their own key air base in the Philippines. Now, three years after the war began, it was the turn of the USAAF to return with armadas of B-24 heavy bombers.

As with the earlier Fifth Air Force air campaigns against the Japanese air base complexes at Wewak and Rabaul in the summer and fall of 1943, the campaign against Clark was designed to consist of a series of maximum-effort raids, with the maximum number of heavy bombers hitting the field for as many consecutive days as possible.

The attacks on the Clark Field and surrounding fields, including the one at Mabalacat, began on December 22 and would continue daily through December 26, except for a weather interruption on December 23. Initially the B-24s were escorted by P-47s out of Mindoro, but on Christmas, the maximum effort by the bombers against Clark would see them chaperoned by the Leyte-based Lightnings of the 49th and 475th fighter groups, the latter including the 431st Hades Fighter Squadron.

On Christmas Eve, as the men of the 431st had toasted the season and looked forward to the following day, Tommy McGuire held his glass high and announced that the Thunderbolts of the 348th had downed thirty-three Japanese fighters that day, and promised his men that they would celebrate the yuletide with a good day of hunting themselves.

Wheels-up for McGuire and the 431st was just before 8:00 A.M. on Christmas morning. Tommy had once told Marilynn that he had hoped to be home for this day, their second Christmas apart, but it hadn't happened.

Across the international date line in San Antonio, it was still Christmas Eve, and Marilynn celebrated alone with a photograph of a smiling Tommy, looking resplendent in a well-pressed uniform that was a far cry from the rumpled khakis he had been wearing for the past two years.

The 431st rendezvoused with the heavy bombers at nine-fifteen and headed north. McGuire was flying lead in Daddy Flight with Lieutenant Alvin Neal on his wing. An hour and twenty minutes later, the strike force was in the airspace north of Manila at twenty-one thousand feet, picking out the landmarks through cracks in a thin layer of clouds.

Suddenly the battle began. Someone in McGuire's Daddy Flight spotted a large number of A6M Zeros diving at the formation from above and to the east, using the glare of the sun to mask their approach.

It was a classic attack against a bomber formation. Interceptors diving from above at maximum power and maximum speed, their guns blazing, slash through the aircraft in horizontal flight like two dozen scythes. Unlike the pilots the Americans may have encountered over Cebu or Mindoro or Leyte lately, the pilots the Japanese had guarding the highest-value targets on Luzon were among their best.

The Lightnings went after the Zeros, and soon a vast, swirling dogfight tumbled across the sky from Clark to Mabalacat.

Tommy McGuire took a deflection shot, and his rounds found their mark. As the Zero exploded, he could see that his wingman also had scored.

Elsewhere, the news was not so good. Two men, including Ricky Provencio, who had scored his first victory on June 16 while flying as Tommy's wingman, reported that they were going down and would attempt to bail out.

As the B-24s began their bomb run against Mabalacat, black puffs of antiaircraft artillery shells began filling the sky, and another seven Zeros appeared.

Tommy McGuire slashed into the attacking aircraft, destroying two almost faster than it takes to tell the story.

Around him, the Hades pilots were killing Zeros, but other Lightnings were among the aircraft mortally wounded.

Floyd Fulkerson, who had flown as Tommy's wingman in the Bong-McGuire dream team just a couple of weeks earlier, announced that his Christmas would not be a happy one. He told his squadron leader that he was going to try to bail out.

At about that moment, another thirty Japanese interceptors piled on.

McGuire made a tight turn and brought a Ki-43 Oscar into the sights of *Pudgy V*.

He thumbed the trigger.

There was a choking sound, and his guns jammed.

Frantically, he hammered at the reset lever, but to no avail. Tommy McGuire was in the midst of one of the biggest aerial battles of his life—and unarmed.

For the next half hour, he did what a brave man would do: he used *Pudgy V* as his only weapon, maneuvering like a madman, dashing at the enemy fighters, chasing them, and drawing them away from the bombers that the 431st was there to protect.

Thanks to the fighters, the bombers left the target area without a loss, and the Americans headed for home. Eight of the Hades Lightnings were saved by their being able to drop into San José to refuel. Only four, including McGuire, were able to get all the way to Dulag without stopping. Three Lightnings—those flown by Fulkerson, Provencio, and Bob Koeck—never returned. Nor did their pilots, although word later reached Dulag that Fulkerson had bailed out successfully and had been picked up by Filipino guerrillas before he could be nabbed by the Japanese.

Christmas had dealt the 431st its worst day of losses in a year.

On the other hand, the two American fighter groups had downed a confirmed total of forty-two Japanese aircraft, including three apiece destroyed by McGuire and Colonel MacDonald.

McGuire's score now stood at thirty-four, matching that of Dave McCampbell, the US Navy's great Hellcat ace, and just half a dozen behind Dick Bong.

The maximum effort resumed again on December 26, with the 475th Fighter Group ground crews having been up all night with the adjective "maximum" also attached to the number of Lightnings that must be available for the day's mission.

Tommy McGuire led his squadron aloft at 8:15 A.M., with Captain Edwin Weaver as his wingman. They rendezvoused with the B-24s forty-five minutes later, leveled out at eighteen thousand feet, and headed north, toward Luzon.

As the armada approached the target area, every fighter pilot in the Satan's Angels Fighter Group had his eyes peeled toward the sun, waiting anxiously for a repeat of the Japanese attack that came at this point during the Christmas raid.

The bombers entered their run, but nothing happened.

The bombers dodged the flak and released their ordnance, but no Japanese interceptors appeared.

As they exited the target area, however, the enemy struck.

Three fighters dropped from above and to the right, heading for the formation. The trio was far short of the number that made the initial attack on Christmas.

The Americans recognized them as Mitsubishi A6M5 Model 52s, a recent development of the ubiquitous Zero that incorporated features designed to make them more competitive with more advanced American fighters such as late-model Hellcats and P-38L Lightnings. Such updates included a more powerful engine and thicker structural components to allow a higher g-force dive.

McGuire ordered his Daddy Flight to skin their tanks and go to work.

Just then, another five A6M5s popped out of the clouds to attack the rear of the bomber force. One Zero set his sights on a lone straggler among the B-24s.

McGuire could see what was happening as the Zero lined up behind the bomber to take his shot, but no Lightning was close enough to take a shot. He slammed his throttles forward, willing *Pudgy V* to cross the distance faster.

In those split seconds as the Zero licked his chops for an easy prey, McGuire saw no return fire from the B-24. The tail gunner's guns must be jammed. He knew the feeling. The same thing had happened to him yesterday.

Finally, at four hundred yards—still too far to hit anything—McGuire could stand it no longer. He took an impossible forty-five-degree deflection shot.

To his amazement, he watched his rounds slam into the unarmored cockpit of the Zero.

To his amazement, the Zero continued to follow the bomber, probably with its pilot dead at the stick.

Tommy closed to nearly point-blank range. A few more rounds and the Zero tumbled out of the sky in a ball of fire.

By now, the air was filled with more Japanese fighters, who had waited until after the bomb run to ambush the Americans. It was a target-rich environment—for both sides.

Fueled by adrenaline and high-octane aviation fuel, Tommy McGuire and *Pudgy V* became, for the next half hour, the sort of amazing fighting machine of which warriors speak with the utmost reverence.

Taking shots at sixty and seventy degrees of deflection, McGuire engaged and destroyed a second Zero. He and *Pudgy V* plowed on, hitting a third Zero with two quick bursts and sending it tumbling out of the sky.

The man and his airplane had maneuvered so hard and so fast that Weaver could not keep up. McGuire was alone, but he hardly noticed. He had eyes only for another A6M5. This Japanese pilot wisely attempted to escape, but the determined war machine went after his tail like a pit bull on methedrine.

Taking shots from wild and impossible angles, McGuire hit the Zero and hit him again, tearing at his wing with a .50-caliber chainsaw.

As a fourth burning A6M5 fell from the sky, Tommy McGuire went hunting again. However, by now the target-rich environment had become the remnants of a rout. Tommy McGuire took a couple of shots at retreating Zeros, but *Pudgy V*'s fuel gauge told him that they had a date with Dulag. The battle was over.

Having now scored seven victories in two back-to-back missions, Tommy McGuire had brought his score to thirty-eight victories, only two behind Dick Bong. Those two days, those seven victories, and especially his having feinted at Japanese fighters for half an hour with jammed guns, also would be the reasons for Tommy McGuire being written up for a Medal of Honor; but that was yet to come.

FOR the moment, General George Kenney had a problem. His Ace of Aces was scheduled to leave for the States in three days with forty victories. Back home, the USAAF publicity machine had announced this, and the press releases were appearing. A photo op with General Hap Arnold at the Pentagon was already on the schedule for January 3.

General George Kenney had a problem. What if Tommy McGuire had a day like he had on Christmas, or on the day after? What would happen is that when Dick Bong reached the United States, he would no longer be America's Ace of Aces.

Kenney had to slow McGuire down until Bong got home!

No maximum-effort missions into the target-rich skies over Clark were scheduled for the next several days. On the day after McGuire's quartet of kills, the B-24s were sent against easier targets on the islands of Negros and Mindanao. That would give Kenney a bit of breathing space.

On December 28, the general summoned Tommy McGuire to his office at Tacloban. He told America's penultimate ace that he "looked tired."

"General, I never felt better in my life," McGuire protested. "I've gained five pounds in the last month. Besides, I'm only two behind, and—"

"That's just it," Kenney interrupted. "You *are* tired and you won't be rested enough to fly again until I hear that Bong has arrived back in the United States and has been greeted as the top-scoring ace of the war. As soon as I get that news, you can go back to work. If I let you go out today, you are liable to knock off another three Nips and spoil Dick's whole party. What do you want him to do, land at San Francisco and have everyone say, 'Hello, number two, how's the war going?'?"

As Kenney recalled, McGuire laughed and agreed that he'd relax, take it easy, get a lot of sleep for a few days, and then go back to work.

That same day, Kenney reassigned McGuire from command of the 431st Hades Fighter Squadron, moving him up a notch to a new job as operations officer for the 475th Fighter Group. Pappy Cline would then move into McGuire's old job.

The reassignment was intended by Kenney as the equivalent of his having allowed Bong to assume freelance status. McGuire was essentially relieved of all duty but aerial combat. Kenney was grooming his next hero, and Tommy McGuire had, in essence, a license to kill.

To end a momentous year on such a note, especially against the backdrop of the talk of a Medal of Honor, should have been the high point of McGuire's career thus far. His career perhaps, but not his life. Life is complex, and so it was for McGuire. The license had an expiration date, and the date was February.

For Tommy McGuire, it was the best of times and the worst of times. His career had reached its apogee, with nowhere to go but the promise of greater glory. Yet he had a wife at home—actually not at home, but in San Antonio, which was certainly not his home—whom he had not seen in two years.

In late December, he had gone to see Kenney and had explained all this, and Kenney had promised that McGuire could go home by the end of February—at the latest.

In McGuire's last conversation with Bong before the Ace of Aces left Leyte on December 29 with six bottles of Coca-Cola courtesy of General Kenney, one of the last things Tommy said was to ask him to phone Marilynn as soon as he reached the United States. He wanted his rival to relay his promise that he *really* was coming home soon.

On New Year's Eve he put pen to the paper of a letter to Marilynn. He did not mention the buzz about a Medal of Honor. He knew that would not be high on Marilynn's list of priorities after nearly two long years. He wrote that he had been expecting to send her a cable by the end of the year telling her to expect him home, but that his plans fell through. He told her that he had gone to see Kenney, and he told her that Kenney's promise about February made it real.

CHAPTER 36

January 1945: Never to Be Forgotten

•SCORE•

BONG: 40
McGUIRE: 38

DICK Bong reached San Francisco on New Year's Eve and continued on to Washington, D.C. As he looked down on the vast continent creeping beneath him on the first dawn of the new year, he knew that he was this nation's Ace of Aces. He knew that when he visited the commanding general of the USAAF at the Pentagon on January 3 that he would still be America's Ace of Aces, but that after that, the title was up for grabs.

He understood that like many things in the rapid flux of wartime, Ace of Aces was a tenuous title. Bong knew as he saw the dome of the nation's Capitol beneath him, that eighty-five hundred miles behind him, Tommy McGuire would soon be flying back into target-rich skies for the final chapter of the Race of Aces.

Wearing a necktie and dress uniform for the first time in many months, Bong sat with Hap Arnold behind the commanding general's desk and posed for photographs. He stood in front of Arnold's situation map with his Medal of Honor around his neck and posed for more photographs.

When the photographers had been ushered out of the inner sanctum, the Ace of Aces handed the USAAF's boss of bosses a letter from George Kenney that he had hand-carried all the way from Leyte. In it, the FEAF commander explained what Arnold and Bong both essentially already knew: his reasons for taking Bong out of combat.

"Bong is still capable of shooting down Nips and is not war weary by any stretch of the imagination," Kenney wrote. "But I believe forty is a good number for him to stop on....The reason that I am sending him home is that he is so popular with the personnel of the Fifth Air Force and so many of them have begun to worry about the possibility of his being shot down that I can no longer take the chance of the loss of morale that would result in case he became a casualty....I am sending Bong home as a courier in order to ensure that he arrives in the United States as your top-ranking ace. I have taken out additional insurance on this matter by putting Major Tommy McGuire on the ground for a week to give him a rest which he really doesn't need and also to keep him from passing Bong's score too soon."

Even as Bong reached Washington, there had already been speculation in the media. On December 27, an article in the *Washington Post* conjectured, "Another day like McGuire had over Clark Field, near Manila, yesterday may lift him to the top."

Nobody knew that this was true better than Dick Bong.

Nobody better than Dick Bong knew that there was another side to Tommy McGuire. The third thing that Bong had done in San Francisco—after phoning Marge and wiring her flowers—was to phone a very sad and bitter Marilynn McGuire and to give her Tommy's message.

In January 1945 there were tens of thousands of young women in the United States who were in Marge's boat and tens of thousands in Marilynn's—and they all were in those boats because of forces beyond their own control.

Marge Vattendahl was the antithesis of sad and bitter. Everything was going her way, but it was the luck of the draw. In her New Year's Eve conversation with "Richie," which Marge later described as "jubilant confusion," they at last set a date for their wedding. They picked February 3, but were later overruled by higher authorities: their mothers. There was too much to do and not enough time, so the date was pushed back a week.

After the anxiety of having the love of her life in harm's way for the past year, Marge Vattendahl relished the fact that her life was filled with certainty. Her man was not home on a furlough, he was home for good—and there was a date set for their wedding.

For Marilynn McGuire, it had been nearly two years of uncertainty, and nothing but uncertainty ahead. Last summer there was talk of her husband coming home by October. In October there was talk of his being home for Christmas. Then he'd said he would be back in her arms by the end of the year. At that moment, Tommy was writing her a letter promising her that he would be home by February, but she would not even see this letter until February. The last she had read in a letter from Tommy was "talk of the end of the year," but now the end of the year had come and gone, and the only talk was of the Race of Aces.

Just after Christmas, John Adams of CBS Radio had interviewed Tommy, and the interview was broadcast nationally. CBS was even so kind as to invite Marilynn to come into the studio of their San Antonio affiliate to listen to the broadcast. Actually, they were most interested in interviewing Marilynn after the broadcast. When the feed from New York did not come through because of a technical snafu, it seemed more than merely disappointing for Marilynn.

"I don't mind telling you I was pretty excited," Tommy said, telling Adams about his December 26 fight in the interview that Marilynn did not hear. "When you run into the Japs it helps a lot if you can fire on them instinctively, like hunting duck or game birds. Hunting Japs is the most dangerous kind of hunting there is."

The adrenaline was driving America's penultimate ace, but he did add thoughtfully, "If you don't have teamwork from your wingman you're liable to be the dead duck instead of the Jap."

He then went on, diplomatically, to credit teamwork for the 507 victories that the 475th Fighter Group had accumulated through the end of the year.

However, Tommy McGuire had already very undiplomatically broken the rules. He had disobeyed General Kenney's orders *twice* by taking *Pudgy V* on fighter sweeps over Luzon on the last two days of the year. Even as Dick Bong was phoning Marilynn, McGuire was hunting for his own numbers thirty-nine and forty. He came up empty, but not for want of trying.

• • •

BY January 6, Kenney's cautionary grounding no longer applied, and Tommy McGuire planned a Daddy Flight sweep for the following morning. Dick Bong had received his hero's welcome. He had been photographed with Hap Arnold, and he had met the Washington press corps. He had dined with—and been photographed with—Wisconsin congressman Alvin O'Konski, who relished the warmth of Dick's glow as any politician in 1945 would relish the glow of a war hero. Dick had made appearances on *Army Hour* radio broadcasts and was headed home at last.

Tommy McGuire was headed for the history books. With luck, America would have a new Ace of Aces before the month was through.

The heavy bombers had flown against Clark and the adjacent air bases on the first three days of the year, and again on January 6. The heavy bombers would repeat the operation on January 7, but McGuire would not be participating in an escort mission that day. Instead, he planned to lead Daddy Flight on a fighter sweep over the Japanese fighter fields on Negros, specifically the one at Fabrica.

While the main air action in the Philippines had moved north, to Luzon, the Japanese were still operating out of a number of airfields on Negros and other islands. The random raids flown by the enemy from these bases were considered more as tactical nuisances than as major strategic threats, but the FEAF was still concerned with eliminating those nuisances.

Jack Rittmeyer would lead the second element as Daddy Three, with Douglas Thropp as his wingman. Edwin Weaver, who'd been run ragged by McGuire on December 26, would again fly as his wingman as Daddy Two.

For some reason, McGuire decided not to fly *Pudgy V*, but rather to borrow Fred Champlin's Block 1 P-38L Lightning, tail number 44-24845, known as *Eileen Ann*. Frank Kish, McGuire's crew chief, later told Charles Martin, McGuire's biographer, that McGuire explained that all the Japanese flags painted on the nose of *Pudgy V* made it stand out. McGuire feared that potential prey would avoid such an aircraft.

Daddy Flight took off at 6:20 A.M. on Sunday, January 7, climbed to ten thousand feet, and set its course toward Fabrica, about forty minutes west of Dulag. As usual, each Lightning was carrying a pair of 160-gallon auxiliary fuel tanks beneath its wings. The fighters flew over solid cloud cover all the way to Negros, and had to descend to seventeen hundred feet before they came out of the clouds about ten miles northeast of Fabrica.

Having orbited Fabrica for about five minutes without encountering enemy opposition, McGuire ordered the flight to head farther west to check out other IJAAF airfields, on the island's western side. On the way, Rittmayer experienced engine trouble, and became separated from the others while flying through a cloud. He caught up again, but ordered Thropp to change places with him in the lead of the second element.

Ten to fifteen miles west of Fabrica, Weaver spotted a Japanese aircraft ahead and below the Americans and heading in the opposite direction. Though he identified it as an A6M5 Zero in his after-action report, the aircraft was actually a Nakajima Ki-43 Oscar fighter piloted by IJAAF warrant officer Akira Sugimoto. As noted earlier, Oscars and Zeros were frequently misidentified as one another by Allied pilots.

McGuire, who had seen the Oscar by this time, dived to the left to attack.

With an enemy fighter in their midst, the pilots would now typically be inclined to drop their auxiliary fuel tanks to be better able to maneuver. However, at some point early in the fight, McGuire specifically ordered that the tanks *not* be jettisoned. Dropping their extra fuel would greatly reduce the amount of time they would have to spend over Negros before making the long flight back. It is theorized that McGuire gave the order because he was anxious to have as much time as possible to hunt for his three decisive kills.

As the Americans reacted to his presence, and as McGuire turned toward him, Sugimoto also made a diving turn to the left, coming out on Thropp's six o'clock, where he took his shot.

Rittmayer, who was now flying as Thropp's wingman, opened fire on Sugimoto. The Japanese pilot banked left, away from Thropp's tail.

As he maneuvered away from Thropp and Rittmayer, Sugimoto found himself on Weaver's tail, and he opened fire again.

Now under attack, Weaver called for McGuire to help him and increased his turn, diving slightly.

As Weaver turned, the very maneuverable Oscar stayed on his tail. Both aircraft were below McGuire and turning inside his turning radius. This meant that McGuire would have to make an extremely tight turn to get on Sugimoto's tail. McGuire had executed such maneuvers in combat before—but never with his two auxiliary tanks attached.

As McGuire turned to go after Sugimoto, *Eileen Ann* started to stall. Instead of backing off the tight turning maneuver, McGuire appeared to turn even tighter.

According to Weaver's after-action report, McGuire "increased his turn tremendously. His plane snap-rolled to the left and stopped in an inverted position with the nose down about thirty degrees. Because of the altitude of my plane, I then lost sight of him momentarily."

Since he was barely more than a thousand feet above the jungle, McGuire had no time to recover control. The tight, fast turn at low altitude—with the heavy fuel tanks still in place—had caused *Eileen Ann* to stall and spin. He was too low to recover, and Tommy McGuire crashed to his death in a ball of fire.

Weaver was sure that McGuire had died trying to save him and that he had not been shot down by Sugimoto.

As Weaver wrote in his after-action report, the Oscar broke off his attack just before McGuire's crash, and climbed to the north.

"It is my opinion that the enemy did not at any time change his attack from me to my leader," Weaver said. "I believe his crash was caused by his violent attempt to thwart my attacker, although it is possible that the major was hit by ground fire, which had now begun."

Rittmayer and Thropp then turned to attack Sugimoto, who managed to escape by ducking his damaged Oscar into a cloud. Heavily damaged, however, the Oscar was doomed and soon crash-landed. Various versions of the story say that Sugimoto either died of bullet wounds suffered in the dogfight or was killed by Filipino guerrillas.

As Sugimoto slipped away, a second Japanese aircraft entered the fight. In his after-action report, Weaver mistook it for the first Japanese fighter, returning for a second go at the Americans. However, it was later determined that the second aircraft was a Nakajima Ki-84 Hayate piloted by Sergeant Mizunori Fukuda. Code-named "Frank" by the Allies, the Ki-84 was similar in appearance to the Ki-43, being built by the same manufacturer and deployed in small numbers as a potential successor to the Ki-43.

Fukuda dived on the Americans from ten o'clock high, scoring a hit or two on Thropp's left engine.

Weaver pulled up and made a short thirty-degree deflection shot from below Fukuda. Finally skinning their fuel tanks, Weaver and Rittmayer attempted to pursue Fukuda, but he outturned them and managed to hit Rittmayer with a fatal burst. He went down not far from where McGuire had crashed.

Again Weaver made a thirty-degree deflection shot from below as Thropp attacked Fukuda from above.

Thropp, whose damaged engine was giving him trouble, broke off and headed eastward. Fukuda made a pass at him just as he entered a cloud, then broke off the attack. Mizunori Fukuda survived the war.

Weaver attempted to go after the Ki-84, but he was far out of range, and Fukuda, too, entered a cloud. Weaver waited for about three minutes for Fukuda to reappear; then he caught up to Thropp, and the two men headed back to Leyte with the news that Tommy McGuire would never be coming back.

The eyewitness accounts confirmed that McGuire had gone down in a crash that could not have been survived, but he would remain officially listed as "missing in action" until his remains were located. This would not occur until 1949.

The news of McGuire's loss would not be released to the public for ten days after the crash. For Marilynn McGuire, this was a blessing. She did not know of Tommy's death until she received a personal letter from General Kenney on January 17, and it would have been hell to have heard it on the radio. The official "regret to inform you" telegram from the War Department would not reach Marilynn until the end of February.

"The word that Tommy had been shot down brought me one of the worst of a number of bad moments I have had to face since the war began," Kenney told the widow of the late Major McGuire in a letter dated the day after he went down. "I have always had a lot of confidence in Tommy. I felt that he would make a name remarkable for command as well as for leadership and great personal courage. Highly intelligent and quick thinking, he had brought himself and his men out of trouble many times when others failed to come through. The accident which left him vulnerable on January 7, in which he met his death, was sheer chance, as Tommy was one of the most capable fighter pilots I have ever known.... Your husband was one of the men the Air Forces can never forget."

Two days later, Marilynn received a note of sympathy from Marge Vattendahl. She told Marilynn that Dick had told her that Tommy was a truly fine person and that he would "always remain as such to those who loved him."

CHAPTER 37

February 1945: The Roses
Were Victory Red

DICK Bong had reached Superior, Wisconsin, three days before news of Tommy McGuire's death was released to the public. The Associated Press reported that he was met at the train station by Sig Vattendahl, Marge's father, who drove him home to see Marge before taking him to Poplar to see his own parents.

When he heard what had happened, he told his brother Carl that he had feared such a thing because McGuire was trying too hard to catch him. Now he never would.

Marge graduated from Superior State on January 26, and she and Dick traveled to Milwaukee at the end of the month to begin a round of public appearances. The headlines in the *Milwaukee Sentinel* read, "Milwaukee Gives Hero's Welcome to Major Bong.... Throngs Line the Streets." By now the media attention was familiar, but it would be a stretch to say that they were used to it. Dick abhorred it, although Marge still found a certain fascination in having her life disrupted by the blistering attention of popping flash bulbs.

The Elks Club staged an enormous banquet, replete with speeches and awards, and the Milwaukee Athletic Club gave Marge a $1,350 fur coat. As Marge wrote later, "The temperature went from a low of eight degrees to a high of twenty degrees. That fur coat was really appreciated!"

Major Richard Ira Bong and Marjorie Ann Vattendahl were married on February 10, 1945, at Concordia Lutheran Church in Superior, Wisconsin, the Vattendahl family's church. Officiating was the Reverend Paul Boe, who had confirmed Marge in that church when she was fourteen. The bride wore a veil described in the news accounts as "a foamy bridal illusion, fingertip length and shirred to a lace calot with graduated back ruffles of lace," and the groom was now getting a lot of use out of his new dress uniform.

The roses in the bridal bouquet were described as "Victory red." There was, after all, still a war to be won.

Dick's sister Jerry, who had facilitated his first date with her friend Marge, was the maid of honor. The best man was Captain Walter Markey, a young New Yorker who had flown with the groom in the 49th Fighter Group. The two men had become friends, and Markey was another of the men who, like Bong, had preferred a furlough to the Queensland beaches rather than the bars and nightspots of Sydney. Markey also was one of the men who was as disparaging of Dick's skill as a bunkhouse clarinet player at Dobodura as he was a champion of his skill as a fighter pilot.

The bride's brother, Sergeant Lowell Vattendahl, and another of the groom's sisters, Nelda Bong, also were in the wedding party.

More than twelve hundred people crowded into the church for what the bride had hoped would be a "simple" wedding, and still more lined up outside to catch a glimpse of the famous couple as they emerged.

The Associated Press reported that nine USAAF officers represented General Hap Arnold, who was "prevented by illness from attending the wedding." He probably would have liked to have been there, and perhaps he even might have attended. However, on January 17, the same date that Tommy McGuire's death was announced, Arnold had suffered his fourth heart attack. When he had not shown up at the Pentagon for three days running, the chief USAAF flight surgeon went to Arnold's quarters to bang on the door. Dragged kicking and screaming—as much as a man in his condition could kick and scream—the boss was shuttled off to Coral Gables, Florida, for nine days of around-the-clock care.

Outside Concordia Lutheran in the freezing Wisconsin air, the Associated Press was joined by Acme and the International News Service, as well as by reporters from many major newspapers and the newsreel cameras of Fox Movietone, Hearst, Pathé, Paramount, and Universal. United Press would later rate the event among the top ten celebrity weddings of the year. Also on the list was that of Humphrey Bogart and Lauren Bacall.

At 7:00 P.M., with soloist Julie Ann Hanson singing "At Dawning," Sig Vattendahl marched his daughter down the aisle to greet the grinning Ace of Aces. In sixteen minutes, by Marge's reckoning, it was all over except for several reenactments by Major and Mrs. Bong for the cameras. An audio recording was broadcast over WLS in Chicago at ten-thirty and over Superior's WEBC half an hour later.

The Walter Butler shipyard donated a bizarre wedding cake, a seven-foot replica, not of a P-38, but of the ship that Dick's mother had helped launch in 1944. The slogan on the side read, "Happy Sailing, Marge and Dick." In the pictures, the bride and groom seem bewildered by the peculiar and massive thing. This being a wedding with military men in uniform, someone had a sword, and Dick used this to cut the cake.

There were toasts, and Dick raised his glass to "the men still overseas, I hope you can come home to as nice a feeling as I have here now."

When it was all over, Marge donned her Elks Club fur coat, and the happy couple headed into the cold night on a four-hour drive to the Hotel Nicollet in Minneapolis, the first leg of their wedded life.

They traveled on to San Francisco, where they spent a few days with one of Dick's cousins. Here they were met by John Gilbert "Tex" Rankin, at whose Rankin Aeronautical Academy Dick had taken some of the earliest steps in his aviation career. Tex and his wife, Shirley, took the newlyweds under their wings and drove them down to Tulare, where Dick spoke with students who were learning the ropes in the same airspace where America's Ace of Aces had once been a student. While guests of the Rankins, Dick also took Marge up in an AT-6 advanced trainer for a forty-five-minute session of slow rolls and spins.

"When he started to hedge-hop and jump the stick, I told him perhaps we shouldn't overdo it and get back to good old terra firma," Marge recalled in her memoirs.

After a brief visit to Sequoia National Park—where Dick and Marge played in the snow they thought they'd never miss when they left the Midwest earlier in the month—Tex and Shirley next drove the Bongs to Hollywood. Dick's celebrity brought them audiences with stars Marge had never imagined meeting. They met Lucille Ball, Judy Garland, and Angela Lansbury on the set of a movie, and they sat in on Art Linkletter's radio show.

As the happy young couple were trading small talk with Bing Crosby and dining at the celebrated Brown Derby, World War II continued to grind on. General Krueger's Sixth Army had made their initial landings on Luzon at Lingayen Gulf, north of Manila, on January 9, two days after McGuire was killed, and by the time Dick and Marge were trading vows in Superior, Clark Field was coming into American hands once again.

As the couple were driving to Tex Rankin's Central Valley ranch, the advance units of two American cavalry divisions had entered Manila itself. After years of the Pacific Theater being an afterthought in Allied strategic planning, MacArthur was getting what he needed. In terms of troops and matériel, the operations to retake Luzon and the rest of the Philippines would be the largest American ground operations in the Pacific. According to official U.S. Army reckoning, it involved more troops even than operations in North Africa, Italy, or southern France.

As more of Luzon was liberated, George Kenney began relocating his FEAF forward bases from Leyte and Negros to Luzon itself. On February 25, Bong's old outfit, the 49th Fighter Group, began operations at Lingayen, and three days later, Tommy McGuire's 475th Fighter Group began flying missions *from* Clark Field rather than *over* it.

Meanwhile, on February 19, the U.S. Marine Corps had gone ashore on a rocky volcanic island in the Pacific called Iwo Jima, beginning an iconic American battle of 1945.

CHAPTER 38

Spring 1945: The Lure of
Jet Planes

WHEN he learned that the Bongs were in Southern California, Lockheed vice president Carl B. Squier invited them to Burbank for a visit to the factory that built the P-38 Lightnings that Dick had flown in combat.

At Lockheed, Bong met Lockheed test pilot Jimmie Mattern. An early barnstormer and Hollywood stunt pilot, Mattern had made a couple of unsuccessful round-the-world flight attempts in the 1930s before going to work for Lockheed as a test pilot on the P-38 program. Among other things, Mattern had been instrumental in developing a piggyback training system whereby both an instructor and a student pilot could squeeze into the single-place cockpit of a P-38. It was during the discussion of this system that an idea arose.

Would Marge be interested in a ride in the famous warhorse in which her ace had scored his forty aerial victories? As she noted in her memoirs, the space was crowded, but she "was not one to pass up such an experience."

Marjorie Vattendahl Bong's first flight in a Lightning was a half-hour jaunt over Los Angeles and the San Fernando Valley on March 9.

"I thought I'd be scared to death but I wasn't at all," she said of the flight.

"I loved it. But, of course, that was because I was with my husband.... My confidence rose with Dick's nonchalance and even more with his ability—and yes, he was singing to me, which helped to allay my initial fears and trepidations—and I relaxed enough to open my eyes to see the world below."

When she quipped upon landing that this had been the nicest buggy ride she ever had, the major said, "Let's not call the Lightning a 'buggy,' honey. She's a lady!"

What interested her husband most at Lockheed was not Lady Lightning but her newest sister—the airplane destined to become America's first operational jet fighter. Every fighter pilot in the USAAF had heard about the Lockheed P-80 Shooting Star, and the subject of this airplane had cropped up in conversations at fighter bases all around the world. For fighter pilots, speed is the performance characteristic they long for most in an aircraft. In aerial combat, speed is frequently the deciding factor between victory and defeat, between life and death. Jet propulsion gave airplanes speed that exceeded anything possible in even the most advanced piston-engine fighters.

In the spring of 1945, jet propulsion as a theory was not new, but practical jet propulsion in operational aircraft was.

The turbojet engine had been invented by Frank Whittle in Britain in 1928, but the first aircraft to fly purely under jet power was the German Heinkel He.178, which first flew in August 1939, powered by an HeS3B engine designed by Hans-Joachim Pabst von Ohain. Recognizing the importance of this new technology to the Luftwaffe, the German Air Ministry had financed the development of the Heinkel He.280 and Dr. Willy Messerschmitt's Me.262 twin-jet fighters even before practical jet engines existed to power them. The He.280 flew in April 1941, powered by two of Ohain's experimental turbojets, which were later replaced by a pair of Junkers Jumo 004 turbojets. The Me.262 made its first flight in July 1942, powered by a pair of BMW 003 turbojets. The He.280 never proceeded past the experimental stage, but the Me.262 would have an interesting service career.

The slow development of the Me.262 in the year after its first flight was due in part to developmental problems with the engines, but also to a general ambivalence in the Air Ministry in Berlin. Fighter pilots—including General Adolf Galland, the head of fighter operations for the Luftwaffe and an ace himself—were delighted with its speed and performance, and wanted it in production as soon as possible. However, the bureaucrats in Berlin saw it as new technology that was of less priority than production of established aircraft—given that in 1942, the Germans still thought that they would win the war. The Me.262 would not be operational until the spring of 1944.

Meanwhile, both the United States and Britain saw the potential of jets and initiated development programs of their own. The first results were the Bell XP-59 Airacomet, which first flew in America in October 1942, and the Gloster Meteor, which first flew in England in March 1943. The USAAF was disappointed with the performance of the Bell XP-59 and turned to Lockheed.

On June 18, 1943, one week after Dick Bong scored his eleventh aerial victory in a Lockheed Lightning, the man who invented the Lightning was summoned to the office of Lockheed president Robert Gross. Clarence "Kelly" Johnson was asked how soon he could design and build a prototype jet fighter. Johnson thought about it and told Bob Gross that it could be done in 180 days—an almost preposterously short time to incorporate all-new technology into an all-new airplane.

Johnson knew that the Germans had a commanding lead in the jet airplane race, and he knew that time could not be wasted. The clock began ticking on June 23 when the USAAF delivered the contract to Burbank, giving the new aircraft the experimental pursuit designation XP-80. The official name, "Shooting Star," was applied later. Johnson and Lockheed chief engineer Hall Hibbard were assigned a staff of 23 engineers and 1,205 shop men, but there was not even a cubbyhole in the sprawling Lockheed complex in which to house the men and the secret activity, so a crude wood and canvas building was slapped together near the wind tunnel and work began.

The drafty shack was a most unlikely site for the home of the nation's most advanced aircraft project. Because of the secrecy surrounding the place, people began to wonder what was going on inside. Kelly Johnson recalls in his autobiography how, when one of his designers was asked what he was doing, he replied that he was "stirring up some kind of brew." As Johnson explains it, this brought to mind the character in Al Capp's *Lil' Abner* comic strip who was regularly seen stirring a big, foul-smelling brew called "Kickapoo Joy Juice," to which he added such ingredients as live skunks. It was from this analogy that Lockheed's most high-technology development center came to be known as the "Skunk Works," a name by which it is still known. The Skunk Works would later be responsible for some of the twentieth century's most remarkable aircraft, from the SR-71 Blackbird to the F-117 stealth fighter.

Working sixty-hour weeks, the Skunk Works crew proceeded quickly on the XP-80 airframe. Even though Johnson had forbidden work on Sunday to make sure the men would get some rest, the "shoemaker's elves" somehow managed to get a lot of work done between Saturday night and Monday morning. A major problem was encountered when the turbojet engine finally arrived seven days before the airframe was completed and was found to be the wrong size! The necessary changes were made and the XP-80 prototype was finished and trucked to Muroc Army Airfield (now Edwards Air Force Base) in the dead of night.

Engine tests were begun on the 139th day, and the prototype was accepted by the USAAF six days later, on November 15, 1943. With Lockheed test pilot Milo Burcham at the controls, the XP-80 made its debut flight on January 5, 1944. The performance of the new Shooting Star was all that had been hoped for, and as the Me.262 entered service, the USAAF anxiously placed an order for thirteen YP-80A service test aircraft.

While the first XP-80 was powered by a British-built deHavilland H1 Goblin engine, two XP-80A prototypes, the YP-80As and later aircraft, were equipped with the J33 turbojet, developed by General Electric from the Rolls-Royce Derwent, the production version of the original jet engine developed in England by Frank Whittle in the early 1940s. Though General Electric had led in the development of the J33, the production license for the engine went to Allison, a division of General Motors that had manufactured 69,305 piston engines during World War II—including the V1710s used in the P-38 Lightnings.

Though at first blush the Shooting Star was a remarkable aircraft, testing during 1944 had shown it to be full of bugs—mainly having to do with the engine and fuel system, rather than the airframe. The dangers of pioneering precarious new technology were grimly illustrated on October 20, 1944, when a main fuel pump failure resulted in the loss of the third YP-80A and the death of Milo Burcham.

Still, fighter pilots everywhere were anxious to get their hands on a jet.

By this time, USAAF bomber and fighter units were beginning to encounter larger numbers of Me.262s, and they were eager for American jets. Across the world, in the South West Pacific, the Lightnings could outperform the Japanese fighters, but there was still a longing for the fastest fighters available.

Dick Bong, like the other pilots, knew that the future of their trade belonged to jets—and they wanted to be there. On November 9, two weeks after the YP-80A crash and a week after he had brought his score to thirty-three aerial victories, America's Ace of Aces pondered his postwar career—and jets.

"The way things look now I may stay in the army after the war, but I'm not at all sold on the idea yet," he wrote in a letter to his mother. "Things are too damned unsettled to try and plan one way or another. I'm just like Nellie [his sister], can't make up my mind as to what I want to do. All I know is that I will continue to fly. I'd really like to fly some fast stuff now and then."

Soon that "fast stuff" would be his.

As Major Bong's honeymoon furlough came to a close, he and his bride bought a used car in California and took an eleven-day cross-country road trip to his new duty station at Wright Field, near Dayton, Ohio. Dick had wanted the fast stuff, and his former boss George Kenney had enthusiastically agreed. Even before Bong left the South West Pacific Area, Kenney had put in a word for him with General Arnold.

"Bong is particularly anxious to get in on the development of the jet-propelled fighter, and I believe that, if possible, he should be given that opportunity," Kenney wrote to Arnold. "With his wide combat experience against every type of aircraft the Japanese possess, he should be invaluable for the development of any special changes in tactics that would result in shifting over to a radically different type of fighter. Bong is a cool, level-headed thinker. From talking to him you get the idea that his thinking apparatus works a little slowly but it has the tremendous virtue of being right most of the time. I would like to see him sent to the Matériel Division and given every opportunity to learn something about the jet engine and the construction and maintenance of both engine and the airplane. While he is not now capable of being a project officer for this airplane, he should be of real value in test work and development of tactics."

And that was exactly what happened.

Early in April, America's Ace of Aces reported for duty at the Flight Test Section of the USAAF Air Technical Services Command (formerly the Air Corps Matériel Division) at Wright Field. Soon the USAAF would be ready to start forming active jet fighter squadrons using the Lockheed P-80. They were anxious to bring the best pilots up to speed in the new weapon.

At Wright Field Dick ran into Captain Don Gentile, who had returned from the European Theater in 1944 as one of the highest-scoring aces in the USAAF Eighth Air Force. Gentile and his wife, Isabella, became close friends with Dick and Marge.

"Having much in common, we enjoyed many evenings together," Marge wrote later. "A picnic outing at an air show turned out to be a tragic one, for a plane exploded in the air before our eyes. Izzi and I were stunned. Perhaps Dick and Don were believers in Kismet, for all they could say about the pilot to console us was 'his number was up.' While that was hardly soothing to two young brides, we were constantly being so reassured by their presence that we both felt it couldn't happen to us. Wrong."

CHAPTER 39

Summer 1945:
Home Sweet Home

I N June, after two months at Wright Field, Dick Bong was reassigned to California, to the Lockheed Air Terminal, where he had first glimpsed the Shooting Star. This time he was going to fly it.

When the news of the transfer came, he was in the midst of a deal to buy a pair of surplus Stearman PT-17 trainers for a total of $1,950. He hoped to sell one and give the other to his brother Bud. Since Bong had to leave town, Don Gentile agreed to help handle the deal for him. He was looking forward to getting his brother a plane.

With this, Dick and Marge packed up the car and headed back down Route 66. At least part of the trip was on the fabled mother road, because by June 17 they were mailing postcards from the Grand Canyon, and Route 66 is the direct route from there to Los Angeles. On the Fourth of July the newlyweds drove out to the Rose Bowl in Pasadena to watch the fireworks show. In a letter to his mother he called the show "quite impressive."

Marge recalled that after rainy Ohio, where Dick had been battling a cold that he could not seem to shake, California looked good again to both of them. However, the housing situation there was difficult, as swarms of service personnel were now returning from overseas. It took them several weeks, but Marge and her young hero finally moved into a furnished bungalow apartment in Hollywood on July 12.

As she wrote home in a letter the following day, Marge spent Friday the thirteenth sprucing up the place, brightening the kitchen with border prints, and hanging a blue print with swans in the bathroom.

"Over the sink I put up a mirror and put a flowered border around it," she wrote. "Almost died of laughter when Dick finally noticed it. He stood in front of it half an hour, but he didn't notice a thing different. Is that a man for you or not?"

However, Dick was indeed pleased with the bungalow that promised to be their home for many months to come. In a letter of his own, America's suddenly domesticated Ace of Aces invited his family to visit, bragging that they had a nice big double wall bed they could pull down. As crowded as the Southern California housing market was in 1945, and as small as the apartment must have been, it was certainly a far cry from the sweaty jungle hovels from Dobodura to Dulag where Dick had once hung his hat.

B Y now, even if you hadn't read a newspaper, you could tell by the mood and number of the soldiers, sailors, airmen, and marines on the street that the war was over in the European Theater. The USAAF had sent a handful of Shooting Stars to Europe during the war's final days, but they never saw action against the badly beaten Luftwaffe. On April 30, surrounded by the Red Army in his Berlin bunker, Adolf Hitler had poisoned his new wife, then shot himself in the head. A week later, on May 7, his generals surrendered the tattered remains of the Third Reich to the Allies, and the Allies celebrated V-E day.

In the Pacific, the Philippines campaign was winding down after the liberation of Manila in early March and the capture of Corregidor in mid-April. By the end of March, Iwo Jima had been secured, and the U.S. Tenth Army had landed on Okinawa, the first actual prefecture of Japan proper to be invaded by the Allies. By the first of June, after some of the bloodiest fighting of the war, nearly all of the island had been secured.

The next step in the Pacific, before V-J day could be celebrated, was to be the final defeat of Japan. To bring this about, Japan's principal home islands would be invaded. Operation Downfall was scheduled to involve the largest major offensive operation of World War II.

The initial phase of Downfall, code-named Operation Olympic, was to be the invasion of Kyushu, the southernmost of the four major islands, on November 1, 1945. Fourteen U.S. Army divisions supported by the largest naval task force in history would seize southern Kyushu as a staging base for the next phase, Operation Coronet. This operation, scheduled for March 1, 1946, was planned to be the largest amphibious operation in history, with twenty-five divisions landing on the island of Honshu and converging on Tokyo.

The airpower component of Operation Downfall was also to be the largest in history. Thousands of B-24 heavy bombers from throughout the Pacific Theater would be concentrated in Okinawa for the campaign, and additional thousands of B-17 and B-24 heavy bombers were being transferred from Europe. Meanwhile, thousands of B-29 *very* heavy bombers were coming off the assembly lines.

The same was happening with fighter units. Both the 49th and 475th fighter groups were scheduled to move from Luzon to Okinawa in August. The two units owned the bragging rights to some of the highest-scoring USAAF aces in the Pacific. In addition to McGuire and Bong, Mac MacDonald had twenty-seven and Jerry Johnson had twenty-two.

Meanwhile, just as the 475th had been created just two years before to specifically operate the then-state-of-the-art P-38, plans were being made for *jet* fighter units. Lockheed would receive orders for three thousand P-80As.

It was expected that Shooting Stars would fight late-model Mitsubishi A6M8 Zeros, Kawasaki Ki-61s, Nakajima Ki-84s, and whatever the Japanese planemakers might have up their sleeves—and fight them in the skies over Japan itself. Arguably more important, the speed of the jets would make them invaluable in chasing kamikazes. After first making their appearance in the Philippines, the massive kamikaze attacks that materialized during the Okinawa campaign wrought havoc on Allied ships.

Dick Bong would not fly in this campaign, but his experience would help to turn others into the effective fighter pilots that would carry the war into the enemy heartland, and defend American lives at sea. He had come to Burbank with experience in combat, and as he learned the nuances of the jet fighter, he would meld the two and pioneer new tactics for the aerial battlefields of the new jet age.

B ONG had made his first flight in the P-80 on July 7, nearly a week before he and Marge settled into their apartment. In a letter he wrote to his family at about that time he told them, "I finally checked out in the P-80 and it is quite an airplane all right."

It was like 1941 and 1942, when Dick had been introduced to a succession of one new aircraft after another, each one incrementally mightier than the last, beginning with Stearman biplanes and culminating in P-38s. Now he was flying an airplane that was significantly mightier even than the Lightning. He liked the feel of the jet beneath him as he streaked through hazy California skies. He liked it a lot.

After his nearly three years in the South West Pacific, his life of commuting to a regular job in Burbank must have been a remarkable contrast. He drove to Lockheed six days a week, noting that it was "not hard work, but it sure takes a lot of time."

The man who once commuted to work in a P-38 and lived in sweltering humidity with cockroaches the size of small dogs now commuted home from work on the Cahuenga Parkway—where soon they would build today's Hollywood Freeway—to a happy home with overstuffed furniture and home cooking. Marge even admitted to often spoiling Dick by giving him breakfast in bed.

At home, Bong often curled up with a Western novel, while Marge dabbled in oil painting. Watching her at work, Marge's young husband took an interest in painting himself—and he actually finished an oil painting of Marge. They also went to the movies, and pursued one of Dick's favorite hobbies by bowling at least once a week.

They also enjoyed listening to hit songs on the radio. Of the songs especially popular on the radio, and on *Your Hit Parade* that summer, and one that perhaps had special meaning for Dick and Marge was the Les Brown

Orchestra and Doris Day recording of "My Dreams Are Getting Better All the Time."

They were beginning to live the peaceful postwar life for which millions of Americans had fought—and for which hundreds of thousands had died—during World War II.

CHAPTER 40

August 1945: By His Example to Inspire

DICK Bong had once alluded to an interest in more of a career in the USAAF, but with people everywhere around him leaving the service, the lure of the private sector must certainly have been there.

"I don't know how long I'll stay in the army," he wrote to his mother in July. "But probably until Christmas anyhow. Got to see what kind of a job I can get now that I'm out here [in California]."

He may have had in mind a job with Lockheed, which would have allowed him to continue flying, but to make a better salary. Of course, there was no shortage of aircraft companies in Southern California. As the home of Lockheed and three major Douglas Aircraft factories, as well as Consolidated Vultee, Hughes, North American Aviation, and Northrop, the Southland was the Detroit of the American aircraft industry.

Test pilots made pretty good money, but they earned it. Flying aircraft that pioneered new technology was a complicated business, and one that was not without risk.

As much as the USAAF desired to now think of the Shooting Star as an operational aircraft, it was really still in its prototype phase, really still an experimental aircraft. Indeed, several had been lost in mishaps since the one that killed Milo Burcham. On March 20, just after Bong had visited Burbank for Marge's P-38 ride, engineering test pilot Tony LeVier had barely escaped when a turbine blade broke, causing a structural failure in the first XP-80 equipped with the J33 engine.

On Monday, August 6, Dick Bong went to work at the Lockheed Air Terminal as usual. He had been invited to play a round of golf with Bing Crosby late in the day, but Dick canceled when he discovered that he had forgotten to put his golf shoes in the car.

Dick had run into Dick Gray, an old pilot friend from the 475th Fighter Group, and had invited him to come out to Burbank that day to see the jets. Dick also invited him to join him and Marge for dinner that night, and Gray accepted.

Bong's job for the day was a routine flight in a production series P-80A. Both he and Ray Crawford, another USAAF pilot, were supposed to fly that day, and they had traded planes in order for Dick to scoot out early to play golf. By the time the golf excursion was canceled, Crawford had already taken off, so Dick decided to fly the other P-80A, tail number 44-85048. After three prototypes and thirteen service test YP-80As, Lockheed was building the first of an eventual 563 production series P-80As. Dick's plane that day was the fifty-sixth Block 1 P-80A. This particular aircraft had been flown once before, for an hour and a half.

By August 6, Bong had made eleven flights in various Shooting Stars, and had logged more than four of his thirteen hundred total flying hours in the new jets.

After his preflight, Bong closed the canopy and taxied out to Runway 33. At about 2:30 P.M., he was given permission by the tower to begin his takeoff roll.

Accelerating to 120 miles per hour, Bong used much of the six thousand feet of runway and lifted off, turning right as he passed over the Southern Pacific rail line that paralleled Vanowen Street. He passed over the Valhalla Memorial Park cemetery as he climbed to two hundred feet. Those watching the flight thought that he climbed out more steeply than usual, and when he banked to the right, he did so at a sharper angle than was his usual practice. Dick Gray was watching, and thought it looked like the right wing dipped suddenly.

Gray also had seen some puffs of black smoke coming out of the tailpipe of the P-80A. He did not have jet experience, but he made a mental note that this didn't look right. Nor did it look right to Frank Bodenhamer, a Lockheed mechanic who had also watched the takeoff.

Mrs. George Zane was in the backyard of her home near the corner of Oxnard Street and Cleon Avenue in North Hollywood, about seven blocks west of the Burbank city limits. She heard an airplane go over. Through the years, especially during the war years, she had heard the piston engines of thousands of planes taking off from the nearby Lockheed Air Terminal, but in recent months she also had heard the distinctly different sound of an increasing number of the new jet planes. Today she heard an unusual popping sound mixed into the engine noise.

As she later explained to a United Press reporter, she looked up and saw the gray jet. Its wings were wobbling and it was rapidly losing altitude. At the moment that she glimpsed the jet, Mrs. Zane saw the pilot emerge, hands above his head, and leap clear. A split second later, as the aircraft was only about three stories above the ground, there was a cloud of smoke and suddenly debris were flying everywhere. She didn't see the pilot anymore.

When an airplane crashes in an urban area, phone calls to news media are instantaneous. Reports broadcast on the radio follow in minutes.

This was how Marge got the news.

The fact that America's Ace of Aces was testing jets at Lockheed was well known, so Dick's name was mentioned in the initial reports.

Her hand trembling, Marge phoned Lockheed, where confusion reigned. Both Crawford and her husband were flying that day, and it wasn't until Crawford landed safely that the terrible facts were made clear.

Several hours later, Lieutenant Colonel Charles Langmack delivered the details to Marge personally, although he could not immediately locate the right bungalow and he had banged on a lot of doors before he found her.

"The shock was great," he later said of the experience of sitting with her in the room filled with the paintings and drawings that the young couple had done of each other.

"What a cruel way I received that news. Alone," Marge wrote later. "The Air Force ordered the news media to 'withhold identity pending notification of next of kin.' One newsman, however, chose to ignore that and revealed the tragic news in its entirety. The Bong family received the information the same way, over the radio. I remember what I did vividly. I ran down the hall screaming, pounding on a friend's door. No one there. Still alone. The next thing I remember is my apartment being filled with Air Force officials, photographers, reporters shoving mikes in my face, one asking if I were pregnant."

She wasn't. There would be no little "towheaded Swedes" for Dick and Marge.

The crash site was in an empty field near what is still the power company right-of-way. It seemed as though Dick Bong had deliberately pointed the aircraft for that spot, an island of nothing in a vast sea of suburban homes.

His broken body was found about a hundred feet from the debris field where the P-80A had disintegrated when it struck the ground and the fuel exploded. He had pulled the rip cord on his parachute, but he had been too low for it to deploy properly. Today's jet fighters are equipped with zero-zero ejection seats that will launch a pilot upward from zero altitude at zero airspeed and save his life, but these did not exist in 1945.

Having heard the news on the radio, Dick's parents drove to the Vattendahl home and the two families tried to come to terms with the tragedy.

It was to be a very personal tragedy in that it was pushed out of the headlines that day by another event with immense implications.

Even as Marge and the family were sinking into a state of shock, the world was reacting to the shock of news that a USAAF B-29 had dropped a nuclear weapon on the Japanese port city of Hiroshima. The following morning, however, beneath the banner headline in the *New York Times* describing the atomic bomb and the Hiroshima attack, was a two-column head that read, "Jet Plane Explosion Kills Major Bong, Top U.S. Ace."

Taking a bit of poetic license, the United Press wire service story said that "with a roaring sigh, the plane, like a giant blowtorch, shot over the airport just before 3 P.M. and then lurched over the trees and nosed down into the field, a mile away."

Out in the Pacific, General Kenney was on his way to General MacArthur's headquarters when he got the news.

"I stopped thinking of the atom bomb, which had wiped out Hiroshima that morning," he said. "I even stopped thinking of the capitulation of Japan, which we all knew was about to take place in a few days. Wherever I landed, I found that the whole Fifth Air Force felt the same, that we had lost a loved one, someone we had been glad to see out of combat and on his way home eight months before. Major Richard I. Bong of Poplar was dead.... We not only loved him, we boasted about him, we were proud of him. That's why each of us got a lump in our throats when we read that telegram about his death. Major Bong, Ace of American Aces in all our wars, is destined to hold the title for all time. With the weapons we possess today, no war of the future will last long enough for any pilot to run up forty victories again.... His country and the Air Force must never forget their number-one fighter pilot, who will inspire other fighter pilots and countless thousands of youngsters who will want to follow in his footsteps every time that any nation or coalition of nations dares to challenge our right to think, speak, and live as a free people."

Harry Truman, the president of the United States, released a statement saying that Dick Bong "stands in the unbroken line of patriots who have dared to die that freedom might live. And grow. And increase its blessings. Freedom lives. And through it, he lives—in a way that humbles the undertakings of most men."

Eddie Rickenbacker, the man who had passed the baton of Ace of Aces to the younger man born two years after his final victory in World War I, commented that Bong was "an example of the tragic and terrible price we must pay to maintain principles of human rights, of greater value than life itself. This gallant Air Force hero will be remembered because he made his final contribution to aviation in the dangerous role of test pilot of an untried experimental plane, a deed that places him among the stout-hearted pioneers who gave their lives in the conquest of sky and space."

Late the following day, the body of that stout-hearted pioneer was placed aboard a USAAF Air Transport Command C-54 at the Lockheed Air Terminal and flown back toward the place of his birth. Marge, still in a state of shock, also boarded the aircraft, although she had not seen the flag-draped casket being loaded. She recalled that she felt his presence on the flight, although she was not consciously aware of the casket being aboard until the plane landed in Duluth.

She was accompanied by her brother, Jerome, and by Major Earl Kingsley, who had known Dick when they were both in flight school and who was serving as guard of honor.

The C-54 touched down at Duluth Airport at eight-thirty on the morning of August 8, where it was met by a crowd of about a thousand, including Dick's parents and several other relatives, including his brother Bud and sisters Jerry and Nelda.

It had to be difficult for all involved to see the coffin taken to Concordia Lutheran Church in Superior, where almost exactly six months earlier, Dick and Marge had exchanged vows to last a lifetime together that they expected to be measured in years, not months.

Leading the service that afternoon was the Reverend Paul Boe, who had married Dick and Marge on that cold February day, and the Reverend Arvid Hoorn, pastor of Bethany Lutheran Church in Poplar. More than two dozen cars formed the funeral procession, but dozens of other vehicles were parked along the route to the cemetery in Poplar where he would be laid to rest. Through their tears, the family must have been overwhelmed by the pageantry of color guards and bands and generals who were sent to the funeral.

Ironically, when it came to the flyover, the USAAF sent P-47s rather than P-38s. It was the thought that counted. Rev. Hoorn read the 91st Psalm, Taps were played, and Marge was handed the folded flag.

Back in Burbank, all P-80s of all variants were grounded—albeit for less than a week. The wreckage of 44-85048 was hauled back to Lockheed, and an inquiry into the crash was undertaken.

The investigation centered on the issue of fuel pressure under the theory that the engine starved and stopped, and the plane stalled as Bong had climbed out. This would have caused the plane to drop suddenly. The aircraft was equipped with an I-16 electric fuel pump as an emergency backup in case of loss of fuel pressure. The one installed in 44-85048 was recovered at the crash site. It was deemed to be in working order, but it was not determined whether Bong had used it during his thirty- to forty-second flight.

It was a fuel line issue that had killed Milo Burcham, and it was a fuel line issue that killed Dick Bong. What caused this fuel line malfunction was a mystery.

There was a theory that the puffs of black smoke seen by several witnesses came from the I-16's motor, but there seemed to be no evidence that it had been burning prior to the crash. Perhaps Bong saw this and shut down the pump manually. Strangely, loose dirt was discovered within the engine gearbox. The mechanism was tested and found to work, but only after the dirt had been removed.

The cause of the crash was determined to be that the engine cut out for lack of fuel, but exactly what caused the interruption in fuel flow was never determined. Subsequent test flights were made by Tony LeVier at Muroc Army Airfield in an attempt to re-create the conditions of Bong's fatal flight, but these failed to shed any light on the mystery.

Shortly after the funeral, General Hap Arnold's letter to Marge reached her. The morning after the momentous day in which one of his airplanes had dropped the atomic bomb and another had killed his Ace of Aces, the commanding general of the USAAF sat down at the desk behind which he had posed for photographs with Dick Bong on a couple of occasions and penned a very personal note:

"I wrote you last February on the occasion of your marriage, I said you were marrying 'one of my best boys,' and I sincerely meant it. Today the sad news of his fatal accident has just arrived. Any urge of the Army Air Forces to rejoice over our latest crushing blow against Japan gives way completely before this loss. All the atomic bombs in the world can never make up for the loss of men like your husband.

"Dick was a true hero, modest in achievement, clean-cut, with the stature of an outstanding American—the type thousands of American boys choose as their ideal. His comrades of the USAAF wanted him to live and by his example to inspire the youth of America. It is impossible to be reconciled to the fact that after surviving so many grueling air battles he has lost his life in service here at home.

"Dick fought and died as a pioneer. In combat, he was always trying something new—something not in the book—to improve not only his own methods but to better prepare his fellow airmen to face the enemy. In a similar manner, he met death while testing, for the Army Air Forces, the newest and fastest plane in the world.

"Dick will take his rightful place in aviation history, but the officers and men of the Army Air Forces will ever grieve at the loss of a most beloved and respected comrade. On their behalf, I send you our deepest sympathy."

PART III

REMEMBRANCE

Oh, I have slipped the surly bonds of earth
And danced the skies on laughter-silvered wings.
Sunward I've climbed and joined the tumbling mirth
Of sun-split clouds—and done a hundred things
You have not dreamed of—wheeled and soared and swung
High in the sunlit silence. Hov'ring there,
I've chased the shouting wind along and flung
My eager craft through footless halls of air,
Up, up the long, delirious, burning blue
I've topped the windswept heights with easy grace
Where never lark or even eagle flew.
And, while with silent, lifting mind I've trod
The high, untrespassed sanctity of space,
Put out my hand and touched the face of God.

—JOHN GILLESPIE McGEE JR.
No. 412 Squadron, RCAF
(McGee was an American who went to Britain
in October 1940 at age eighteen to fly against
the Luftwaffe in the Battle of Britain.
He was killed on December 11, 1941.
His famous poem was a favorite
of Dick Bong's widow.)

CHAPTER 41

Aces High

NEITHER Tommy McGuire nor Dick Bong lived to celebrate his twenty-fifth birthday. Two young men who were born in 1920—that hopeful first year of the first decade after the war that was supposed to have ended all wars—had both died in 1945, the hopeful year during which their nation prevailed in mankind's biggest and most terrible war.

Great literature is filled with the tragedy of great warriors who die young, yet in this they never age. They remain "forever young," always remembered as they were in their prime.

Major Raoul Lufbery—a great World War I ace and the man whom Eddie Rickenbacker called his inspiration—had a saying. When asked about what he would do after the Great War had ended, he replied, "There won't be any after-the-war for a fighter pilot."

A few weeks later, on May 19, 1918, he was killed in action.

We still remember Lufbery as we remember Bong and McGuire, as a young warrior who had lived life with an almost unparalleled intensity.

In the last two years of the short lives of Bong and McGuire, they experienced more of a warrior's life than most career military personnel experience in their lifetimes. They also had more to show for their time than most of their fellow fighter pilots. They were the two top-scoring American aces of World War II—though they were so close in their scores that to rank one above the other is a slippery slope.

On December 26, 1943, coincidentally one year before his heroic Medal of Honor engagement over Luzon, McGuire shot down four Japanese aircraft over Cape Gloucester, but lost one in a cut of cards. Had this not happened, McGuire's final score would have been thirty-nine instead of thirty-eight.

On April 12, 1944, Dick Bong shot down three planes off the northern coast of New Guinea, but one was not verified until General Kenney made a special effort to locate the wreckage in exactly the same place that Bong said it was. Had this not happened, Bong's final score would have been thirty-nine instead of forty.

These are just two examples. With both Bong and McGuire, there are numerous other cases where gun cameras failed, or where victories were downgraded to "probables" when they should have been confirmed. There are still others where later examination of Japanese records reveal that aircraft not credited by the Americans to have been destroyed actually *were* lost. For example, on April 14, 1943, Dick Bong attacked three Mitsubishi G4M bombers over Milne Bay. He was credited with a confirmed victory and with one of his seven probables, yet the Japanese records show that none of the three G4Ms survived.

History lists Dick Bong with forty and Tommy McGuire with thirty-eight, but no one should think of one as a more historically important ace, or a better combat pilot, than the other. They were certainly *different* as combat pilots, but neither should be regarded as superior. McGuire was a master of maneuver and of impossible deflection shots, while Bong's style was to bore in tight to get his kills. While a theoretician may criticize either approach, the fact is that they both worked—not because of the approach, but because of the skills of the men.

Who won the Race of the Aces?

They both did.

The two men were remarkably similar and strikingly different. They were born just a few weeks apart, both played the clarinet, and both were very skilled P-38 pilots. The phrase "personal courage" fits easily in the same sentence with both of their names. Each is among the select few to have received the Medal of Honor.

On the other hand, just as their styles of fighting differed, so, too, did their style of personality. Bong was perceived as a shy and retiring man when on the ground—although those who knew him well begged to differ—while McGuire was an outgoing, "mile a minute" talker. Bong was described as a loner, probably because nearly half of his victories were scored while he "freelanced," while McGuire was a leader, first as an operations officer and later as commander of the 431st Fighter Squadron.

Some theorize that McGuire would have exceeded Bong's score early on had he not had command responsibilities tying him down. Others insist that Bong could have easily reached a score of fifty or higher had it not been for Kenney's repeated nervous interference. Such speculation takes on the trappings of mere quibbling. Both men were remarkable combat pilots with very different styles.

In speculating what "might have been," people often wonder what would have happened to Dick Bong and Tommy McGuire had they lived.

Based on what Bong was doing during the last few months of his life, we could easily see a career as an industry test pilot. He and Marge would almost certainly have had some of the little "towheaded Swedes" George Kenney referred to back in December 1944—and raising them would have gone more smoothly on an industry paycheck than on an Army officer's salary. They had grown to like Southern California, and they probably would have remained there. Marge stayed on after Dick was killed.

As for McGuire, Kenney wrote in his epitaph for Tommy that he would have made "a name remarkable for command as well as for leadership." One could easily imagine him in command of a postwar fighter group as the USAAF became the fully independent U.S. Air Force in 1947. Kenney, his mentor, served two years as commander of the newly formed Strategic Air Command, and he might have taken McGuire with him, although we could better imagine Tommy remaining with fighters. It takes no stretch of the imagination to picture Colonel Tommy McGuire leading a dozen F-86 Sabre Jets up to MiG Alley in 1951, or General Tommy McGuire commanding F-102s in the Air Defense Command a few years later.

· · ·

WHAT of the other top American aces? Dave McCampbell ended the war in number-three place with thirty-four victories, and remained in the U.S. Navy. He commanded the carrier USS *Bon Homme Richard* during the Korean War and ended his career in 1964 on the staff of the Joint Chiefs of Staff in the Pentagon. An Arleigh Burke class destroyer commissioned in 2002 bears his name.

Pappy Boyington, the Marine Corps' "Black Sheep" ace, was presumed dead, but a few weeks after Dick Bong died, he was discovered at a prison-of-war camp in Japan. As a colorful Medal of Honor hero and twenty-eight-victory air ace who had just "returned from the dead," Boyington became the object of intense media attention as soon as he arrived in the United States. The Marine Corps used Boyington—now promoted to lieutenant colonel—in a campaign to sell bonds, but on the last night of a nationwide speaking tour, he appeared in public very drunk and very incorrigible. Having embarrassed himself and the Marine Corps, much of the glory of his triumphal return quickly faded. Discharged as a colonel in 1947, Boyington spent most of the next decade battling alcoholism and drifting from job to job, which included being a draft beer salesman and a referee for wrestling matches. His life began to turn around by the late 1950s, though, as he got a job flying for a charter airline out of Burbank, California. He also completed his best-selling autobiography, *Baa Baa, Black Sheep*, which was published in 1957 and which became the basis for a made-for-television movie and a network series.

Joe Foss, Boyington's fellow marine who was the first American to match Rickenbacker, went on to be elected governor of his home state of South Dakota.

Francis "Gabby" Gabreski, who scored twenty-eight victories to be the highest-scoring USAAF ace in Europe, was shot down on his last mission and languished in a German stalag for nine months. He continued his career in the postwar U.S. Air Force and flew Sabre Jets during the Korean War. He scored 6.5 victories against the Communist MiGs to raise his cumulative score to 34.5, edging out McCampbell as the third-highest-scoring American ace of all time. After his retirement in 1967, Gabreski worked in public relations and customer relations at the Grumman Corporation, and later as president of the Long Island Rail Road.

Bob Johnson, who had been the top-scoring USAAF ace in the European Theater at the time he appeared with Dick Bong and Hap Arnold at the Pentagon photo op in June 1944, ended his combat career with twenty-seven. He left the service and joined Republic Aviation—makers of the P-47 Thunderbolt—as a test pilot and had an eighteen-year career with the company.

Mac MacDonald, the third-highest-scoring USAAF Pacific Theater ace after Bong and McGuire with twenty-seven victories, commanded the 475th Fighter Group until July 1945. He remained in the postwar U.S. Air Force and retired in 1966.

WHAT then of the aces in other air forces during World War II?

The highest-scoring ace of World War II was the German pilot Erich Hartmann, who scored 352 well-documented aerial victories. Behind him there were more than 100 aces in the German Luftwaffe who scored more than 100 victories each. Gerhard Barkhorn was second with 301. After World War II, Hartmann spent more than ten years in a Soviet gulag. Released in 1955, he served with the postwar Luftwaffe.

Germany's Luftwaffe aces outscored the aces of other countries for many reasons, including the fact that they fought the Soviet Red Air Force at a time when it had many aircraft but poorly trained and poorly equipped pilots. Compared to the USAAF, the Luftwaffe also had fewer pilots who flew more missions for more years. The average USAAF tour of duty was much shorter than that of the Luftwaffe. No air force ever came closer to matching the 2.37 million personnel that were in the uniform of the USAAF in June 1944. Nor did the Luftwaffe high command withdraw its aces from service for long periods of time, as George Kenney did with his pilots, especially Dick Bong.

The highest number of confirmed victories outside the Luftwaffe is the score of 94 credited to Eino Ilmari Juutilainen of Finland, who also flew against the Soviets.

The leading Soviet ace is known to have been Ivan Kozhedub, and his score of 62 is generally accepted by most sources. After the war ended,

Kozhedub remained in the Red Air Force and was among the Soviet contingent that secretly flew with the Chinese Air Force against the U.S. Air Force during the Korean War. Though he had command responsibility among these shadowy Soviet regiments, it is generally believed that he flew no actual combat missions over Korea himself.

The highest-scoring British Commonwealth ace in World War II was a South African, Marmaduke "Pat" Pattle, whose score is known to have been at least 40 but possibly as high as 51. The relevant records for his unit, Royal Air Force No. 33 Squadron, were lost in the British evacuation of Greece in 1940, and Pattle himself was killed during this operation.

James Edgar "Johnny" Johnson is remembered as not only the highest-scoring Englishman in the Royal Air Force but also as having survived the war with his aircraft being hit only once—by a single shell—in an aerial combat career that ended with 38 aerial victories, the same as Tommy McGuire. After World War II he had a long career in the Royal Air Force, retiring as an air vice marshal.

Among the Japanese, Tetsuzo Iwamoto is credited with having scored 66 victories in World War II and 14 during the Sino-Japanese War for a total of 80. Hiroyoshi Nishizawa is credited with 87 in World War II alone. However, because of Japan's official record-keeping practices—or the lack thereof—these totals are regarded as "best guesses." Nishizawa met his end over Luzon on October 26, 1944, at the hands of a pair of U.S. Navy Hellcats. Iwamoto survived the war but found it hard to get a job, and he died in obscurity in 1955.

In all the wars that have been fought in all the world since 1945—from Korea to Southeast Asia to the Middle East—no ace of any nation has scored more victories than Bong or McGuire. In the Korean War, Joe McConnell scored sixteen victories to be the highest-scoring American ace of that conflict, while only two pilots on the opposing side had scores in the twenties. Over Vietnam, Chuck DeBellvue, a weapons system operator in F-4 Phantoms, scored six as the highest-scoring of only five American aces in that conflict. No North Vietnamese aces are believed to have scored in double digits. Since then there have been no American aces, although two U.S. Air Force pilots had three victories each in the first Gulf War.

As the years have gone by, the names of the hundreds of men—and a handful of women in the Red Air Force—who became aces during World War II have faded from the headlines and from the currency of popular culture. Many have been, or will be, forgotten.

Others, however, such as Dick Bong and Tommy McGuire, remain an indelible part of the history and valor that is part of the legacy of mankind's most terrible war.

CHAPTER 42

Those Who Remember Them

AFTER Dick's funeral, Marjorie Vattendahl Bong chose to return to Southern California rather than to go back to her hometown. In retrospect, it seems a counterintuitive decision for a twenty-one-year-old girl who had never traveled far from Wisconsin before she met the dashing young airman whose easy smile was at its easiest in her presence.

Before he died, Marge had started to secretly write a book about the love of her life. He died without knowing about it, and she never finished it. She took it out and reworked it, though, selling it in 1946 as a syndicated article titled "An Angel Flew Piggy-Back."

In their brief time together, California's Southland had become their home, the place where they would have lived and where they would have raised their little "towheaded Swedes." So Marge went back, seemingly a fish out of water in a strange land. She went home to the empty bungalow, where she and he had lived their lives and dreamed their dreams. The lonely girl lived with the ghost of a household name. What could the lonely girl alone in Hollywood do next?

How many starry-eyed twentysomethings have traveled to Hollywood in search of the impossible dream of a glamorous career since that day in 1937 when Lana Turner skipped her high school typing class to get a Coke at the Top Hat Café on Sunset Boulevard and was discovered by William R. Wilkerson, publisher of the *Hollywood Reporter*? The answer is in the tens of millions. Marge soon found that through her association with Dick, then a household name, she had already been "discovered."

The summer of 1945 in Hollywood was a time of handsome heroes. Audie Murphy, the twenty-year-old infantryman who had become the most decorated American combat soldier of World War II, appeared on the cover of *Life* magazine on July 16. Among the millions who saw his smiling face that week was screen legend James Cagney, who invited him to Hollywood for a screen test. Though nagged by personal demons, booze, and posttraumatic stress, Murphy eventually went on to a stellar film career, starting by essentially playing himself.

Dick Bong was another of the handsome heroes whose story seemed tailor-made for Hollywood. Even on the day when a nuclear strike brought the promise of an end to World War II, his name was above the fold in the *New York Times*.

In the fall of 1945, as Hollywood was celebrating these handsome heroes who had won the war, Marge got a call. Then another. Several major studios wanted to do his story, and they wanted her involved. She recalled later that Paramount was especially interested. The reclusive and aviation-obsessed Howard Hughes even sent an emissary to discuss a film—but he swore her to secrecy. That was Hughes's way of doing things. So, too, was indecision. He never followed through.

Marge went to several meetings, including at least one in which she had to wrestle herself off of a "casting couch." She closed her mind to any notion of a movie about Dick, just as she was locking his very memory away.

She found herself living on the dark side of the Hollywood stereotype, complete with the desperation of running short of money as she waited for Dick's military life insurance to come through. Having earned a teaching degree, she applied for a teaching job with the Los Angeles High School District, but the shy midwestern girl was told that the Los Angeles high schoolers would "eat you alive."

The famous media columnist and radio talk-show hostess, Hedda

Hopper, heard about Marge's dilemma and took the poor girl under her wing. She loaned Marge some money and made some calls. At last Marge got a teaching job, but unlike anything for which she had trained at Superior State Teachers College. She found herself training models at the Dorothy Preble Model Agency in Los Angeles. Amazingly, it was a job at which she would remain for the next ten years.

In October 1946, Marge remarried, exchanging vows with James Baird of Beverly Hills, a woolen goods salesman, at Hollywood Lutheran Church. It had been a year of deep loneliness for Marge. In her memoirs she described "the endless search of trying to find out who I really was, what I wanted my life to become." The search was slow and painful.

"I was unsophisticated, naive and made mistakes," she admitted.

She ranked her second marriage among those mistakes, describing it as "a marriage that turned out to be a series of separations, finally ending in divorce."

As she put it, the only good thing that resulted from the marriage was her first daughter.

Marge threw herself into her work with Dorothy Preble, doing ramp work for famous designers, trunk shows for French couturiers, shows for New York milliners, and "counseling those with problems in facing an audience." At the same time, she was building her own self-confidence.

Soon she married a third time, to a magazine publisher named Murray Drucker, with whom she had another daughter and to whom she remained married until his death in 1991. Through the years she worked with him on a number of his magazines, covering topics from California fashion to show dogs.

As Marge Bong was finding her feet in Hollywood, Marilynn Geisler "Pudgy" McGuire remained in San Antonio, although she made several trips to New Jersey. The first came in 1946. At last it had come time to award the long-awaited posthumous Medal of Honor, which had been recommended for Tommy by General Kenney after his heroic missions over Luzon in December 1944.

As Charles Martin points out, Marilynn could have arranged to receive the medal on Tommy's behalf in San Antonio, but she chose to ask that the ceremony take place in New Jersey out of deference to Thomas Buchanan McGuire Sr. If Tommy's father appreciated the gesture, he never admitted it.

On May 8, 1946, General Kenney handed it to her personally at the City Hall in Paterson. Tommy's father and Mayor William Furrey reportedly wore white tie and tails to the midafternoon event. Also present were Governor William Edge and both of New Jersey's U.S. senators, Howard Alexander Smith and William Wahl Hawkes. Congressman John Parnell Thomas, the friend of Tommy's father who once read an embellished variation of Tommy's war record into the *Congressional Record*, also was on hand.

In the back of the room, scarcely noticed by the preening politicians, was a tall man who had flown with Tommy in New Guinea. By this time Charles Lindbergh had closed himself off completely from the world. He almost never appeared in public. On May 8, he made an exception.

In a letter he had written to Marilynn a year earlier after Tommy's death, he recalled their time together and told her: "I had hoped to see your husband again in this country, and to continue the friendship which began in that Hollandia jungle camp. The announcement of his death came to me as a great shock; and with it, I felt a keen personal loss."

Like Marge, Marilynn also remarried twice after the death of her war hero. Her second marriage was to Clem Stankowski, with whom she would have a son and with whom she would remain until his death thirty-five years later. Shortly thereafter she married her third husband, Robert Beatty.

As their widows were picking up the pieces of their lives, both Tommy McGuire and Dick Bong received what can be described as the ultimate tribute by which an airman could be remembered by the U.S. Air Force: each had an air force base named after him.

In New Jersey, the U.S. Army's Fort Dix opened in 1917 as a staging base for troops going overseas in World War I, and opened its first airstrip, Rudd Field, in 1937. During World War II, this landing strip evolved into the much larger Fort Dix Army Airfield. By 1949, as the assets of the former USAAF were being transferred to the U.S. Air Force, the new service took title to the former Fort Dix Army Airfield. The property needed a name, and what better name—insisted Congressman John Parnell Thomas—than that of a true New Jersey war hero?

Technically, Tommy McGuire was a war hero who happened to be the son of a New Jersey man, and he had not lived in New Jersey since he was seven years old. To Thomas, this was splitting hairs. On September 17, 1949,

Marilynn McGuire made her next trip to New Jersey to attend the formal dedication of McGuire Air Force Base.

While McGuire Air Force Base was to become a busy and important hub for the U.S. Air Force's Military Air Transport Service (later the Military Airlift Command and now the Air Mobility Command), the base that was named for Dick Bong had a much different story.

The idea of naming a base after both of America's top two World War II aces certainly had to have been discussed as early as 1949, but Richard Bong Air Force Base was not formally designated until December 1955. Unlike McGuire Air Force Base, Richard Bong Air Force Base was not an existing base but was intended to be an all-new construction, initiated as part of a comprehensive program by the U.S. Air Force's Air Defense Command to protect the United States from Soviet bomber attack.

The idea was to base F-102 (and later F-106) interceptors at bases across the northern tier of the country. These delta-winged, supersonic interceptors were considered "point defense" interceptors, meaning that they were designed to be based close to the targets they were intended to protect. They were very fast and had an exceptional rate of climb, but the trade-off was that they had a relatively short range. This translated as a need for many bases, and Richard Bong Air Force Base was such a base.

The location selected for the base was in far southeastern Wisconsin, diagonally across the state from Dick's hometown. It was to be roughly halfway between Milwaukee and Chicago to provide air cover for these two cities in the event that the Soviets decided to start World War III with a "midwestern Pearl Harbor."

For the next several years, little happened at the 4,515-acre site of Richard Bong Air Force Base. Surveys were made, but no runway was built. By 1957 the U.S. Air Force changed its mind, deciding to use the base not for interceptors but as an emergency dispersal site for Strategic Air Command bombers, specifically the new B-58 Hustler supersonic bombers. On June 5 the base was formally transferred, and the Strategic Air Command's 4040th Air Base Squadron arrived on August 1, 1958. In 1959 a 12,900-foot runway was graded, buildings were constructed, and concrete was scheduled to be poured for the runway on October 5.

Suddenly, three days before the pour date, work was halted. Construction never resumed, leaving the base with what is probably the longest gravel runway in Wisconsin. During the Vietnam War the base was used for Special Forces training, but no permanent facility was located there. Richard Bong Air Force Base sat frozen in time until 1974, when the state bought the land, renaming it the Richard Bong State Recreation Area.

FOR four decades, neither Marge nor Marilynn spoke publicly of the young airmen they had lost in 1945. For both, the memories were, as Marge put it, "difficult."

"I didn't talk about Richard," she wrote in 1995. "I was suspicious about anyone who brought up his name to me. I locked all of those memories deep in my heart—the precious ones—the painful ones when I lost him."

For Marilynn, it was more complicated. Tommy's father had never accepted her. From his vantage point, she was merely a woman with whom Tommy had lived for a couple of months during the war. He had never even met her while his son was alive. He consistently snubbed her. He snubbed her at the Medal of Honor ceremony in 1946, and at the McGuire Air Force Base dedication three years later, he specifically made sure that she was excluded from the reviewing stand.

In May 1950, when Tommy's mortal remains were finally brought home to be buried at Arlington National Cemetery, Thomas McGuire Sr. told the Air Force that no special accommodations need be made for Marilynn. She wound up having to hitch a ride to the funeral from Tommy's aunt, Stella Tolson, who had owned the hotel at Lake Hopatcong where Tommy had once spent his summers.

After the elder McGuire died, Marilynn learned from Joan Mallon, his longtime girlfriend, that he had been given the use of the special VIP suite at McGuire Air Force Base, and he used it frequently over a period of two decades. Marilynn was unaware that the "McGuire Suite" existed, or that she would have been entitled to use it as well.

Through the 1950s and into the 1960s, Marge had received numerous invitations from aviation organizations, and even from the Air Force Academy, to speak in public about Dick—and she had refused them all. Eventually the number of requests petered out.

It was not until 1985 that Marge Bong Drucker decided to insert the "Bong" back into her name and to speak publicly about her first husband. She was invited to the dedication of the Richard Ira Bong Memorial Bridge, connecting Duluth and Superior, and she decided to attend. Her response was that she had stayed in the closet long enough, and "why not?"

In the process of returning to Superior, she was invited to a Bong family reunion and welcomed as "Aunt Marge."

In July 1986, Marge accepted an invitation to Dick's enshrinement in the National Aviation Hall of Fame, at Wright-Patterson Air Force Base in Ohio—the former Wright Field, where she and Dick had lived briefly in the spring of 1945. Once again she ran into old friends, and was glad to have been accepted.

A few months later, Marilynn McGuire Beatty had a similar opportunity to pick up the long-untouched but not forgotten thread of her relationship with Tommy and with the Air Force. Colonel E. M. Leete phoned from McGuire Air Force Base in New Jersey. He explained that had been trying—with some difficulty—to track her down because he wanted to invite her to attend the dedication of a memorial to Tommy. As with Marge Bong Drucker a year earlier, Marilynn decided that it was time, and she accepted the invitation.

The centerpiece of the memorial was one of the relatively few P-38 Lightnings still in existence, which had been acquired for display at the base. Only about 30 of the 9,925 Lightnings that Lockheed built still existed at the time, so it was quite a coup for the base to be able to find one. It was a P-38L-5 that had never gone overseas. Converted to F-5G configuration as a photoreconnaissance aircraft, it was stored until March 1946, when it was sold as surplus. It went through a succession of owners, including race driver Rex Mays, and later vintage aircraft enthusiast Dave Tallichet, who removed the large F-5G reconnaissance nose and restored the aircraft to fighter configuration. The Air Force Museum acquired the aircraft specifically to be loaned to McGuire Air Force Base, and Tallichet flew it to New Jersey personally.

At McGuire Air Force Base, the aircraft was stripped of its camouflage paint, restored, and repainted to replicate Tommy's last P-38L, *Pudgy V*, complete with his thirty-eight victory markings. The original *Pudgy V*, which he had not been flying on his fateful last mission, was apparently scrapped in the

Philippines, as were most surplus USAAF aircraft that remained there at the end of World War II. It was cheaper than bringing them home.

Secretary of Defense Caspar Weinberger made the formal dedication of the Lightning and the memorial to Tommy McGuire in November 1986. With her husband, Robert Beatty, Marilynn flew in from San Antonio to be the guest of honor. At last, after all the years, Marilynn was accommodated in the "McGuire Suite." As Charles Martin recalls, "It was her first public recognition as the widow of Tommy McGuire since she had received the Medal of Honor for Tommy, forty years before."

Since the turn of the twenty-first century, there has been an increasing interest in the crash site where Tommy McGuire went down. In early 2001, Captain David Mason, a pilot with World Airways, led an expedition to Negros Island. Here, on January 7, the fifty-sixth anniversary of the crash, he interviewed an elderly man named Vincente Bedoria. He had observed the crash and the removal of a body from the wreckage. His description of a ring the deceased man was wearing matches the ring visible in a photograph of Tommy McGuire taken a few days before the fatal flight. Bedoria explained how the local people hid the body from the Japanese, and how they approached U.S. Army personnel in 1947 to tell them of the gravesite. Mason was then taken to the actual crash site, where he recovered several artifacts that are definitely P-38 parts.

As at McGuire Air Force Base, there is also a P-38 on display in Superior, Wisconsin. Acquired by American Legion Post 435 as part of a plan to memorialize their hometown hero, the Lightning had been flown into Duluth's airport in 1948 by 23rd Fighter Group ace Don Lopez. It was trucked to Superior and finally placed on display in May 1955, and repainted to replicate Dick Bong's P-38J, tail number 42-103993, to which he had attached Marge's portrait.

Four decades of Wisconsin winters took their toll on the rare old warbird, and by the 1990s there was a move afoot to raise money for a permanent museum that could display the aircraft indoors. The idea was to create not just a place to house the Lightning but also a center that would contain interactive exhibits to tell the story of World War II, a facility with not just displays but also a theater, a research library, and a classroom for visiting school groups.

In the meantime, the P-38 was trucked back to Duluth in 1994, where it was restored by Minnesota Air National Guard volunteers, and in 1997 it went on temporary display at the Polar Aviation Museum in Blaine, Minnesota.

Marge threw herself into a tireless fund-raising effort for the museum in Superior, logging more than forty thousand miles on behalf of the project. The woman who had, for four decades, kept her silence about Dick, was now speaking publicly at events from air shows to rubber chicken dinners, from the Air Force Academy to the Museum of Flight in Seattle, and at the Congressional Medal of Honor Convention in Philadelphia on the fiftieth anniversary of World War II.

The Richard Ira Bong Heritage Center on the bayfront in Superior was formally dedicated on September 24, 2002—on what would have been his eighty-second birthday. Don Lopez, now the deputy director of the Smithsonian National Air and Space Museum in Washington, D.C., was the keynote speaker for the dedication.

Standing near the replica of the airplane that Dick had named for her fifty-eight years before, Marge also spoke, telling the assembled dignitaries, "When Dick was killed in 1945 just six months after our wedding, I was devastated, along with the rest of the country. For forty years I couldn't talk about it. But when the heritage center was commissioned in 1989, I had to get involved—to honor both Dick, my first love, and all the brave veterans who never saw themselves as heroes but truly defined the word 'hero.' I feel a great release with the opening of this center, and I know that other people from my era will feel similarly. This is our place, our story, our chance to help younger generations understand what we did and what it means to them today."

A year later, shortly before Marge lost her own last battle with cancer, she added, "People have often asked me what Richard would have thought about the heritage center. I always explain that I think he would have been very upset if this was just for him. But the heritage center brings in all veterans, all aspects of the war. Dick's favorite phrase was 'We are just doing our job.' Well, with the heritage center we are doing our job by providing a very fitting tribute to all the heroes who came out of World War II. We have done our job for them, and I am very proud."

EPILOGUE

Heroes

EACH January 7, as the anniversaries of Tommy McGuire's death come and go, so, too, do the snows that settle on the P-38 that guards the gate at McGuire Air Force Base. As with that other P-38 that once stood as a lone sentinel in the Wisconsin snows, this Lightning stands today as a silent reminder of a war long ago, and of the brave young airmen who sacrificed their lives to win it.

They were remarkable men, all the American pilots who battled the Axis air forces in the skies all over the world. They were part of that selfless generation of whom a grateful nation will be forever proud.

Among these warriors were the fighter pilots, a breed apart from the others who fought the war, because they fought alone. They flew in the company of others, but when the bullets flew, they were alone, facing another lone enemy in a contest that was likely a duel from which only one would emerge.

In those duels from which only one man emerged we celebrate the aces, the fighter pilots whose victories numbered five or more. The ones whom we celebrate most are those whose victories number most. For Americans, those two men were Bong and McGuire, close enough in their final totals that they deserve to be listed as a pair, with neither more preeminent than the other.

So often in eulogies, we hear the phrase "never again will there be a man such as he was." Often this is hyperbole. In the case of Dick Bong and Tommy McGuire, it is true. You should never say "never," of course, but it is a virtual certainty that no American ace will ever match the score of these two heroes.

As time passes, and as the snows come and go in New Jersey and Wisconsin, and the monsoons come and go over the islands in the South West Pacific, memories of battles long ago change but do not fade. Increasingly, they are the memories of those who were not there but who remember because the lives of the knights who fought those battles have been preserved as stories and legends for all time, preserved to make those knights of long ago immortal.

Dick Bong and Tommy McGuire have achieved immortality. They are forever young. Recalling the words of Walter Clifford Meller and John Gillespie McGee, we sigh for our own lost youth as we think of Bong and McGuire. We see them as they stood at the threshold of their adventures on "laughter-silvered wings" within "the tumbling mirth of sun-split clouds." We see them with all the world before them.

We imagine them as they explored that world, with all its possibilities of wild adventure and romantic fortune. We imagine them as Meller imagined the medieval knights in the age of chivalry. We see them in their world of "knights to overthrow at spear-point and distressed damsels to succor and a princess's smile to win."

We take delight in their immortality and in the "rank and fame gained by prowess and hardihood, under the eye of kings, in some great stricken field."

Both Marge and Marilynn—their damsels, their princesses—are gone now as well. They each had their decades of reflection, followed by the opportunity to reclaim that slice of their identity that will link them forever to their young—very young—war heroes.

As we have imagined the knights, perhaps we can image them now with their princesses—in the high, untrespassed sanctity of the heavens, where one might stretch out a hand to touch the face of God.

Once the media called them rivals, and rivals they were. However, it is probable that whether Tommy had scored three more or not, if the two men had met again in the years after the war, there would have been smiles and a handshake.

That's the mark of true heroes.

BIBLIOGRAPHY

Berg, A. Scott. *Lindbergh.* New York: Charles Putnam's Sons, 1998.

Bong, Carl. *Dear Mom: So We Have a War.* Edina, MN: Burgess, 1991.

Bong, Carl, and Mike O'Connor. *Ace of Aces: The Dick Bong Story.* Osseo, WI: Privately published, 1985.

Boyington, Gregory. *Baa Baa, Black Sheep.* New York: Bantam, 1958.

Drucker, Marge Bong. *Memories: The Story of Dick and Marge Bong (Major Richard Bong, America's All-Time Fighter Ace): A Love Story.* Los Angeles: Drucker, 1995.

Jennings, Peter, and Todd Brewster. *The Century.* New York: Doubleday, 1998.

Johnson, Clarence L. "Kelly", and Maggie Smith. *Kelly: More Than My Share of It All.* Washington, D.C.: Smithsonian, 1985.

Kenney, George C. *Ace of Aces: The Dick Bong Story.* New York: Duell, Sloan, & Pearce, 1960.

———. *General Kenney Reports: A Personal History of the Pacific War.* New York: Duell, Sloan, & Pearce, 1949.

Martin, Charles A. *The Last Great Ace: The Life of Major Thomas B. McGuire, Jr.* Fruit Cove, FL: Fruit Cove, 1998.

Meller, Walter Clifford. *A Knight's Life in the Days of Chivalry.* London: T. Werner Laurie, 1924.

New York Times. Various issues, 1943–1946.

Rickenbacker, Edward Vernon. *Fighting The Flying Circus.* 1919. Reprint, Garden City, NY: Doubleday, 1965.

Sakai, Saburo, with Martin Caidin and Fred Sato. *Samurai.* New York: Simon & Schuster, 1957.

Sebring American. Various issues, 1943–1946.

Stanaway, John, and Tom Tullis. *P-38 Lightning Aces of the Pacific and CBI* (Osprey Aircraft of the Aces No 14). New York: Osprey, 1997.

Ward, John William. *From Prosperity to Collapse.* Amherst, MA: Amherst College, 1958.

Washington Post. Various issues, 1943–1946.

Yenne, Bill. *Aces: True Stories of Victory and Valor in the Skies of World War II.* New York: Penguin, 2000.

———. *Lockheed.* New York: Crown, 1987.

WIDELY USED ACRONYMS

FEAF   Far East Air Forces (formed in 1944 as a component of the USAAF and containing the Fifth, Seventh, and Thirteenth air forces)*

IJAAF   Imperial Japanese Army Air Force

IJNAF   Imperial Japanese Navy Air Force

SOPAC   South Pacific Area (an administrative division of the Allied Pacific Theater of Operations)*

USAAF   U.S. Army Air Forces*

*See the sidebar to chapter 9 for a full description.

APPENDIX 1

Cumulative Scores

	BONG	McGUIRE*		BONG	McGUIRE*
1942			**1944**		
December	2	—	January	21	16
			February	22	16
1943			March	24	16
January	5	—	April	28	16
February	5	—	May	28	18
March	9	—	June	28	20
April	10	—	July	28	21
May	10	—	August	28	21
June	11	—	September	28	21
July	16	—	October	33	24
August	16	7	November	36	28
September	16	10	December	40	38
October	19	13			
November	21	13			
December	21	16			

*McGuire flew his first combat missions in August 1943

APPENDIX 2

Official Texts of
Medal of Honor Citations

BONG, RICHARD I. (Air Mission)
Rank and organization: Major, U.S. Army Air Corps. Place and date: Over Borneo and Leyte, 10 October to 15 November 1944. Entered service at: Poplar, Wis. Birth: Poplar, Wis. G.O. No.: 90, 8 December 1944. Citation: For conspicuous gallantry and intrepidity in action above and beyond the call of duty in the Southwest Pacific area from 10 October to 15 November 1944. Though assigned to duty as gunnery instructor and neither required nor expected to perform combat duty, Maj. Bong voluntarily and at his own urgent request engaged in repeated combat missions, including unusually hazardous sorties over Balikpapan, Borneo, and in the Leyte area of the Philippines. His aggressiveness and daring resulted in his shooting down 8 enemy airplanes during this period.

McGUIRE, THOMAS B. JR. (Air Mission) (Posthumous)
Rank and organization: Major, U.S. Army Air Corps, Thirteenth Air Force. Place and date: Over Luzon, Philippine Islands, 25–26 December 1944. Entered service at: Sebring, Fla. Birth: Ridgewood, N.J. G.O. No.: 24, 7 March 1946. Citation: He fought with conspicuous gallantry and intrepidity over Luzon, Philippine Islands. Voluntarily, he led a squadron of 15 P-38s as top cover for heavy bombers striking Mabalacat Airdrome, where his formation was attacked by 20 aggressive Japanese fighters. In the ensuing action he repeatedly flew to the aid of embattled comrades, driving off enemy assaults while himself under attack and at times outnumbered 3 to 1, and even after his guns jammed, continuing the fight by forcing a hostile plane into his wingman's line of fire. Before he started back to his base he had shot down 3 Zeros. The next day he again volunteered to lead escort fighters on a mission to strongly defend Clark Field. During the resultant engagement he again exposed himself to attacks so that he might rescue a crippled bomber. In rapid succession he shot down 1

aircraft, parried the attack of 4 enemy fighters, 1 of which he shot down, single-handedly engaged 3 more Japanese, destroying 1, and then shot down still another, his 38th victory in aerial combat. On 7 January 1945, while leading a voluntary fighter sweep over Negros Island, he risked an extremely hazardous maneuver at low altitude in an attempt to save a fellow flyer from attack, crashed, and was reported missing in action. With gallant initiative, deep and unselfish concern for the safety of others, and heroic determination to destroy the enemy at all costs, Maj. McGuire set an inspiring example in keeping with the highest traditions of the military service.

INDEX

Page numbers in *italic* indicate maps; those in **bold** indicate tables.

ABOUT THE AUTHOR

Bill Yenne is the author of more than two dozen books on military, aviation, and historical topics. The *New Yorker* wrote of his bestselling biography of the Lakota leader Sitting Bull, that it "excels as a study in leadership." Amazon named the same book to the Number 5 place for nonfiction in its Top 100 list. The *Wall Street Journal* recently called one of Mr. Yenne's military histories "splendid" and went on to say that it "has the rare quality of being both an excellent reference work and a pleasure to read." The reviewer also wrote that Mr. Yenne writes with "cinematic vividness."

His books include *Aces: True Stories of Victory & Valor in the Skies of World War II*, *The B-17 at War*, *Attack of the Drones: A History of Unmanned Aerial Combat*, *The History of the U.S. Air Force*, and *SAC: A Primer of Strategic Air Power*. Of the latter, Major Michael Perini wrote in *Air Force Magazine*: "This book deserves a place on any airman's bookshelf and in the stacks of serious military libraries."

Mr. Yenne worked with the legendary U.S. Air Force commander General Curtis E. LeMay to produce the recently rereleased *Superfortress: The B-29 and American Airpower in World War II*, which *Publishers Weekly* described as "An eloquent tribute." Meanwhile, *FlyPast*, the United Kingdom's leading aviation monthly, said that his *The American Aircraft Factory in World War II* "knits a careful narrative around the imagery."

Mr. Yenne has also written corporate histories of America's greatest planemakers, specifically Boeing, Convair, Lockheed, McDonnell Douglas, and North American Aviation. He is an occasional contributor to *International Air Power Review*.

1/19

PO #: 0003260230